HISTORIC KERN COUNTY

An Illustrated History of Bakersfield and Kern County

by Chris Brewer

Enjoy Kern County's Past!

Chris Brewer
2-19-02

Judy,
I hope you enjoy the book. Thanks for your help at the museum.
Jeff Nickell
2-19-02

Published by the Kern County Museum & Foundation

Historical Publishing Network
A division of Lammert Publications, Inc.
San Antonio, Texas

CONTENTS

First Edition

Copyright © 2001 Historical Publishing Network

ISBN: 1-893619-14-1
Library of Congress Card Catalog Number: 2001088368

Historic Kern County: An Illustrated History of Bakersfield and Kern County

author:	Chris Brewer
photo editor:	Jeff Nickell
cover artist:	Calhoun Collins
contributing writer for "sharing the heritage":	Sean Steele
	Marie Beth Jones

Historical Publishing Network

president:	Ron Lammert
vice president:	Barry Black
project representatives:	Ron Franke
	Bari Nessel
	Robert Steidle
director of operations:	Charles A. Newton, III
administration:	Angela Lake
	Donna M. Mata
	Dee Steidle
graphic production:	Colin Hart
	John Barr

PRINTED IN SINGAPORE

ACKNOWLEDGMENTS

This book was created as the result of the effort of a number of people who are dedicated to the preservation of history. First and foremost, I thank my wife Sally, who watched me get through this project, showing great support and understanding that these manuscripts take due diligence and concentration, something that is not easy for me. She has always supported my love of Kern County history, many times to her own detriment.

I also wish to express my sincere appreciation to Shirley McFadzean, of Bakersfield, without whose careful and well-trained eye for editing, content, and form, this book may have not been completed. Shirley is one of those rare individuals who remain in the background, giving way to allow others to shine. Shirley deserves more credit for this effort than I can possibly give her.

David Adalian also worked on editing my draft manuscript and was the first to work it over. Dave has been the editor of the newspaper here in Exeter and writes a column for internet web page Streetmail.com.

Caltrans Architectural Historian Juti Winchester, Ph.D., was responsible for final outside edits and adjustments. Juti took the time and care to work the manuscript over and adjust the text and punctuation. I owe her a great debt of gratitude for what must have seemed like a never-ending task.

All have been supportive of the work, and came to the fore when the effort bogged down under the weight of the thousands of words that had to be reviewed and edited. They are good writers in their own right, and containing their exuberance toward the project was, in its own way, a special effort.

Although we didn't use her images in this book, I owe a special debt of gratitude to Exeter's.May Marshall, who is a fine darkroom technician, and has been a tireless supporter of my efforts. May has had some health problems, but the energy level at her age is something to behold. Her images may be seen in many of my other books, both past and future.

The black and white images and artifacts shown in this book came from the archives of the Kern County Museum, which houses perhaps the largest collection of Kern County imagery. The staff of the Kern County Museum selected the images, and Curator Jeff Nickell tirelessly wrote the original captions and provided final editing for the book.

Finally, special thanks go to Shadow, my office cat, without whose ceaseless and relentless pestering, I would have finished this book sooner. Shadow has his own agenda.

Chris Brewer
September 2001

✧
The Jewett Brothers built the original Rio Bravo ranch house near the mouth of the Kern River in the 1850s. Here the ranch is shown in the 1890s when it was owned by Captain John Barker.

FOREWORD

When I came to Kern County in 1965 to teach at Bakersfield College, I came for a job and found a life. Sharon and I married and raised our family here. We have made Kern County our home.

Kern County is a remarkable place. Kern is one of the premier counties in the nation, known as an agricultural, trade, and energy leader. Annually, Kern's agricultural yield exceeds $2 billion in products that feed and clothe the world. Kern's annual oil production exceeds that of all but three states. The Air and Space Museum in the nation's capital is filled with Kern's contributions to aviation firsts.

Although these facts tell the story of Kern's physical riches, it is not the enduring story. Because the people who migrated here, who were born and raised here, and who worked to provide a better life for themselves and their families, are the real wealth of Kern County.

I commend the Kern County Museum, the Kern Superintendent of Schools, and all those who helped produce **HISTORIC KERN COUNTY**. Author and Kern native Chris Brewer takes us on an interesting and educational journey through Kern's past. His balanced use of historical photos and narrative make the founding fathers, who many may know only as city or town or street names, come alive.

HISTORIC KERN COUNTY enables us to better appreciate the ordinary people who often engaged in extraordinary efforts to make a better life for themselves.

As good as **HISTORIC KERN COUNTY** is, it can tell us nothing of the future. The future is up to us.

This foreword is being written following the tragic events of September 11, 2001.

President Bush has challenged us to join him in a war between Freedom and Fear. I know the people of Kern stand ready to write a new chapter in our treasured history. Indeed, we have already begun.

A Kern fire-fighting crew has been assisting in the rescue and recovery operation at the Pentagon. Our military is ready because of the efforts of Edwards Air Force Base and the Navy's China Lake facility in eastern Kern County.

As always, our future will be written by the efforts and aspirations, and the sweat and blood of the people who live free in the home of the brave. I know that as in the past, the people of Kern County stand ready and willing.

Congressman Bill Thomas
September 2001

The Lakeview Gusher, which blew out near Maricopa in 1910, is still one of the largest gushers ever recorded.

THE LAND AND ITS EARLY PEOPLE

Kern County, with its diverse geographical divisions and geological formations, has a rich and varied history. The early Spanish explorers were the first non-natives to look upon and name the great expanse of Kern's southern San Joaquin Valley. Buena Vista or "good view" they called it, describing rolling hillsides ablaze with fields of orange and golden poppies intermixed with the blues and purples of lupine.

At the beginning of this twenty-first century there are still many acres of this wild land in the county, where masses of flowers bloom. But Kern's once renowned wildflower fields are gradually disappearing, as is much of its wild game. There is a direct correlation with this disappearance and the spread of agriculture, the oil industry, and mostly the building of towns and cities.

Kern is the third largest county in California, with a tremendous variety of geologic features. Nearly every type of climate exists in Kern, from the nearly sub-tropical regions of the San Joaquin Valley, to the sub-alpine areas of the high Sierra Nevada, and the wonders of the great Mojave Desert.

Half of Kern County is mountainous; a bit over a fourth is valley and plains, and the remainder is desert. The lower section of the Coast Range serves as the boundary for most of western Kern. These Temblor Mountains create a natural barrier to the Pacific Coast, with the county line running through them in a zigzag direction. The Tehachapi Mountains form part of the southern boundary, and the middle of the Mojave Desert is the east boundary. One-fourth of the county is east of the Tehachapis and Southern Sierra Nevadas, and the rest is in or near the San Joaquin Valley.

The desert is far from flat, with rolling hills, picturesque solitary hills, and buttes with names like Soledad and Black Mountain. All Kern County desert communities exist as a result of the area's natural resources with the exception of Mojave, which was a railroad terminus. Even Ridgecrest, in Kern's northeast corner, and home of the China Lake Naval Ordinance Test Station, was founded as a result of the dairy operated in the area by Robert and James Crum, after whom the original town was named Crumville.

✧

Trapper Thomas Fitzgerald built this thatched home in the 1850s. Christian Bohna, who purchased the house from Fitzgerald, eventually sold the house to Colonel Thomas Baker.

Isabella before the days of Isabella Dam. The Kern continues into the San Joaquin Valley, eventually ending up in Buena Vista Lake, which sometimes overflows northward into Goose Lake Slough. In high water years, waterways have been shown navigable to the San Francisco Bay area through the rivers and sloughs, beginning at Buena Vista Lake.

Piute Mountain, at an elevation of 8,440 feet, is the highest peak in the southernmost Sierra, with Owens Peak, at 8,475 feet, to the northeast. Communities such as Alta Sierra and Glennville, in the Greenhorn Mountains, are popular winter havens. Many more towns and resorts have been created since the completion of Isabella Dam and its reservoir. The old town of Kernville disappeared under the waters of Isabella Lake, while new communities sprung up around its banks.

The second area of mountains, the Tehachapi Range, includes the 8,826-foot Mt. Pinos in the county's southwest corner. This peak is considered the junction of the Temblor or Coast and Tehachapi Mountain Ranges. The Temblor Range, on Kern County's western boundary, rises gently out of the valley, which is covered with oil wells. Here are towns with names like McKittrick, Lost Hills, Taft, Fellows, Keck's Corner, Maricopa, and Tupman. These towns make up the western edge of the county in the valley, as it makes its ascent toward the top of the western mountain range.

The San Joaquin Valley makes up the rest of the county, lying between the Coast Range and the Sierra Nevadas. As part of what is called California's Great Central Valley, it is land ideally suited to agriculture. Here are also located the county's most traveled highways as well as its principal cities. Bakersfield, the county seat, lies in the center of the area, with less populated communities like Arvin, Shafter, Wasco, Lamont, McFarland, Delano, and others nearby.

The recorded history of Kern County begins with the native people or Indians. Kern was the one-time home of the tribes of three main Indian groupings: Yokuts communities; a number of Shoshonean or Tubatalabal and Kawaiisu groups sometimes referred to as Piutes; and a western group of the coastal Chumash people.

The towns of Randsburg, Johannesburg, and their neighbors are located in Kern's rich gold, silver and tungsten country, known as the Rand Mining District. Boron is Kern's easternmost community and is located near a huge Borax supply operated by the U.S. Borax and Chemical Corporation. Willow Springs, on the southeast edge of the Tehachapi Mountains, is a natural water hole, and Kern's Edwards Air Force Base is located in a flat area, some of which is known as Rogers Dry Lake. It has proved to be a perfect site for testing airplanes and landing space shuttles.

Kern's mountains are divided into three parts, with the Sierra Nevada dominating. Two forks of the Kern River flow through the Sierra Nevada canyons, once joining east of

Several Yokuts tribes, in time, developed their own names and dialects and lived in specific locations. The Yokuts did not migrate out of their surrounding area, and their village sites are commonly known.

Major village sites include a huge village on the western edge of old Buena Vista Lake, known as Tulamniu. Wogitiu, was another Tulamni village, located near the McKittrick area, northwest of Buena Vista Lake. The Halaumne lived close to the point where the Kern River entered the old channel connecting Kern and Buena Vista Lakes, with other villages on the north and south shore of Kern Lake. Around Poso Creek were the Paleumne, and further up Greenhorn Mountain were the Bancalache. The Yowlumne were among the largest of the Yokuts group, and were located at the south end of the Valley, from the Bakersfield area and the village of Woilu, south to the Tejon. They were also found up Caliente Creek.

The word "Yokuts" itself can be misleading, since it is an Indian word meaning simply "people." Probably more than twenty thousand Indians were living in the valley and foothills of Kern County. Yokuts villages were usually beside bodies of water or streams. Kern River was a particularly important source of food. When it was high, the fishing was good and food plentiful. The river furnished some transportation in its lower channels. Yokuts vessels were crude canoes and rafts constructed mostly of tule reeds. The reeds were tied together in tight bundles.

Each group had a headman who resided in the central village. He held his title by hereditary right and the succession could be passed to a female descendant. Each of the smaller villages within the group had its own leader who was appointed by the headman.

Further south are the Tejon Indians, who were actually a part of the coastal Chumash. They lived in the San Emigdio Mountains, on the south end of the San Joaquin Valley and were called the San Emigdiano tribe.

Within the boundaries of Kern County and having different customs from the Yokuts, were a Shoshonean people known as the Tubatalabal. They lived in the mountains and valleys in the area of what is now the Kern River Valley to Tehachapi Pass. The Kawaiisu laid claim to the

drier eastward slopes of the Tehachapi Mountains, as well as part of the Mojave Desert.

With the expansion of the Spanish into Alta California, the early explorers came into what is now Kern County. Over two and a quarter centuries ago in 1772, Don Pedro Fages became the first white man to look upon that southern-most region of the San Joaquin Valley, a land which makes up a part of Kern County. He saw the endless panorama of the valley, exclaiming it to be *Buena Vista* or "good view."

Ahead of Fages and his men were miles of level valley in every direction as far as the eye could see. Smoke from Indian villages drifted skyward. Herds of deer, elk, and antelope moved about effortlessly from one pasture to another. Rivers and sloughs were slender rivulets winding their way sluggishly through the valley, losing themselves in the blue depths of Kern and Buena Vista Lakes. The floor of the valley was dotted with swamps and water holes, all but hidden in the clumps of tule reeds growing in great abundance around their edges.

Fages came to the future site of Kern County by accident and, despite his inspired comment on its beauty, had no real interest in the area. He was attached to a pioneering expedition traveling northward along the Pacific shore under the leadership of Gaspar de Portola. The trek started in San Diego, and its destination was San Francisco Bay. The present-day Kern County area was neither their destination nor

✧

A Yokuts hooded baby cradle with milkweed fiber strap, no date given, but most of the collection dates to the 1890s.

their route, as they had been traveling along the coast. Fages made brief notes on his travels into the southern valley, and gave us its first European place name, Buena Vista.

To obtain any substantial record of early Kern, Father Francisco Garces is the one to whom we turn. Father Garces trekked into the area in 1776, as our Anglo forefathers were declaring independence from the tyranny of England. Spanish colonization around the world had a decidedly religious objective. Besides acquiring lands in the New World for the crown rulers of Spain, colonists had the duty to convert the natives of the strange land.

Garces left the Mojave villages on the banks of the Colorado River with four Indians as guides. He crossed the hot sands of the Mojave Desert and continued west across Antelope Valley, into the hills and down Cottonwood Creek into the San Joaquin Valley.

Garces' path took him to the north of that of Don Pedro Fages, and along his way he encountered what he called "a large stream," undoubtedly the Kern River. He couldn't swim and encamped on the right bank of the river. Local natives then assisted him across the Kern, which he named Rio de San Felipe.

Garces continued his journey into northern Kern County, where he performed the first recorded baptism in the San Joaquin Valley. Turning back in the area of White River, Garces retraced his steps and traveled through the area of what is now Bakersfield. Here he re-crossed the Kern and left the valley, apparently through Bird Springs Pass, reaching the Mojave Desert. He was killed in 1781 in an uprising of the Yuma Indians. Garces is honored in several places in today's Kern County, the most notable being the Garces Memorial Circle in Bakersfield.

More Spaniards came to the San Joaquin Valley, but recorded visits aren't known to have occurred until the beginning of the nineteenth century. Diaries were kept by a number of priests who traveled with contingents of the Spanish army. Between 1804 and 1816 no fewer than five accounts were made of the area, but none is as dramatic as the earlier accounts of the very first Europeans to enter the area.

To connect the missions and presidios, an old Indian trail came into use. El Camino Viejo, as it was called, was used after 1800 to traverse between Los Angeles and San Francisco Bay. This skirted the western part of present-day Kern County from what is now Lake of the Woods north along the foothills. It was also a trail for refugees and allowed Spanish fugitives to make their way into the San Joaquin Valley unseen by the people of the more thickly populated coastal areas.

Lieutenant Francisco Ruiz was sent out from the Santa Barbara Mission on July 19, 1806, to explore the interior of Alta California. The work of his diarist, Father José María Zalvidea, is important as it describes the trek through the Santa Inez area and Cuyama Valley into the Buena Vista Lake area, during a wet year when Buena Vista Lake and Kern Lake were joined. They then followed the mountains along the south valley, turning north toward the what is now Bakersfield, finally making camp along the banks of the Kern. On the fourth day, they again turned south, departing the valley by Tejon Pass.

Also in 1806, Gabriel Moraga, with Father Pedro Muñoz as chaplain and diarist, led twenty-five men into California's interior. On this eventful journey they traversed Kern County from north to south. Moraga, in 1813, gave the San Joaquin Valley its name, also happening upon the San Joaquin River, which he also named. He also discovered and named the Tuolumne, Merced, Calaveras, Mokelumne, and Stanislaus Rivers.

As a result of his treks into the valley, he made definite recommendations to his superiors that a mission and presidio be established in the interior. Its purpose was to keep the local Indians in check.

In 1816, an expedition led by Father Luis Martínez set out from San Luis Obispo Mission. He was accompanied by the usual troop of soldiers. As was then customary, this Spanish expedition stopped on the shores of Buena Vista Lake, where they made an effort to convince the Indians that they should change their wild customs for those of the mission. Having little success, they moved on. During their next stop they so frightened the natives they were attacked with a shower of arrows. The soldiers promptly put the village to the torch, sealing away any opportunity to convert the Indians to the mission life.

By 1819 the missionaries had figured out that the Indians were a menace to their way of life. Runaways from the missions were able to find asylum among the non-mission Indians, and it was all too frequent to lose livestock to them. The California Indian had now mastered the art of riding horses. Considerable fear of attack by the Indians was felt at the mission settlements.

As a result, Governor Pablo Vincente Sola sent three large expeditions into the San Joaquin Valley. These did little more than make a show of strength, which apparently had the desired affect. By 1822 the area had become territory of Mexico. However, in 1824 there was a ferocious battle at San Emigdio between the Mexican soldiers and the tribes at San Emigdio, with mixed results. Fighting would continue sporadically for some time.

Once Mexico gained its independence in 1822, Alta California was governed by a different set of rules. The Mexican government granted ranchos, often of huge dimensions, in a patronage fashion to those whom it favored. What is now Kern County had five such land grants: San Emigdio, La Liebre, El Tejón, Rancho de los Castac, and Los Alamos y Agua Caliente.

Governor Juan B. Alvarado granted the first of these on July 14, 1842. He granted José Antonio Dominquez the four-square-league Rancho San Emigdio, at the south end of the San Joaquin Valley. Years later a half interest of the Rancho was purchased by John C. Fremont. The ranch eventually ended up in the holdings of the Kern County Land Company. The four other ranchos in what is now Kern County were granted to individuals between 1842 and 1846.

No Spanish or Mexican missions were ever established in the Kern area, but it is said an attempt was made to settle and develop an Extensionada at San Emigdio. This was to help convert the local Indians and try to diminish the impact of settlers coming into the area. However, although foundations of large adobe buildings have been found in the past, no record appears to exist of a successful establishment of any mission church at San Emigdio.

In 1827 the first American made his way into the area entering the San Joaquin Valley in February, just below what was to be known as Kern Lake. Camping in the area of what is now Bakersfield, Jedediah Smith entered the Valley to trap, like many others would in later years. He trapped throughout the San Joaquin Valley on and off for the next two years. Other frontiersmen like Kit Carson, Ewing Young, and Grizzly Adams traversed the wild territory of what would become Kern County.

Joseph Reddeford Walker traversed into the future Kern County in 1834 on an exploration trek. His party left the San Joaquin Valley through what is now known as Walker Pass, east of Lake Isabella, traversing the Mojave Desert. Walker Pass has been known as the northernmost all-weather pass in the Sierra Nevadas. Walker would return with the first group of American settlers, the Joseph B. Chiles party. Walker led the party over the Rocky Mountains and through the great desert. He went down the eastern side of the Sierras and over the pass he

✧

The old Walker's Pass road, seen in the middle of this photograph, led travelers toward Kernville and the other mountain communities created by the Kern River Gold Rush in the mid-1850s.

discovered in 1834. The party entered the San Joaquin Valley, but traveled north and settled in what would become the Gilroy area.

In the late 1890s a group calling itself the Foxtail Rangers would stumble upon an obscure part of Kern County's history long forgotten over time. The Rangers were an informal group of friends who came together for excursions into the hinterlands of the county. Living in the Bakersfield area, they would meet for picnics and other socializing. At one of their gatherings at Fort Tejon, a heavy piece of bark was peeled from a giant oak tree, showing an inscription behind the outer bark. They had uncovered the tombstone of Peter Lebeck, a French trapper thought to be connected with the Hudson Bay Company. On a fateful day, October 17, 1837, Lebeck had the misfortune to run into a bear that would ultimately take his life. Nothing is truly known of the incident other than the inscription in the bark of the tree that states "In memory of Peter Lebeck, killed by a X Bear, October 17, 1837." The Tejon was known in the nineteenth century as having a heavy concentration of grizzly bears. Apparently Lebeck found out the hard way. Whether he was indeed with the French fur company, or actually an American-born trapper is still a mystery, but the find would go down in the annals of Kern County history as a great discovery and mystery.

In 1843 the American government commissioned John C. Fremont to explore the western territories, mapping the area as he went. Fremont mapped the Oregon Territory, turning south and entered the San Joaquin Valley in 1844. It was Fremont who was responsible for naming several of the county's place names, including the county itself. Fremont was sent on another western expedition in 1845 with a number of frontiersmen, including Joseph Walker, Kit Carson, and Alexis Godey. This time Fremont split up his party at the Truckee River in northern California with Fremont going west, eventually joining with the Americans fighting the Californios at San Jose in the San Francisco Bay region.

The rest of the party again followed the lead of Joseph Walker and crossed the Sierra through Walker Pass, encamping on the Kern

River at what is now Lake Isabella. The party eventually decamped and trekked north, finding Fremont in San Jose. He had been selected to guide the new so-called California Republic until American troops could arrive from the east. With the defeat of Mexico and subsequent Treaty of Guadalupe Hidalgo, California became part of the United States, but not before gold would be discovered and reported to Washington, D.C. by none other than Lieutenant Edward F. Beale, who carried samples of the find to the East Coast.

Alexis Godey ended up in Bakersfield, becoming a developer of one of the community's first subdivisions. He bought eighty acres in Bakersfield in what was known as the Kruse Tract, later subdividing them, and selling off lots for residences and business sites. One home he was connected with is the Alphonse Weill house on the corner of Seventeenth and H Streets. Godey sold Weill the lot. The house is now on display in Pioneer Village. Godey built his own residence on the north side of Nineteenth Street, described in later years, as "the first house East of the Kern Island Canal." After Godey's death, his widow married Edward Salcido and continued to live in the old home. Following Mrs. Salcido's death, the house was destroyed by fire. The state has placed an historical marker on the site, on Nineteenth Street in Bakersfield, where it may be seen today.

✧

Western pathfinder Alexis Godey's last home was on the site of the current Coca-Cola Bottling Company next to Central Park on Ninteenth Street in Bakersfield.

KERN'S EARLY SETTLEMENTS AND AGRICULTURAL HERITAGE

Encroachment into the San Joaquin Valley by the Spanish, Mexicans, and finally, Americans, caused early aggression in defense of their territory on the part of the Native Americans of the valley. By the time the United States incorporated California as a state in 1850, this intrusion into Indian territory had become a problem, sometimes addressed by aggression on the part of both parties. Up and down the new state, small skirmishes were fought between the newly arrived Americans and some of the Indian tribes. The southern valley was no exception.

While there were no true Indian wars, a number of isolated incidents caused the government to try to deal with the indigenous people. In 1850 and 1851, the tribes south of the Kings River appeared to have made an effort to jointly attack foreigners in the south valley. To settle the issues at hand, a peace commission was created, and a treaty with the Indians around Kern Lake was agreed upon. But jealousy among the commissioners caused them to divide up the state, with one of them getting the San Joaquin Valley.

Mismanagement ensued and in the spring of 1852, Lieutenant Edward Fitzgerald Beale, who four years prior had carried the first California gold to Washington D.C., was made superintendent of Indian Affairs in California and Nevada. Beale was able to control the Indians and created the Sebastian Indian Reservation. Although successful in quelling the Indian problems in the southern San Joaquin Valley, the reservation became ineffectual in its original intent. With the logistical difficulties of the War Between the States, it only lasted until 1864, when many of its residents were moved further north. Numerous Indians remained with Beale, who gave them land to live on, and jobs at his ranchos.

Meanwhile Beale had also become involved in one of the more unusual experiments of the U.S. Army. Beale made the suggestion to Secretary of War Jefferson Davis that camels should be utilized for the southwest explorations and army posts. As a result, David Dixon Porter was sent to northern Africa and began the process of buying camels for the corps. By April 1856, he had a group of thirty-three camels and shipped them to Indianola, Texas, where Beale was put in charge of the corps. Porter was immediately dispatched to the orient for more animals. Once all were together, Beale set out across the southwest desert, arriving with the camels in Los Angeles in January 1858.

✧

This 1900s photograph of Tehachapi is a good example of the type of parades held throughout Kern County to celebrate Independence Day.

Beale took the corps to Fort Tejon, where they spent a lackluster short career as the U.S. Camel Corps. Beale used them in 1858 and 1859 to survey for wagon roads in the west. However, the experiment failed due to a number of factors, including the lack of good camel drivers and the inability to mingle with pack animals, especially mules. By 1861 Beale turned over the herd of twenty-eight to the quartermaster of California for dispersal. After this time, more camels arrived in San Francisco for use in the west. However, none of these groups of camels ever succeeded in their assigned tasks. Besides those left at Camp Verde, Texas, camels were seen in California, Nevada, and Arizona for years after the dispersal by the government. Beale kept a small number at Tejon Ranch and would occasionally take some into Los Angeles, pulling a sulky.

One of the great sagas of the early west is that of the Jayhawkers and the Bennett-Arcane party, who ventured southwest via Utah, stumbling into Death Valley in 1849. They made the fateful decision at Mountain Meadows, Utah to follow the route directly west into the San Joaquin Valley, following Fremont's route. The party divided and both unknowingly headed directly into the valley. Parties split even more and passed each other frequently as they trekked on. Eventually they

were forced to encamp and send out William Lewis Manly and John Rogers for help. The two entered what would become Kern County down Indian Wells Valley into Red Rock Canyon, eventually ending up at Willow Springs, where they found water. They then traveled south to Newhall Valley where they were able to find enough provisions and horses to return for the rest of the party. After twenty-six days they returned to camp, finding what appeared to be four abandoned,

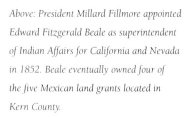

Above: President Millard Fillmore appointed Edward Fitzgerald Beale as superintendent of Indian Affairs for California and Nevada in 1852. Beale eventually owned four of the five Mexican land grants located in Kern County.

Right: This is an adobe home located on the Sebastian Indian Reservation, started by Edward F. Beale near the old Rancho El Tejón headquarters.

Birds Eye View of San Emidio
From Hills at Mouth of Cañon

Bakersfield, Cal.,
Nov. 16, 1895.

topless wagons. But the Bennett and Arcane families were still in camp and were taken back via Red Rock Canyon, where a two-inch snowfall provided the essential moisture to get them to civilization. Other parties met similar fates in Death Valley, but none suffered as much as the Jayhawkers and Bennett-Arcane parties.

By the early 1850s disgruntled prospectors moved south from the gold fields of northern California, seeking the riches of the rivers in the southern Sierras. The first real strike was at White River in southern Tulare County, where several hundred miners discovered good gold ore. The area was also known as Tailholt and was the first major mining effort in the southern Sierras.

Miners soon found their way south, eventually crossing the Greenhorn Mountains into the Kern River Valley. They settled areas on Greenhorn with names like Petersburg, after Peter Gardette and his supply store, and Glennville, named after James Madison Glenn. Keyesville, named after Richard Keyes who located the nearby Keyes mine, was located on the Kern River slope.

By the early 1860s mining camps with names like Williamsburg, Washington, Quartzburg, and Whisky Flat sprung up. Most of these merged into what was soon called Kernville, now located beneath the waters and silt of Lake Isabella. Huge mines with strong names like Big Blue, the Sumner, and the Mammoth were discovered and laid in. Further mining efforts spread south toward the Walker Basin area.

Here, in 1864, gold was discovered ,and a town named Havilah sprung up. A character named Asbury Harpending, known by some as "The Father of Kern County" founded the community eight miles south of what is now Bodfish. Harpending was undoubtedly an opportunist and saw a chance to take advantage of people wanting to settle near the far southern mines. He is probably best known for his scheme called "The Great Diamond Hoax," where he allegedly salted the mines and ground in the area. Harpending was a strong supporter of the Confederacy, actually having a commission in the Confederate Navy, and was among those who worked to obtain California gold for the Southern cause. It is not truly known whether any sizable amounts of local gold actually reached the south, but strong rumors and stories of Confederate gun-runners in the area persist to this day. The Southern cause was strong in the south valley.

Farther south of Havilah were the Piute Mines, a number of mining operations, some of which still run today. This mining area was discovered in the 1860s and, by the end of the decade, became the center of mining activity in the county, including communities like Claraville, named after Clara Munckton, the first white child in camp. The community was later known as Kelso, named after one of the creeks that run through the area.

A foothill district was formed about the same time of the formation of Kern County. Called the Rio Bravo Mining District, it was organized after shepherds working for

✧

San Edmidgio was home to many early agricultural workers in Kern County. Here, a wide range of marketable produce was grown. This photo was taken November 16, 1895. Rancho San Emidgio was one of Kern County's five Mexican land grants.

Solomon and Philo Jewett found rock indicating a gold deposit. A stamp mill was put into place, but deposits were found to be on the slim side. By 1867 the area was being mined by Chinese miners who worked the claim for a number of years.

By 1866 Havilah was in its heyday, with dozens of mines, stamp mills, and thirteen saloons. The community became the center of population in the southern Sierras, and soon an effort was being made to separate this area from the rest of Tulare County. In 1856 a proposal was made to split Tulare County into two separate counties, the southernmost being Buena Vista County. The effort failed, but subsequent efforts succeeded and, on April 2, 1866, parts of Los Angeles and Tulare Counties became Kern County, named after the river that flows through the area. Havilah was the first county seat, remaining so until 1874, when the governmental center was moved to Bakersfield.

The State Legislature appointed Michael Erskine, Daniel W. Walser, John M. Brite, Eli Smith, and Thomas Baker as the commission to organize the county. Baker was named to

chair the commission and operated it efficiently and effectively. The first county officials were appointed by the state legislature in July, with three supervisorial districts. With the county seat in Havilah, representation of outlying areas was difficult at best, but the next year saw great improvements in the transportation system with the Baker Toll Road winding its way up, the hills between what is now Bena and Walker Basin. Vestiges of it still remain today, on private property.

The Baker Toll Road helped move people and supplies to and from the county seat of Havilah in the early days. But before the settlement in the Kern Island area, what is now Bakersfield, supply lines were a different matter. Early supplies and stages had to cross the mountains from the nearest supply center, Visalia, several days to the north. The old stage road ran through White River and up the side of the mountains through Linn's Valley and into Glennville. By 1857, William P. Lynn completed what was called the "Bull Road" over Greenhorn Mountain, into the gold camps of the Kern River. This road continued on into Havilah and then further south. Later, in 1864, Andrew McFarlane completed a toll road over Greenhorn Mountain between Glennville and Kernville, replacing the old Bull Road to the south. Part of it is now Highway 155.

✧

Right: The founder of Bakersfield, Colonel Thomas A. Baker, was responsible for the early reclamation of the land in and around the site of present-day Bakersfield, as well as in the rest of the southern San Joaquin Valley.

Below: Colonel Thomas Baker's revolver was made by Samuel Colt and is a Navy model from 1851.
COURTESY OF GREG IGER.

Bottom: Colonel Thomas Baker's .50 caliber rifle, made by Slotter and Company of Philadelphia, Pennsylvania, is in the collection of the Kern County Museum.
COURTESY OF GREG IGER.

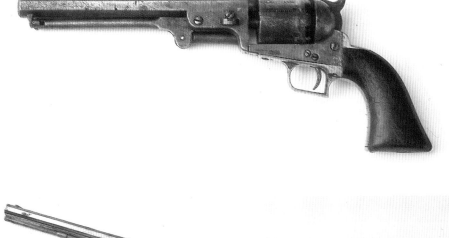

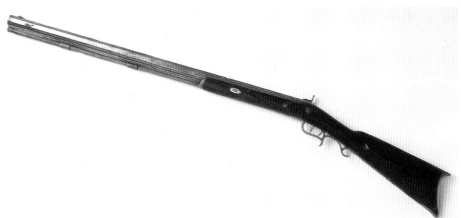

In 1863 Thomas Baker settled in the Kern Island area that would later bear his name. Bakersfield in its early days was a sleepy settlement in the middle of a swampy underbrush. It was settled directly on the Los Angeles to Stockton Road, a feature that would soon be an important asset.

In the early days of Kern Island several families had settled prior to Baker's permanent arrival. One of the prominent names that still remains in the area was that of the Jewett brothers, Solomon and Philo. In 1860, they settled along the Kern River at the mouth of Kern Canyon, calling it Rio Bravo. The ranch and part of the original house still exist there.

Although the Jewetts and other families had settled in the southern valley by around 1860, many of the mountain areas had already been claimed by former miners and others. A. T. Lightner, Sr., settled in Walker Basin in 1858, commuting to Havilah for supplies. One of his daughters married Walker Rankin, who had purchased land in the area from pioneer Daniel W. Walser. The Rankin Ranch still operates in Walker Basin.

The South Fork Valley of the Kern River was settled early on by William Scodie and William Weldon, both of whose names are borne by local communities. Later names in the area include W. W. Landers, J. L. Mack, and George Clancy.

Linn's Valley was named after William P. Lynn, who settled in and is said to have built the first mill on Poso Creek. David Lavers settled in 1855, building a hotel on the stage road from White River to Glennville. Thomas

Lavers, a cousin of David, built a home there in 1860, and the Engle family came soon after, later marrying into the Stockton family, which is still in the area. Other early pioneers included the Carver and Hughes families. The Hughes originally settled in Linn's Valley in 1869.

The foothills north of Bakersfield were the new location of the Christian Bohna family, who first settled in the Kern Island area in 1860. Although they had farmed on the "Island" they were washed out by the great flood of 1862. The family moved, with Sparrell W. Woody marrying Louisa Bohna and relocating into the foothills at the location of the present town of Woody.

The Carver family also married into the Woody family. In 1891 the town of Woody was renamed Weringdale after Joseph Werringer, who operated the Greenback copper mine nearby. A short time later it reverted to its old name.

In the Tehachapi area was to be found the John Moore Brite family, which moved into the area in 1854, building the first house. Brite had five sons who eventually owned most of Brite, Bear, and Cummings Valleys. They raised cattle, alfalfa, and other grains. G. P. Cuddeback settled in Tehachapi in 1858 and frequently served as a mediator between the local Indians and the settlers. Cuddeback's name became synonymous with cattle raising

in Kern County. Also in the area by 1858 was Josiah Hart, who settled the area known as Hart Flat.

All these families of Kern's mountains still reside in Kern County, many retaining their early names. The mountains of Kern are rich with history and lore, most of which still remains to be discovered.

Kern County has always been agrarian, its occupants growing everything from grain to pistachios. Agriculture in Kern County has been the number one industry since the beginning of the county, with only brief periods under the veil of the mighty oil discoveries. The variety of crops planted and livestock raised is virtually unlimited, making agriculture king in Kern County.

Before the days of Thomas Baker, crops planted by settlers were those needed for their own survival. Still having family farms, the region's agriculture has changed, with megalithic farms producing thousands of acres of crops.

The Yokuts were first to produce crops in Kern County. Harvesters and not farmers, they reaped the abundant seed, roots, and fruit from local plants, especially enjoying one type of wild rice that grew in the area. They hunted game and fished in the valley and gathered acorns in the surrounding mountains. The one thing they did not do, prior to outside intervention, was cultivate the soil.

A young priest from the Mission San Luis Rey, Father José María Zalvidea, is credited with starting the first agricultural practice in the southern valley area. Doing so unknowingly, he taught the Indians how to raise crops of corn, pumpkins, and melons. When many of the Indians fled the Missions to the San Joaquin Valley they brought with them the teachings of Zalvidea, and some seed, planting it where they settled.

Mexicans from the Southland were the first to come to settle Kern County. In the late 1840s, prior to the arrival of the first Americans in the area, they settled in the old Panama area calling it Rio Bravo, what we now call the Kern River. They raised vegetables and cattle as needed on Kern Island in the area of present-day Bakersfield. Edward F. Beale introduced agricultural practices to the Indians at the Tejon early in the 1850s.

Kern County's agricultural start followed somewhat the discovery of gold in the southern Sierra Nevada. In the Kernville area where transportation of produce was difficult, farming was a necessity to keep a sustainable food source nearby. Farmlands were located along the valley floors near the Kern River and other streams. There was also farming in the mountains of the upper Kern. William P. Lynn and John Brite, both of whom have small valleys named after them, were probably the first farmers in the future Kern County, starting their cultivation in the mid 1850s. Many of the early farmers raised wheat, alfalfa, potatoes, and other vegetables and fruits, as well as cattle and sheep.

Bakersfield has long been the center of Kern County's agriculture industry. Innumerable changes have been made in the method of operation of local agriculture, but one thing is constant: agriculture and Bakersfield are inseparably linked.

Prior to the permanent arrival of Thomas Baker in 1863, numerous settlers were living around the present-day Bakersfield area. The late 1840s Rio Bravo settlement at what is now old Panama was fairly self-sustaining long before Baker. Other than transient trappers like Thomas Fitzgerald, early American settlers didn't arrive until around 1859, when the John McCray family moved

into the area just north of Greenfield, introducing short-horned Durham cattle to the area. This allowed interbreeding with the local wild herds, producing a better steer.

By 1860 Thomas Barnes and his family, as well as Wellington Canfield, lived west of old Rio Bravo. Barnes began constructing a ditch for irrigation when the flood of 1862 widened it into a channel of the river. James Harvey Skiles and his family also lived on the south end of Kern Island, further north of the others but southwest of the Gilberts at Reeder Lake. Walker Shirley's family lived east of the Gilberts near the south fork of the Kern River. Other early settlers included James McKenzie, Corbin Wicker's family, Bill Daugherty, Dr. Sparrell W. Woody, Jeff and Jim Harris, Allen Rose, and the Lovelace family. Captain Elisha Stephens settled in the area near present Columbus and Union Avenues on thirty-eight acres, and became the first permanent settler of future Bakersfield.

✦

Kern County was the final home of many early western pioneers including Captain Elisha Stephens, who became the first permanent white resident of what would later become Bakersfield. Stephens moved onto thirty-eight acres near present-day Columbus Street and Union Avenue.

Almost without exception, all of the early settlers planted potatoes, corn, and grain as staple foods. These early plantings were the foundation for some of the largest producing crops in the area. Settlers also had poultry and livestock for both tillage and food.

In 1860 the Rio Bravo Ranch was started by Solomon and Philo Jewett, on the Kern River just outside the mouth of Kern Canyon. It was operated as a sheep ranch, with availability of more than forty thousand acres for grazing. Later, in 1874, it was sold to the Kern County Woolgrowers Association, and then to Louis B. Olcese and Captain John Barker. The ranch continued raising sheep well into the twentieth century. The Jewetts relocated to the area north of present Thirty-fourth Street, where they introduced purebred Merino sheep to Kern County, cross-breeding them with existing flocks. Through their sales, the Jewetts were responsible for improving the quality of flocks throughout the West. Philo Jewett's son, Hugh, became a prominent farmer and philanthropist, and is still remembered by many in Bakersfield.

Colonel Baker purchased Christian Bohna's homestead rights on Kern Island in 1862 for $200 and moved down to the area from Visalia. By that time, Baker was well into a reclamation project in the southern valley, the result of which was the drainage of much of the area's swamplands.

Due to the large number of sheep in the area, numerous French and Spanish Basque families came to the Bakersfield area and became important in its rich agricultural heritage. Names such as Berges, Eyraud, Vieux, Faure, Villard, Bimat, Lambert, Pauly, Mon, Clerou, Iriart, Gerard, Ansolabehere, Bidart, Echenique, Etcheverry, Eyrhabide, Mendiburu, Othart, and Iribarren were the foundation of the Kern County Wool-growers Association.

Cattle were not an uncommon sight in the pre-statehood days. They gathered and grazed around the rivers and lakes of present Kern County. The first recorded integration of pure bred cattle into the Kern Island area was by Alexander McCray, who brought between 150 and 200 head of Durhams (or Shorthorns) from Indiana in 1852. He grazed the cattle

around Kern Island and later drove them up to Poso Creek. The only other cattleman known to be in the southern San Joaquin at that time was David Alexander, who headquartered at San Emigdio. He had twenty thousand head of wild Spanish cattle that ranged over the San Emigdio hills and around the entire Kern Delta. Their cattle interbred, mostly because Alexander had scrawny range cattle. He purchased all of the bull calves of purebred stock from McCray and gradually built up the quality of his herd.

Early cattle ranchers in the valley included Thomas Barnes, who brought forty head of cattle when he settled on Kern Island west of old Panama. Jerry Bush, Ferdinand A. Tracy, and Wellington Canfield ran herds around Jerry's (now Jerry) Slough. The cattle industry grew in the flat lands and soon became one of the mainstays of the Miller & Lux empire, which had land holdings in excess of fifteen million acres through the West. But the largest cattle ranch in the county belonged to Haggin, Tevis, and Carr—the Kern County Land Company. At one time, it owned sixty thousand head of cattle in the county.

Irrigation has been the true reason that agriculture has flourished around Bakersfield and Kern County. What is now Bakersfield was intermittently wet and dry, causing the necessity of creating some type of irrigation system to either bring sorely needed water from the river in dry years, or take it away in

wet years. The first successful system was constructed by Colonel Baker, who had thirty Indian workers put a head gate on the remnant of the old south fork of the Kern River. The south fork, west of the Kern Island Canal, meandered around the large hill and bluffs (Panorama Drive) to the northeast of present-day Bakersfield.

Much of the southwest section of the bluffs above Bakersfield have now been removed and the area leveled, so the topography is considerably changed from its appearance in the 1860s. The Indian crew constructed a levee along a watercourse which become known as the Town Ditch, providing water to occupants of the area. The ditch ran along a southwesterly course, ending south of what is now Brundage Lane and A streets. Secondarily, it provided some overflow relief for the Kern River.

Beginning in the 1880s, water around Bakersfield would become the focus of a legendary legal battle between two giant land holders, Miller & Lux, and Haggin, Tevis, and Carr, later known as the Kern County Land Company. This most historic battle over riparian water rights was to change water law in the western United States. Though the issue has never really been settled, the rights of landholders to water is defined in the Riparian Water Right Law of 1888, and later

what has become known as the Shaw Decree. The issue went all the way to the State Supreme Court and was decided only after all 31 corporations and 58 individuals owning rights on the Kern River agreed to give Henry Miller, whose land the river ran through, one-third of the water from March through August, while allowing the rest to continue downstream for the other parties. George Nickel, Jr., is a descendent of Henry Miller and, over a hundred years later, is still fighting the battle over Kern River water rights.

Cotton, the county's number two crop, traces its roots to James Harvey Skiles, who in 1862 planted a small patch on the Kern River Delta. In 1865 Solomon Jewett planted the first commercial cotton in Kern County. Jewett had the foresight and finances to construct a gin and ship his product to Alameda, where it became the first manufactured cotton material in California.

San Francisco investors were soon hiring Chinese labor to tend valley fields. It was noted in the *Tulare Record* of 1865 that "the lower Kern River is being settled by San Francisco families for cultivation of cotton. Work is being done by Chinese." Jewett imported one ton of cottonseed from Tennessee and a second ton from Sonora, Mexico. He planted over two hundred acres in the area north of today's Thirty-fourth Street.

❖

Artesian wells were a commonplace sight on the ranches of the San Joaquin Valley in the 1880s and 1890s. An artesian belt was located down the middle of the valley. This photo of the Stockton Ranch was taken by Carleton Watkins in 1899.

the merchandising and transportation business of Livermore and Chester, and an improved farm of one thousand acres with tools, teams, and buildings.

The eventual outcome of the company was for it to go under the trusteeship of Celsus Brower and S. J. Lansing to untangle the web of financial dealings. Brower was later to challenge the title of Thomas Baker's property and lose the case. Lansing was the clerk of the Kern Valley Bank, and became famous for robbing the bank (hitting himself in the face, to make it look good) and after being caught, jumping the bail put up by the bank president and Brower. Things just weren't meant to be easy for the early cotton industry.

Fortunately, others took up the slack in the industry when the Cotton Growers Association folded. Haggin, Tevis, and Carr purchased property from the association and continued to grow cotton. In 1885 they decided to import Southern labor as a means of improving local cotton farming. The *St. Louis Chronicle* of November 13, 1885, boasted the fact that F. M. Ownby was in St. Louis on that date arranging to bring to Kern County eleven hundred negroes to work on Haggin and Carr lands. They were to be paid at the rate of twelve dollars per month for men, eight dollars for women, and six dollars for boys and girls. It didn't take long for them to realize that they could earn higher wages, and most took other jobs in Bakersfield and around the state.

Kern County cotton growers have been at the forefront of new developments in the cotton industry. The discovery of the first Acala cotton in 1906 and the subsequent developments of newer strains have kept Kern County's cotton ahead of the game. The Shafter Experiment Farm, which continues to work on improving the old Acala strain and newer strains, has kept Kern County and California among the top cotton-producing regions in the world. Another key to the overall success of the cotton industry was the one-variety cotton law, which was enacted by the California Legislature in 1925. In 1927 the California Cotton Cooperative Association, now Calcot, Ltd., was created by area cotton growers to increase sales and strengthen the cotton market. It continues to operate in an ever-broadening market.

Unfortunately, the experiment failed because of the high cost of transportation to the Bay Area and the severe drop in cotton prices to twenty-five cents, a quarter of its former price.

That wasn't the end of cotton in Kern County, however. In 1871 the California Cotton Growers Association was formed in Bakersfield. It was organized by Julius Chester, Horatio Livermore, and James D. Johnston, with Johnston as secretary and Chester was its first president. The new company was a mechanism for transforming the property of Livermore and Chester into another entity. They stated that the acreage held by the company would be planted in 50 to 100 acres of cotton each, surrounded by hedges of mulberries, with rows of fruit trees.

The association's holdings added up to ten thousand acres. Unfortunately it was mismanaged, and the operation soon failed. In the association's ambitious beginning it purchased property from Livermore and Chester including the townsite of Bakersfield. This included sixteen houses, a large brick store (Livermore and Chester) and warehouse, the motive power and privileges of the Kern Island Irrigation Company's canal, the new flour mill,

Even though the potato industry centers in Shafter, to the north of Bakersfield, it is important to remember that potatoes were planted first in the Bakersfield area around 1860. In 1915 Bakersfield's Yen Ming sold his potato crop for ten thousand dollars through brokers Keester and Smith, getting $1.57 per one hundred pounds. Ming was one of many early Chinese settlers in Bakersfield, coming in 1874 with the Central Pacific Railroad. Ming Avenue is named after him and his fields were located on the site of present-day Valley Plaza Regional Shopping Center. The Kern County potato industry started successfully operating in about 1920 around Shafter, to the north of Bakersfield. Today potatoes are grown throughout the area.

In modern times, there have been two defining eras. One was in the 1930s and 1940s when due to severe weather and soil conditions, thousands of people migrated from the Midwest to California. This was during the time of the Depression, when jobs for locals were scarce. The people who became known as "Arkies" and "Okies" flowed into Kern County in such numbers they had to be housed in camps. From Missouri, Kansas, Oklahoma, Arkansas, Texas, Alabama, Mississippi, and other states they came to Kern County and Bakersfield, and they were willing to work the fields of Kern County and the Central Valley. Though they struggled against the merciless times, many of these migrants became important business people in Bakersfield and Kern County.

The second defining era began in the 1960s, but peaked in the 1970s. This was after the bracero program had ended and Mexican field workers began to organize. The Agricultural Workers Organizing Committee first struck in Delano vineyards for increased wages. They went to Cesar Chavez of the National Farm Workers Association for support. Eventually the two groups joined to become the United Farm Workers. Throughout the 1970s and '80s, the organization was active and responsible for gaining wage and benefit packages for the farm worker. The UFW revolutionized the farm labor industry not only in California but the entire United States. After Chavez died in 1993, his son took over leadership of the UFW. Along with the AFL-CIO, the UFW continues to fight for what it perceives as being equitable work conditions and benefits for its members.

✧

Protestors are seen being taken to the Kern County Courthouse after the Arvin Cotton Riot of 1938, which ended with seventy-two people being charged in district court. The protesters wanted a fair wage for an honest day's work.

With all the agriculture around Bakersfield, Kern County vies with Monterey County for the number three spot in agricultural production in the United States, behind Fresno and Tulare Counties, respectively. Grapes, cotton, citrus, and almonds are the big crops grown on Kern's eight hundred and forty thousand acres of farmland. Additionally, more than two million acres are range land.

Kern is ranked number one in the state in the production of almonds, pistachios, carrots, potatoes, apples, watermelons, sheep, and wool. In 1995 Kern County led the nation in almond, pistachio, and carrot production.

The first fruit mentioned in Kern County's early history was grapes. Notes and papers of Don Pedro Fages refer to the numerous grapevines in the upper San Joaquin Valley in 1772. Geologist William P. Blake, working on the Railroad surveys in the early 1850s, reported as early as 1853 on the valley's grapes. Indeed, the wild grape is responsible for the naming of places like Grapevine Canyon, Grapevine Peak, Grapevine Creek, and the Grapevine itself.

In 1863 Thomas Barnes planted an acre of producing peach trees south of Bakersfield. Various fruit trees had been previously planted in mountain communities, but peaches were the first commercial fruit grown in Kern County by white settlers.

In the 1870s, Simon Wible had planted one hundred and twenty acres of Georgia cling peaches on his land twelve miles west of Bakersfield. In 1880 the Wible Orchards gathered 7,731 boxes of fruit on 23 acres and sold them in the east for $1.40 to $2 a box. Also in the 1870s, noted explorer Alexis Godey planted figs on his 320-acre ranch near San Emigdio. In addition, in the San Emigdio area were orange and lemon trees, planted as early as the 1870s.

Driving along Rosedale Highway, a person can still see the tall palm-lined driveways of the Rosedale Ranch and other ranches on which the English colonists began growing grapes and other fruit trees around 1890.

Though commercial orchards wouldn't be planted for another thirty years, by the 1880s apple orchards were thriving in Tehachapi. Grapes are number one in Kern County today, and citrus (a transplant from Southland urbanization) is number three. Much tree fruit was planted in Kern County Land Company colonies such as Rosedale and Union. Even though the colonies failed, the concept of planting trees for commercial crops did not.

Kern County owes its status as a giant among agricultural counties to the diligence and foresight of its early pioneers and their successors.

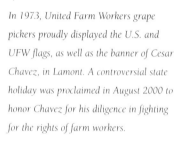

✧

In 1973, United Farm Workers grape pickers proudly displayed the U.S. and UFW flags, as well as the banner of Cesar Chavez, in Lamont. A controversial state holiday was proclaimed in August 2000 to honor Chavez for his diligence in fighting for the rights of farm workers.

EARLY KERN COUNTY TRANSPORTATION

Before the settlement of Kern Island in the 1850s, few ventured west into the area. They did, however, travel along the western foothills of the San Joaquin Valley before 1800. By the 1820s travel along what was called *El Camino Viejo a Los Angeles* (The Old Road to Los Angeles) was becoming more common as refugees from the southern California missions streamed into the valley. The road followed old Indian and game trails and circumnavigated the eastern Temblor Range foothills, running from one water hole to another.

Many would cross into the valley from Pueblo de Los Angeles by way of San Fernando and San Emigdio Canyon into the San Joaquin Valley. The Yokuts Indians of the San Joaquin were peaceful, but travelers, knowing of hostile tribes elsewhere, made the 250-mile trek through the valley in terror. They skirted the Tule Lakes, hiding in the tules by day and traveling by night, using every means to avoid discovery.

Once gold was discovered in California, sections of the road were made usable for wagon transportation. The Hudgins Immigrant Party, given credit for bringing the first vehicles into the San Joaquin Valley from the south, actually reconstructed the old trail.

✧

Workers who built the 1898 San Francisco and San Joaquin Valley Railroad over the Kern River posed for this wonderful image, which shows the rig used to drive pilings into the river bottom.

In the early 1850s Los Angeles was several hundred miles from the southern mines. By the mid-1850s, quite a bit of traffic was crossing the Tehachapi Mountains into the San Joaquin Valley via what was called "New" Tejon Pass, between San Emigdio and Tejon Passes.

In September 1854, the people of Los Angeles raised $6,000 by public subscription for the construction of a wagon road from their city to Fort Tejon, then newly established. Work was completed in December of the same year, with the road leading through San Fernando into Santa Clarita Valley. It passed through San Francisquito Canyon to Elizabeth Lake, then by way of Crane Lake (now Quail Lake) to Gorman Station and Tejon Pass.

The Los Angeles and Stockton Road skirted the eastern foothills of the Sierra Nevadas, going around the swampy lowlands such as Kern Island. The road crossed the Kern River at Gordon's Ferry and the Kings River at Poole's Ferry (later known as Smith's Ferry). The

Indians of the valley were controlled by federal troops, and those remaining were placed in reservations such as that of the Sebastian Reservation in Tejon Canyon. Construction of Fort Tejon in Grapevine began in August of 1854. Transportation of a commercial nature began moving northward to the fort and soon into the San Joaquin Valley to serve the Kern River mines.

In 1854 Los Angeles businessmen David W. Alexander and Phineas Banning operated a stage and freight business between San Pedro and Los Angeles. By January 1855 they advertised stage and freight service between San Pedro and the Sebastian Indian Reservation. They also falsely advertised that their stages went to the Kern River gold mines, when in fact they dumped their passengers off quite a distance from the diggings.

There was stage service to the mines in the early 1860s by way of Visalia, and the mail was delivered by riders who traveled between Los Angeles and Visalia round about through

Keyesville. Keyesville was a booming mining town near the junction of the two forks of the Kern River.

The first mountain roads were generally constructed on natural trails that had been traversed for years by native inhabitants. A number of these roads were built by individuals as toll roads. One such road was the McFarlane Toll Road, completed by Andy McFarlane in 1864. It crossed Greenhorn Mountain between Glennville and the Kern River Valley. It replaced the old Bull Road, built years before to accommodate the oxen used in freighting. Another important early road was "Baker Grade," built by Colonel Thomas Baker from near Caliente Creek below what is now Bena, up the Walker Creek into Walker Basin. This allowed freighting between the San Joaquin Valley and Kern's county seat, Havilah. It also connected with the old road into Havilah and the Kern River mines. That road descended from the mountains east of Baker's road, through White Wolf Grade into what is now the Arvin area, a road still in use today as a county road.

On modern maps "Tollgate Canyon" serves to mark the general course of a road built in the mid-1860s from near Tehachapi to Loraine on Caliente Creek. The county seat and Kernville were linked with Linn's Valley by a good stage road when the McFarlane Toll Road was built.

The need for a state highway down the San Joaquin Valley was projected in the 1850s. Baker eventually ended up holding the Montgomery patent that originally stipulated that those recovering the swamp lands were obligated to build a canal system capable of floating eighty-ton steamers from San Francisco Bay to Kern Lake. Not only that, but they were to place a two hundred-foot right-of-way along the canal to permit a portion to be used as a public highway.

In September 1857 a group of New Yorkers, with John Butterfield among them, organized, and a year later the Overland Mail Company began operation with a federal subsidy to support passenger and mail service between the Mississippi and San Francisco. In August 1858, stages were running on the road between Los Angeles and San Francisco. Leaving Los Angeles, the stages reached Fort

Tejon on the route taken earlier by the Alexander and Banning wagons. Moving north, they descended into the valley via Grapevine Canyon, turning northeast through the Sinks of the Tejon to Gordon's Ferry on the Kern River. The stage then crossed through the low foothills and the plains to Visalia. It then turned northwest to Whitmore's Ferry on the Kings River, Firebaugh's Ferry on the San Joaquin, and over Pacheco Pass to Gilroy. By May 1860 Concord stages were running the route between San Jose and Visalia.

In May 1860, John Butterfield, president of the company, was succeeded by William B. Dinsmore, who operated the company in the San Joaquin Valley until April 1861, when it ceased to run in the Valley.

Later in the 1860s, when the local livestock men were discouraging settlement in the valley, an agricultural community was growing along the lower Kern River. Bakersfield was emerging as a commercial trading center in the southern valley.

In April 1870 Horatio P. Livermore and Julius Chester began operating a wagon line between Bakersfield and White River, connecting with the Telegraph Stage Company's line running between Visalia and the Kern River mines. By March 1871, they began stage service between Bakersfield and Visalia by way of a new, more direct road.

✧

The Southern Pacific roundhouse and yard located in East Bakersfield as seen in 1940. Notice the plume of smoke and steam coming from the locomotives.

George W. Andrews, who operated stages between Los Angeles and Havilah, rerouted them through Fort Tejon and Bakersfield in May 1871. Entering the valley, the stages traveled north through the Hudson and Rosemyre Ranches (Rose Station), Adobe Station, and then to Bakersfield. At Bakersfield they turned southeast, going up Baker Grade to Walker Basin, turning north to Havilah.

By July 1872 the southbound construction of the Southern Pacific Railroad had reached Tipton, twenty miles south of Visalia. Now the owners of the Telegraph Stage Company developed plans to extend their operations to Los Angeles, purchasing Livermore and Chester's operation. The company's General Manager Amos O. Thoms began stage service to Los Angeles through Fort Tejon, Elizabeth Lake and San Fernando, continuing to send stages from Visalia to the Kern River mines through Linn's Valley. A new line was inaugurated to Lone Pine and the eastern mines from Bakersfield through Baker Grade to Havilah and Kernville.

In July 1873 partner Henry M. Newhall had enough of the stage company and sold his interest to William Hamilton. Hamilton and co-owner William G. Roberts shared the management of the company, providing regular delivery of the mails.

With the loss of mail contracts, the Telegraph Stage Company was divided into three parts in a sellout in June 1874. Cyrus H. Cotter bought the stages and the route connecting the Southern Pacific railheads at Delano and San Fernando. William Buckley purchased the line between Bakersfield and Lone Pine, and John Aliman bought the service between Visalia and Kernville.

The construction on the Southern Pacific from the north, brought the railhead to Bakersfield in the fall of 1874, with the line running to Caliente by April 1875. The trains were running to Caliente, at the foot of Tehachapi Pass. Bakersfield lost two stage lines with this occurrence, but it was felt that the railroad made up for the loss of stage service. The stage did continue to operate to Tehachapi and over the hill through Oak Creek Pass. William Buckley's stages to Havilah and Lone Pine ran over the newly built road to Walker Basin.

By July 1876, the Southern Pacific Railroad Company completed its construction up Tehachapi Pass and over the hill to Mojave. This was the beginning of the end of the era of stage operation in Bakersfield. Minor companies operated between Bakersfield and the mountain communities, but no longer would there be the bouncing and swaying of the Concords and mud wagons through Bakersfield.

In the early 1850s the United States Congress sent out exploration parties to survey and map out the best routes for a railroad line from the Mississippi River to California. The surveyors entered the San Joaquin Valley in

1853, mapping the way for the initial route. The R. S. Williamson party was responsible for surveying and mapping out the southern San Joaquin Valley. As this work proceeded Williamson made a brief examination of the mountain passes which led eastward out of the San Joaquin Valley.

The party explored Walker Pass through Kern River Canyon, which he called "the worst of all known passes in the Sierra Nevada." Williamson also surveyed Tejon Pass but condemned this too, saying its only claim to merit was that it was not quite so impracticable as Walker Pass. San Francisquito and Grapevine Canyons, both of which open into Tejon Pass, were also considered possibilities. These were found to be impractical. In the end, Williamson recommended that the railroad builders utilize either the Tehachapi or Grapevine Canyon.

It was ten years before the plan for a transcontinental railroad was placed into the hands of the engineers. President Abraham Lincoln signed the Pacific Railroad Bill, authorizing the construction of two separate railroads. The Union Pacific started in Omaha and went to the eastern California border. The Central Pacific built eastward from Sacramento across the Sierras. The Central Pacific was to play a key role in the development of the San Joaquin Valley and Bakersfield.

The CP was owned by four giants of early California industry. Leland Stanford was president; Collis P. Huntington, vice-president; Mark Hopkins acted as treasurer; and James Bailey as secretary. Charles Crocker was the real power of the railroad. Huntington, Stanford, Hopkins, and Crocker made up what was called "the Big Four." The railroad's chief engineer was Theodore B. Judah.

The question of why businessmen would risk huge investments on a railroad when none existed is answered simply: government subsidy. The United States government granted huge amounts of land for railroad use throughout the Sierra Nevada and California. Counties and cities granted land, bonds, and cash to the railroad. The concept was soundly backed from the start. The Big Four took a minimum risk, which made them even greater multi-millionaires.

In 1867, it was announced that a new railroad, the Southern Pacific, would build a railroad through the San Joaquin Valley, and across the desert via Tehachapi Pass. Curiously, the same partners who controlled the Central Pacific also ran the Southern Pacific. This, of course, created a rail monopoly in California. In the then-new small town of Bakersfield, community leaders were planning for the day when the railroad arrived.

The construction of the line down the valley and into Kern County was a jerky proceeding. By 1873 track had been laid only as far as Tipton in the southern part of Tulare County, and, so far as anyone could tell, this was to be the end of the line. However, by July 1873 work continued until the line reached a point four miles below the Kern-Tulare border. Once again, all were convinced that Delano was the end of the line.

Work on the tracks did continue, however, and by the summer of 1874 the line had reached the Kern River. Here the line stalled again until a bridge could be built. Passengers unloaded on the north side of the river and were transported into Bakersfield by wagon or other conveyance.

Numerous problems existed in building the line through Bakersfield, not the least of which was the refusal of the town to grant a two-block right of way or to come up with financial incentives. Interestingly, in the days after

✧

The Tehachapi Loop, constructed in 1876, is an engineering landmark that allowed Kern County farms and oil companies to transport commodities over the Tehachapi Mountains to the rest of the United States.

A simple dirt road leads through Grapevine Pass (far right) in 1912. Imagine traveling this route and how long trips to the Southland took to complete.

Baker's death, when other "big shots" were controlling the interests of the town, the railroad surveyed its line across Ellen Baker's cotton farm northeast of town. Through that property they laid their line straight into a new community of their own, named Sumner.

The Southern Pacific claimed that the line was built to avoid the risk of washouts and to gain the best possible location for a bridge to cross the river. If the line had been kept on that elevation, it would not have been practical to run directly into Bakersfield. The location of the proposed railroad town was at a higher elevation than Bakersfield, thus avoiding the recurring flooding of the Kern River.

Before the middle of 1874, the railway had laid out the town of Sumner, begun selling lots, and established its station. It had already started on its way up the hill toward Greenwich (west of Tehachapi) and Tehachapi. The main construction camp east of Bakersfield was Caliente, which became the base camp for the entire effort up the hill.

The Southern Pacific Depot was not initially constructed. A building on the northwest corner of Baker and Sumner Streets was used as a depot. This later became solely a telegraph office and was demolished in the early 1970s.

The first permanent railroad building to be constructed on the site was the machine shop, with ground being broken on July 21, 1888. The shop was at that time one of the largest on the West Coast. On October 1, 1888, as soon as the shop was completed, construction of the depot and hotel began. Bricks for both projects were furnished by Curran and Swan (predecessor to Sandstone Brick). Work continued for nine months, and the hotel and depot opened on June 27, 1889. E. G. Ashmun, formerly of the Mojave Railroad House, was manager of the hotel.

The Southern Pacific Depot and Hotel building was constructed at the corner of Baker and Sumner Streets. Several remodels have taken place to alter its original Richardsonian Romanesque architecture, including work in 1895 upon the nearing of the completion of the San Francisco and San Joaquin Valley Railroad (1898), and again in 1941. In one sense, the building is an architectural disaster. It is a combination of several different architectural styles including Richardsonian Romanesque, Spanish Colonial Revival, and Moderne. The roofline and arcade are the only elements that have original architecture somewhat intact. It is, however, still the most elegant depot in the southern valley, and one of only a few remaining.

The Southern Pacific Depot and Hotel was constructed in 1888-89 as a result of the expansion of the valley line. In 1888 the Southern Pacific Company expanded into the east side of the San Joaquin Valley, establishing a line from Fresno to Porterville and then on to the main line. That year, the Southern Pacific Company established the east side line, which ran through the towns of Dinuba, Kaweah, Exeter, Lindsay, and Porterville. Continuing pressure from the citizens and business people utilizing the Southern Pacific Depot in Sumner and the need to create a yard closer to the Tehachapi Loop caused the company to expand finally its facilities in the Bakersfield area.

East Bakersfield began as the town of Sumner in 1874, when the Southern Pacific Railroad bypassed Bakersfield with its line from the north. Sumner, named after Charles Sumner, an influential senator from Massachusetts, was soon to become a thriving village, nearly destroying the commercial trade in Bakersfield. Though commercial and

passenger traffic commenced in 1874, it was not until 1876 that the Southern Pacific linked its line over the Tehachapi Mountains with the main line to Los Angeles.

Sumner was laid out with all lots being 25-by-150, and it wasn't long until it had a substantial population. By 1883 it had two hotels, six saloons, two restaurants, and three stores. It also had a livery and feed stable, a barber, a blacksmith, a post office, a telegraph office, and an express office. In 1893 Sumner was officially incorporated as Kern, which it remained until its consolidation into Bakersfield in 1909. Familiar names of additions to Kern City include the 1893 Bernard Addition to the north, the 1893 and 1901 Drury Additions to the northeast, and the 1907 Ardizzi-Olcese Addition in the lower La Cresta area.

Twenty-two years of transportation dominance by the Southern Pacific would end with one of the biggest celebrations in Bakersfield's history. It took place on May 27, 1898 and commemorated the arrival of the "People's Railroad" and its first steam passenger train.

The San Francisco and San Joaquin Valley Railroad connected Stockton with Bakersfield, its southern terminus. The difficult engineering feat of tunneling through the Contra Costa Hills to connect the railroad from Bakersfield to the port of Richmond near San Francisco wasn't completed until after 1898. By this time, the Santa Fe Railroad had openly taken over the line.

It seems odd that a second rail line would be built into the southern San Joaquin Valley, as the Southern Pacific Railroad already provided services to the area. However, the Southern Pacific had a habit of gouging the farmers and merchants with exorbitant fees for shipping on their line. The Southern Pacific was also known to have a controlling interest in California politics.

In San Francisco there was determined opposition to the Southern Pacific Railroad by the Traffic Association of California dating back to 1891. Its members were quite aware of the risky nature of their purpose, and they were determined to fight the Southern Pacific Railroad's monopoly.

Fund collections were begun in 1893 to build the San Francisco and San Joaquin Valley Railroad, but true funding didn't begin until 1894. New shareholders, including Claus Spreckels, joined the effort to bring affordable transportation to the valley. Spreckels had a great deal at stake with his agricultural and manufacturing holdings, and he showed his interest with enough investment money to push the project forward.

With enough subscriptions toward the project, and with William B. Storey as chief engineer, ground was broken at Stockton on July 22, 1895. This marked the beginning of the railroad, which was to terminate in Bakersfield.

As the railroad got closer to completion, the Southern Pacific reduced its rates on freight and passenger service, added train service, and arranged for more convenient schedules. They even cleaned up the area around their depot, and put on a flyer, or fast passenger train, between San Francisco and Bakersfield.

✧

In the 1920s advertisements for the Lebec Hotel pointed out that the hotel was three hours from Los Angeles and boasted of visitors from every state in the Union.

On May 9, 1898, work on the final section of the valley road was begun. Track followed in the next few days to the end of the franchise's right of way, just east of Q Street.

The Santa Fe Railroad actually fronted the railroad and soon bought out its stock. The Santa Fe Railroad served Bakersfield for nearly one hundred years, using the city as the southern hub of its transportation system until the 1970s, when operations shifted east to the large automated Barstow switching yard. In 1994 the Burlington Northern merged with the Santa Fe Railroad, and operations again shifted away from Bakersfield. The Santa Fe tracks to the north of the city currently serve freight and Amtrak passenger service.

The McKittrick Sunset Railroad to the west side oil fields was constructed in 1892 and 1893 to McKittrick under an agreement between the Southern Pacific Railroad and the partnership of Solomon Jewett and Hugh Blodget. Jewett and Blodget were to secure the right of way lands, and the railroad was to build the railroad. They also guaranteed sufficient business to pay the operating expenses. The Standard Asphalt Company was formed, and both were equal partners. The railroad agreed to construct the rail line to haul the asphalt and other oil products from the west side area. The line was to initially run to McKittrick, which it did in 1893. Then it was to be extended to Sunset to handle the Jewett and Blodget oil. Unfortunately the Great Panic of 1893 caused the demand for the asphalt and other oil products to dwindle. The partnership was dissolved and the railroad retained the railroad line to its terminus in

McKittrick. In 1901 the line was extended west to Olig.

By 1902 Solomon Jewett, Hugh Blodget, L. P. St. Clair, C. N. Beal, and F. T. Worff incorporated as the Sunset Railroad Company, and Beal managed to coerce the Santa Fe Railroad to build a line out to Sunset. By the time all the financing was in place, the Southern Pacific and Santa Fe Railroads made an agreement that they would jointly build and operate all feeder lines that terminated at common points. The road was laid from Gosford and Miller's Siding, later called Buttonwillow, to Asphalto, near McKittrick.

The Sunset Western Railroad was another branch railroad running to the Midway area of Kern's oil fields. By 1908 the line was being constructed by both the Southern Pacific and the Santa Fe Railroads, with its beginning west of Bakersfield at Pentland near Hazelton. The line was laid into the west side to Moro, later to become Taft. It was then run up to a siding at Fellows. Later it was extended south as more oil was discovered on the west side. The Sunset Western and the Sunset Railroad were merged in 1912 into the Sunset Railroad.

The Southern Pacific ran another line into the east side of the San Joaquin Valley in the late 1880s. This line brought east side produce to markets across the nation and was completed to Spottiswood (originally Poso, now Famoso) in 1890. The Arvin branch was a spur line run off the Southern Pacific tracks with construction beginning in 1923 at Magunden. Arthur J. McFadden laid out Lamont on this line, and the line was completed to Arvin in December 1923. The Arvin district was then ready to compete with the outside markets.

LAND AND WATER DEVELOPMENT

The tale of Kern County's rich history would not be complete without a discussion of its early land and water development. In the days before Kern was a county, the area was thought to be a swampy marshland, rife with mosquitoes and disease. The first to truly realize the opportunity offered by the Kern River Delta was Thomas Baker, who is said to have been Kern's first land owner in the valley to hold more land than he needed to supply his own living by farming it.

In Tulare County, old timers and their descendants alike credit Baker with laying out the town of Visalia for Nathaniel Vice, its credited founder. In 1855, Baker was elected to the California State Assembly representing Tulare County, serving in 1856. He was also appointed receiver for the United States Land Office by President James Buchanan, serving during his term. In 1861 he was elected to represent Tulare and Fresno Counties in the state senate, serving in the session of 1861. During this time period, Baker had the opportunity to observe the land and settlement opportunities of the southern San Joaquin Valley.

In 1856 Baker was involved in a legislative act that created an opportunity to reclaim swamp and overflow lands in the southern valley. Eventually known as the Montgomery Act, it offered the right to reclaim all the swamp and overflow lands belonging to the state located in the San Joaquin Valley. For the reclamation work, the contractors would be deeded a percentage of the recovered land. This act would later become the basis of Baker's activities in the southern San Joaquin Valley. In 1857, Captain Elisha Stephens first took Baker and his son James to the Kern Island area. Though not the original contractor for the project, Baker and a partner, Harvey S. Brown, purchased the rights to fulfill the contract. Baker then moved onto Kern Island in 1863, having purchased Christian Bohna's property in what is now downtown Bakersfield.

Although normally a swampy area, by 1864 the southern San Joaquin Valley was suffering from the worst drought since California was settled by Americans. Baker was able to construct a dam across the outlet of Buena Vista Lake to control the flow of water. The area further dried up in the summer of 1865 due to the lack of rain as well as the construction of several irrigation ditches that had diverted much water from Kern, Buena Vista, and Tulare Lakes. After inspection of the drainage by the state, Baker was issued a patent for just over eighty-seven thousand acres of land

✧

This 1895 image of Buena Vista Lake's Pelican Island illustrates the abundance of wildlife that was commonplace in the southern San Joaquin Valley.

✧

The pelts seen hanging on this hunter's shack show the amount of game found near Buena Vista Lake at the turn of the century.

in Kern, Tulare, and Fresno Counties, his part of the reclaimed land under the agreement.

He laid out what would become the town of Bakersfield in 1868. It was situated mostly on Baker's land, although by that time he had already sold much of what would become downtown Bakersfield. Baker continued in his endeavors to bring settlers into the area by selling his land at rock bottom prices, sometimes giving it away.

In 1869, he ran again for the state senate but was defeated. He then turned his attention to the settlement of Bakersfield, opening a real estate office in town. He also built several city facilities including a flour mill and brick works, the latter of which he didn't live to see in operation.

In November 1872, an epidemic of typhoid fever ravaged Bakersfield, and among the first stricken was the sixty-two-year-old Baker. Upon his death from pneumonia, all activity ceased in the stunned community he had founded until after his funeral. He was buried in what later became Union Cemetery, on land he donated.

Unfortunately for the first settlers on lower Kern River, the period during which they settled was one of the wettest times on the delta. The winters between 1849 and 1860 were seasons of extremely heavy rainfall. Although there were some drier years, the massive rainfall in other years more than made up for the lost precipitation. The sloughs and swamps remained full of stagnant water. Then came two comparatively dry winters.

During these dry years the Bohna, Fried, Woody, and other families arrived in the delta area where Bakersfield is located. In 1861-2, they were flooded out, and some families left the area for higher ground.

Several ditches existed prior to the 1862 flood, but most were washed away at that time. In the Kern Delta, Baker constructed the Town Ditch to create a system of water delivery for the community. This ditch ran from the old south fork channel, its head gate near where Thirty-second Street would cross the channel, just west of what is now Union Avenue. It ran a bit southwest, eventually crossing Brundage Lane about three hundred feet west of A Street.

The main waterway through the Bakersfield area was Panama Slough. It was formed during the flood of 1862 and ran diagonally through what is now downtown Bakersfield. It left the old south fork channel north of the town ditch, passing near the north end of Jewett Lane. Once reaching the Twenty-third and L Street area, it turned down present-day Twenty-third Street, making a southwest jog at D Street. The slough ran diagonally through what is now being called, though a misnomer, Old Westchester. It continued south close to the intersection of Twenty-first and D Streets and backed up into a body of water commonly called Reeder Lake, around Cedar and Eighteenth streets. The Old River channel, or Panama Slough, was used into the twentieth century for irrigation. It continued south past the present community of Old River.

The Old River channel entered Kern Slough, which connected Kern and Buena Vista Lakes, midway between the two bodies of water. Agriculture and development have destroyed the remains of the channel. In places there were remnants of the Indian population in the area. Mortars, pestles, and other artifacts used to be discovered along the old channels with some frequency. Now it's all gone.

Baker constructed the old Mill Ditch, which was actually east of the old south fork, quite a bit north of the town ditch. It ran down to the millpond between Seventeenth Street and Railroad Avenue (Truxtun) at R Street. Here the first Kern River Flour Mill was later built.

The network of sloughs that laced Kern Island (Bakersfield) in every direction were filled almost year-round with stagnant water.

This was thought to pollute the drinking water, which came from wells. Most of these wells were shallow, less than ten to fifteen feet deep.

In the early 1870s Bakersfield's water was hauled from wells dug on higher ground at the Bull residence in what was then called Sumner, now East Bakersfield. Since the water was better from the "hill" it was transported into Bakersfield by A. P. Bernard's hack. He had his drivers haul water in ten-gallon cans for regular customers in Bakersfield. Drinking water cost twenty-five cents per delivered can. This continued until as late as the 1880s.

By the time of his death in 1872, Baker had sold nearly all his land, leaving Beale's expansive ranchos obtained from Mexican land grants, Fremont's Rancho San Emigdio, and the holdings of Livermore and Chester as the only large land holdings prior to the rise and expansion of what became known as the Kern County Land Company, the Tejon Land and Cattle Company, and Miller and Lux.

Once mining waned in Kern's mountains, it was inevitable that there would be growth in the delta. By the mid-1870s, two large companies had been formed, and the struggle for the control of Kern River water was at hand.

By 1874 James Ben Ali Haggin, a San Francisco capitalist, had a firm hold in the county. He purchased what was called the Galtes Tract, which was fifty-two thousand acres of prime bottom lands in the Kern Delta. Haggin formed the Bellevue and McClung Ranches on this property. He then purchased large tracts of land around Kern and Buena Vista Lakes, getting them for nearly nothing due to the threat of malaria in the area.

Three years later, through his connections with the Southern Pacific Railroad, W. B. "Billy" Carr joined Haggin and became active in obtaining railroad lands. The referral to Haggin and Carr is a bit of a misnomer as truly it should be called Haggin, Tevis, and Carr. Lloyd Tevis, a San Franciscan, was actually a full partner, and Billy Carr appears to have held a lesser interest in the company. But in the formative days of the company, Carr played an important role in building the empire. Later, after the water wars, when William S. Tevis was coming into power, Carr was forced out of the company.

The cheaply bought railroad land became the basis of the great land holdings of Haggin & Carr. Livermore and Chester came into their land by buying up swamp lands from Baker's Montgomery patents, lands which Colonel Baker had earlier sold at ridiculously low prices. Within a year or two it had become obvious to all that there was no love lost between the two groups. It was a natural enmity, as both sought to control land in Kern County.

The importance of water in Kern County cannot be overstated. Crops will not grow on Kern County's semi-arid land unless there is water with which to irrigate. Although problems arose from time to time between the large land-holders, it took the drought of 1877 to bring it to a head. Livermore and Chester, who did business as the Kern Island Canal Company, tried to assure themselves of sufficient water for their lands by putting up a shaky dam across the Kern River bed at the foot of the bluffs, just north of Bakersfield. Small farmers reacted strongly to this, and Haggin and his fellow entrepreneurs took full advantage of their resentment. Haggin fought along side the small farmers appearing to help them. Meanwhile, work on the dam continued and lawsuits and bitter arguments interrupted its progress. Finally the dam was blown up, although the perpetrators of the explosion were never apprehended.

Livermore and Chester ended up in financial failure and hoped to rescue the company

✧

Friant-Kern Canal excavation and lining equipment of Peter Kiewet Sons Co. are seen in this May 6, 1947, photograph. The trimming machine seen here was used to build the canal, weighed approximately 130 tons, and was eighty feet wide at the top.

operation by selling land tracts to prospective colonists. These contained forty to eighty acres and were located on Kern Island, but the effort would be of no value to them. Celsus Brower made the first satisfactory plan for the colonization of the county as selling agent. However, this too was short-lived as Haggin & Carr bought up the remainder of Livermore's and his new partner J. H. Reddington's holdings in 1879.

Prior to obtaining the land of Livermore and Reddington, Haggin and Carr had gotten control of smaller, unincorporated canal companies that had rights to the water of Kern River. They also filed for whatever swamp lands remained available from the state, and started reclamation of almost fifty thousand acres of unwatered lands to the north and west of Bakersfield. This land became part of the area known as the Rosedale District. They had a plan to colonize that district, which it was to receive its water supply from a large irrigation system,

which was installed. However, the actual colonization plan ran afoul amidst questions of the legality of the means by which the land was obtained in the first place. This caused the activity to cease and not be resumed until 1891.

At a time when the most effusive land acquisition was occurring, Haggin and Carr were very active. They were always in the news and operated in a brasher manner than did their eventual nemesis, Henry Miller. While Haggin and Carr were in the public eye, busily engaged in acquiring as much land as possible along the south side of Kern River, the determined Miller, through his agent J. C. Crocker, was buying up thousands of acres further to the north and west. As far back as 1873, Miller experimented in the raising of alfalfa, then a crop not well known to grain farmers (even though the first alfalfa in Kern County was grown by Thomas Barnes in 1863).

Miller came to California several years prior to the gold rush directly from Germany. Upon arriving in San Francisco in 1849, he went to work as a butcher, his former trade. By 1852, he met another youthful butcher, Charles Lux, and their friendship eventually formed one of the largest land holding companies in the Unites States. They started as a retail meat business, and then changed to wholesale. This led them to look for their own cheap land on which they could raise the beef and lamb they were selling.

They plowed their receipts back into the business, immediately reinvesting earnings throughout the west in land, slaughterhouses, butcher shops, banks and hotels. Their holdings were so vast it was said that Miller & Lux could round up a market-bound herd of cattle on their Arizona acreage and drive them

✧

Above: Tule Elk once roamed the southern San Joaquin Valley, but were hunted to near extinction. The elk population has increased dramatically since the creation of the Tule Elk State Reserve.

Below: Land giant Miller & Lux Company built more than just offices in their town of Buttonwillow. Also seen in this 1920 photograph are the general store, water storage district office, barbershop, and a place to wet your whistle.

to the Oregon border, camping on their own land every night of the journey.

Miller & Lux had one very inflexible rule: Never sell any of the land. At one time, they held nearly twenty-three thousand square miles (over 14.5 million acres) of land and were able to pay the property taxes by making their other investments profitable. It was stocked with 150,000 head of cattle and 100,000 sheep, operated by hundreds of superintendents, with the number of vaqueros in the thousands.

Charles Lux died in 1877, but Henry Miller lived until 1916. Much of the Miller & Lux Company lands were sold off soon after. The premier parcel was the large area of the company's Buttonwillow tract. In 1929 the company sold 115,000 acres of the 187,000 they held in the San Joaquin Valley.

Livermore and Haggin were battling it out in Bakersfield while Miller & Lux quietly purchased west side land. When Livermore's Kern Valley Water Company was dissolved, Miller & Lux obtained its holdings including a multi-ditched canal system covering one hundred thousand acres on the western border of the swamp lands. Two of Livermore and Chester's top executives, S. W. Wible and Celsus Brower, resigned to go with Miller & Lux. Wible was made general superintendent for Miller & Lux.

When the irrigation of the Rosedale acreage began with water diverted from the Kern River into Haggin, Tevis,m and Carr's recently constructed Calloway Canal, the lower forks of the river nearly dried up. The downstream holdings of Miller & Lux were left without surface water. This was the foundation of the issue of the great water suit that, when finally agreed upon in the Shaw Decree, has truly never been settled.

The two monoliths of the Kern River Country squared off against each other in court and left no stone unturned. They showed no mercy, and with great craft, worked behind the scenes on politicians and anyone else who could influence the outcome. This was probably the most vicious civil suit seen in the county, with Miller & Lux as the plaintiff, and Haggin & Tevis as the defendant. The plaintiff's case was based on the ancient and honored riparian laws found

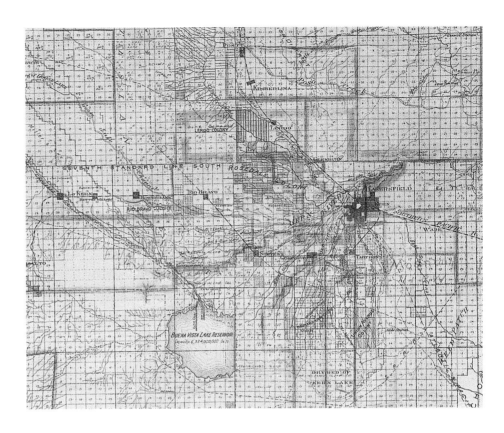

in English Common Law. This doctrine assumes that brooks, creeks and rivers are valuable only for waterpower, navigation, or personal pleasure. Any additional use to which waterways might conceivably be put was declared a misuse. Those residing along the shores of a natural water course were privileged to have the stream flow past the property undiminished in volume, save for domestic uses and watering stock, and unimpaired in quality by any person or persons living above him.

Were the doctrine to have been left standing, Miller & Lux, with their holdings along the mouth of the Kern River, would have owned water rights to the river. Haggin, Tevis, and Carr claimed the right of "first appropriation," a law they claimed was in effect in California prior to that immediate period. English Common Law was designed for the streams of England, but was unsuited to California, where there is almost no navigation on its small streams. The laws were especially unsuited where the most important use of the water would be farm irrigation.

Judge Benjamin Brundage had jurisdiction over the original suit. On November 3, 1881, Brundage handed down his decision favoring Haggin, Tevis, and Carr. Miller & Lux

✦

Buena Vista Lake, at one time, was among the largest lakes in the western United States. During wet seasons it would merge with the smaller Kern Lake to the east, forming a huge body of water.
COURTESY OF GREG IGER.

immediately appealed and, at the same time, began campaigning to bring about Brundage's defeat for another term of office.

On October 27, 1884, the Supreme Court of California handed down its momentous decision establishing the English interpretation of riparian rights as the governing factor for preempting the flow of natural waterways. With the first Supreme Court decision handed down, the issue still wasn't settled. The rights of landholders to water were again defined in the Riparian Water Right Law of 1888 and, later, the Shaw Decree.

The battle between the two Kern County giants was long and difficult. It became apparent that to continue the legal battle would result in nothing but bankruptcy for both, so compromise was necessary. On July 28, 1888, an agreement was signed with Miller & Lux that guaranteed one-third of the run-off of the Kern River from the months of March to August, inclusive, and Haggin & Tevis received the remainder. The agreement ultimately was legally ratified and has become California law.

In 1928 the citizens of California voted on an amendment to restore to the state all waters in excess of those actually used beneficially by riparian owners. Further water efforts to satisfy the needs of California and Kern County have shaped today's water image.

To protect bottomlands from flood, levees had been constructed. In May 1884, it was a Haggin & Tevis levee that broke, releasing a torrential flood that reclaimed the beds of both Kern and Buena Vista Lakes. A small area of

land in the Buena Vista Lake bed belonged to Henry Miller, who quickly invoked the newly handed-down doctrine of riparian rights, obtaining an injunction forbidding the repair of the broken levee. The rationale was it would allow the water of Kern River to flow past his property unimpaired in quantity. Legal minds throughout California tried in vain to win a decision favorable to their clients, and five hundred men worked around the clock trying to replace the flood-wrecked dam, but could not manage to get up a structure strong enough to stem the flood waters. In the end, Haggin & Tevis finally yielded their choice bottomlands.

With the water rights issue behind them, Haggin, Tevis, and Carr returned to their colonization efforts in the county. They hoped to recover at least a part of the huge expenditures from the legal battles. Haggin was somewhat of an idealist in the colonization effort and thought they should not only sell land to would-be settlers, but also instruct them as to the crops and methods of farm operation best suited to the San Joaquin Valley.

S. W. Fergusson was made manager for the company, and, as a result, several colonies were formed including Union Avenue, Lerdo, Rosedale, and Mountain View. The most active were Union Avenue and Rosedale. The other two were eventually sold off for other colonization efforts. The Rosedale Colony consisted mostly of

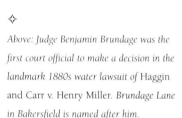

Above: Judge Benjamin Brundage was the first court official to make a decision in the landmark 1880s water lawsuit of Haggin and Carr v. Henry Miller. *Brundage Lane in Bakersfield is named after him.*

Below: The Souther Ditch Plow, once the largest plow in the world, pulled by eighty oxen, was commissioned to be built to dig the Kern Island Canal by Horatio Livermore. The plow is currently being restored at the Kern County Museum.

truck farmers and remittance men from England. Many toiled at their land, eking out a meager living. Families came and went, but many of the early Rosedale settlers are still there.

Rosedale Colony was not a success because it was too far from the markets for colonists' crops. Settlers were willing enough to work, but they were unable to overcome the great obstacles placed before them. Eventually the colony plans were abandoned, and the Rosedale colonization idea failed. Once Henry A. Jastro assumed the office of general manager of Kern County Land Company in 1903, its properties, at least for the time being, were taken off the market.

Carr never gave up his expansion ideas and was not happy with the colonization plan. With the pressure from the newly appointed manager, S. W. Fergusson, and Tevis' son William, Carr resigned his post and sold out his interests in the company.

After the Carr separation, Tevis and Haggin reorganized as the Kern County Land Company. It lasted until 1967, when it was sold to Tenneco. Later it was sold to Castle and Cooke, which has developed much of the colony lands southwest of Bakersfield.

Subsequent to the great water wars in the San Joaquin Valley, efforts were made to tame the Kern River. All were futile, and the State of California and the Corps of Engineers, in an effort to quell the raging waters of western rivers, conducted a series of studies. By the 1930s, with the Great Depression raging and massive unemployment, the government created projects for agencies like the Works Project Administration and the Civilian Conservation Corps. It was during this time that massive studies were undertaken to demonstrate whether man-made control of rivers was feasible and was an effective method of flood control.

The construction of the Isabella Dam by the Corps of Engineers culminated years of effort on the part of local interests to control the river. The initial plan for a dam dated back many years and was proposed for the conservation of water. It was not until the 1930s that such a plan was given serious consideration. At that time, a project based on water conservation alone never seemed to be economically justified, but the passage of the 1936 Flood Control Act by Congress made possible the realization of the project. Its major element was now the protection of life and property from hazardous floods.

Prior to the construction of the dam, the strengthening and maintenance of the system of levees to protect the rich urban, agricultural, and industrial properties on the Kern Delta cost millions of dollars and was still inadequate.

The responsibility of maintaining and operating the physical works required to

✧

Frames for the main control gates are seen being installed in the outlet tunnel of Isabella Dam, August 22, 1950. The construction of the dam has spared the residents of Bakersfield and the surrounding areas from countless floods. The dam has also helped to provide a steady flow of water to Kern County's communities and farmlands.

✧

With its massive pumps, the A. D. Edmonston Pumping Plant, part of the California State Water Project, provided the vital link between the California Aqueduct in the San Joaquin Valley and the continuation of the aqueduct into Southern California.

control and utilize the waters of Kern River was a near impossible task without some kind of development of a large regulatory storage area. It was known there was a great topographic basin lying at the junction of the north and south forks of the Kern. This suggested the site for a reservoir of adequate capacity to regulate all floods of the Kern.

There was a twenty-one-year dry cycle (1917-1936) in Kern County, when local residents forgot the danger of floods. They were rudely awakened during the period of years 1937 through 1943, when a series of flash floods and extremely high and long stream flows caused great property loss in Kern and other counties. In 1937 the Corps of Engineers, under authority granted by the 1936 Act, began an investigation of conditions on the Kern River and developed a report completed in 1940. Because of the beginning of World War II, the report was not made public until 1944.

The report disclosed that the heart of the business district of Bakersfield lay seventeen feet below the flood crest of the February 1937 flood. It also indicated in general that an average annual flood control saving of more than $700,000 would result from the construction of the proposed dam. It was also found there was an average benefit of $185,000 to irrigation and existing power facilities. This information was to prove itself once the dam was built, but in 1943 it was estimated that in the Tulare Lake Basin in

Kings County, damage to agriculture due to flooding was estimated at $10 million. The Kern River contributed forty-five percent of the flow causing this damage.

After the filing of the report of the Corps of Engineers in the spring of 1944, Congress included the Isabella Project in the 1944 Flood Control Authorization Act. The first direct appropriations for the project came in the 1948 fiscal year appropriation, when $1.25 million was made available. The Appropriation Act for fiscal year 1949 was finally passed by both houses of Congress containing $2.5 million for the project.

Isabella Dam is a multiple arch reinforced concrete structure approximately 160 feet above the streambed. An auxiliary dam of earthen construction and less height was required to close the gap on the crest of Hot Springs Valley. The Kern River had a variance in its annual flow from nearly two million acre-feet to as little as 185,000 acre-feet. The construction of the works for impounding the run-off of both forks of Kern River initially developed a storage capacity of 570,000 acre feet with a surface area of over one thousand acres. Ground was broken for the dam on May 29, 1948, and it was completed in 1953.

Friant Dam in Fresno County is a part of California's vast Central Valley Project, the state's largest water development. The Central Valley Project extends from the Cascade Range in the north to the semi-arid but highly fertile plains of Kern County in the south. It was created to move water from the northern part of the state where the water supplies are far greater than the requirements, to the water-short San Joaquin Valley.

From the time California achieved statehood in 1850, many studies of ways to develop canals and water exchanges to move water to the San Joaquin Valley had been completed.

As early as the 1870s investigations were made by both the state and federal governments to develop a program coordinating the use of the water resources in the Central Valley. One such study, the Alexander Commission (1873-74), came up with the concept of the Central Valley Project. Numerous investigations led to the establishment of a state legislative committee in 1921 to devise a plan for the solution of the state's water problems.

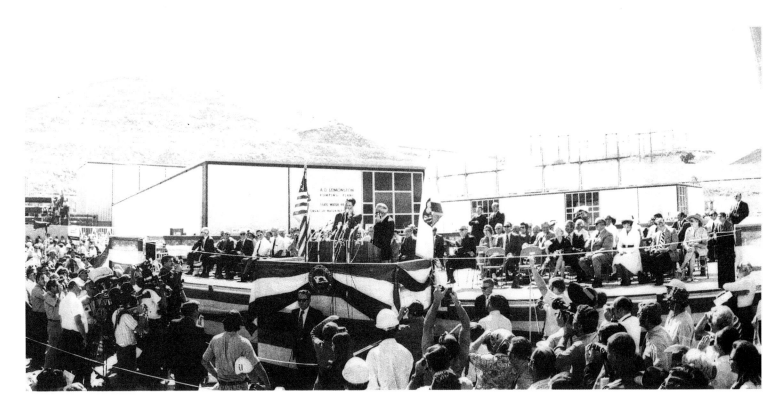

During the following decade both the state and federal governments cooperated in the development of a suitable water program for California. By the 1920s San Joaquin Valley water and farm production conditions were deteriorating because of rapidly declining groundwater resources. To the north, salt water was encroaching on the delta. A federal-state commission in 1931 recommended a solution in the Central Valley Project.

In 1931 the California State Water Plan was adopted. It called for linking many principal CVP features as a comprehensive system. Out of this action came the most complete plan ever devised by any state. From this plan came the program adopted by the state in 1933 for the Central Valley Project. However, California was unable to launch the CVP due to the Depression. In December 1933 a $170-million revenue bond issue was narrowly approved by state voters. However, state efforts to win a large-scale federal grant for the project were unsuccessful, and no market could be found in the depths of the Great Depression for the sale of the state bonds. In 1935 the federal government adopted the program as a project of the United States Department of the Interior's Bureau of Reclamation.

Meanwhile, the federal government became interested in building the Central Valley Project as part of its Depression-era public works program, following the state's basic plan. This time it would be a federal project under the Reclamation Act of 1902.

Initial project features were authorized in 1935-36 by Congress and President Roosevelt and were reauthorized by Congress on August 26, 1937, placing the project under the U.S. Bureau of Reclamation. The 1937 law declared the Central Valley Project's purposes to be improving navigation, regulating river flows, controlling floods, providing for storage and delivery of water, construction of distribution systems, reclamation of arid and semi-arid lands, and power generation.

Among the principal features of the Central Valley Project are Shasta Dam on the Sacramento River and Friant Dam on the San Joaquin River. The diversion of water from the Sacramento Valley to the San Joaquin Valley is accomplished by means of the Delta Cross-Channel. The Contra Costa Canal, Delta-Mendota Canal, Madera Canal, and Friant-Kern Canal serve to distribute the water over the Central Valley. More than 150 miles in length, the Friant-Kern Canal diverts water southward from Friant Dam for use in the southern San Joaquin Valley. Begun in 1945, the Friant-Kern Canal was completed to the Kern River early in 1951.

✧

Governor Ronald Reagan presided over the dedication ceremony of the A. D. Edmondston Pumping Plant, which marked the first time the California State Water Project delivered Northern California water to the thirsty Southland.

The Tracy Pumping Plant and Delta-Mendota Canal were constructed to transfer surplus Sacramento River water 113 miles from the Delta to the San Joaquin River at Mendota Pool, thirty-five miles west of Fresno. The Delta water would then be exchanged for San Joaquin River water diverted at Friant.

The Contra Costa Canal was developed in the north, and the Madera and Friant-Kern Canals were constructed in the San Joaquin Valley. By 1951 the project was fully operational. Several other units were later developed that greatly increased project efficiency.

Because of Friant Dam in Fresno County, the later Terminus Dam on the Kaweah River in Tulare County, and Isabella Dam on the Kern River, flooding has been controlled, and a great deal of damage has been prevented.

Friant Dam's construction was nothing short of a miraculous occurrence for the water-short east side of the San Joaquin Valley. Madera County interests in the late 1880s made the first proposal for a San Joaquin River dam. That plan failed. Beginning in 1915, Madera County irrigation leaders launched an effort to bring San Joaquin River water to its farms. In 1939, under agreement with the government, the Madera Irrigation District presented the site of Friant Dam to the Interior Department.

In Tulare and Kern Counties, much of the Friant-Kern Canal's service area faced a continual water shortage crisis. It had been developed decades earlier into fertile, productive farms. They were plagued by inadequate or non-existent surface water and groundwater supplies, much like the problems experienced by the colonists at the Rosedale Colony years before.

At the dedication of the Friant Dam, Secretary of the Interior Harold Ickes stated the dam was "but a lifeline to preserve and enhance our American civilization. This is a line of creation, built to unlock the fertility of the rich soil, to resist drought, to overcome floods, to provide outdoor recreation, and to generate cheap power that will improve the living conditions of millions of our citizens."

Although all of Ickes' forecasts came true, the area is faced with a problem greater than the mere supply of water. With the political climate in Washington, D.C. focused more toward international trade, the Department of Interior's focus had changed as well. Within the next twenty years, a profound change in the surface water deliveries to the south valley will be seen.

With the introduction of the CALFED project and its many alternate water-use plans, it seems likely that the water users of the Arvin-Edison, Kern River Water, East Niles, and other smaller districts will be making radical adjustments in their water allocations.

Friant Division development by the U.S. Bureau of Reclamation, which operates the dam and reservoir, cost $180 million. The project made possible deliveries of municipal water supplies from the Friant system to Fresno, Friant, Orange Cove, Lindsay, Strathmore, and East Niles (near Bakersfield), and to Fresno, Madera, and Tulare Counties.

Its construction was eagerly anticipated and applauded because of the region's acute water shortages. On July 9, 1949, three thousand valley residents watched the first water release from Friant Dam into the canal. Governor Earl Warren called the canal "one of the outstanding accomplishments of the nation in the last half century." He added: "The most precious natural resource the state has is water, and we do not have an over abundance of it. We need every drop that falls on the mountains and the plains." What true and prophetic words.

The Central Valley Project grew from turbulent times and continual water shortages in the Central Valley. More water projects will appear in the future, and hopefully Kern County will continue to receive an adequate surface water supply to satisfy its thirsty agricultural industry.

Since October 1, 1986, the Friant-Kern Canal has been maintained and operated by the Friant Water Users Authority, a public joint-powers agency formed in 1985.

The locally financed Cross Valley Canal was completed in 1975. Through a series of six lift pumps, it conveys supplemental water from the California Aqueduct to the Bakersfield area. The Arvin-Edison Water Storage District and eight other entities contract for Central Valley Project water from Shasta Dam. This allows the exchange of equal amounts of water between Cross Valley contractors who take delivery of allotments of Arvin-Edison's San Joaquin River or Friant supply. It makes available an additional nearly 130,000-acre feet of water annually into the Friant service area.

The State Water Project was authorized in 1951, when the legislature authorized construction of a water storage and supply system. The intent was to capture and store rainfall in Northern California and deliver it throughout the state. It would be eight years before the legislature passed the Burns-Porter Act, providing the mechanism for the funding to construct the initial facilities. In 1960 California voters approved the issuance of $1.75 billion in general obligation bonds, completing the cycle as authorized in the act. This allowed for the funds to build the State Water Project.

Today's State Water Project is the largest state-built, multipurpose water project in the country. Managed by the State Department of Water Resources, it serves about 20 million of California's 32 million residents with at least part of their water. Project water irrigates nearly six hundred thousand acres of farmland. It is designed to control flooding, generate power, and provide recreational facilities. The project is also intended to enhance fish and wildlife habitats.

The State Water Project relies on numerous aqueducts, reservoirs, dams, power plants, canals, and pumping plants to deliver water.

The first deliveries from the project were made in Northern California in 1962. Initially, the plan included 22 dams and reservoirs, 4 hydroelectric power plants, 3 pumping-generating plants, 14 pumping plants, and 550 miles of pipelines and aqueducts. The facilities are part of a distribution system that, once completed, would be capable of delivering the more than four million acre-feet of water forecast to be needed in the year 2020.

The State Water Project is designed around three small recreational lakes on Feather River tributaries in Plumas County—Lake Davis, Frenchman Lake, and Antelope Lake. The branches and forks of the Feather River flow into Lake Oroville, the project's principal

✧

Above: Then California Governor, and later Chief Justice of the United States Supreme Court, Earl Warren came back to Bakersfield in 1948 to help honor legendary Bakersfield High Coach Goldie Griffith.

Below: The Frazier Park communities have become home to many people from Bakersfield and Southern California. This photo was taken above the Lake of the Woods in the 1920s.

reservoir, with a capacity of about 3.5 million acre-feet of water (An acre-foot consists of about 326,000 gallons.)

From Lake Oroville water flows through three hydroelectric power plants, then down the Feather and Sacramento Rivers before reaching the San Joaquin Delta. From the northern Delta, water is supplied to Napa and Solano Counties through the North Bay Aqueduct, which was completed in 1988.

In the southern Delta, near Byron, the Harvey O. Banks Delta Pumping Plant lifts water into the small Bethany Reservoir. From here, the South Bay Pumping Plant lifts the water into the South Bay Aqueduct, completed in 1962. Through the South Bay Aqueduct, water is supplied to Alameda and Santa Clara Counties. Most of the water from the Bethany Reservoir flows into the Governor Edmund G. Brown California Aqueduct, which is a familiar scene to those who drive through the valley's west side. From the north, the aqueduct flows into the O'Neill Forebay, west of Los Banos. From O'Neill Forebay part of the water is pumped through the William R. Gianelli Pumping-Generating Plant for storage in San Luis Reservoir until needed.

The San Luis Reservoir has a storage capacity of more than two million acre-feet. It and the B. F. Sisk San Luis Dam are jointly owned by the California Water Department and the U.S. Bureau of Reclamation, which has a gross storage share in the reservoir of more than one million acre-feet of water.

Water flowing out of the San Luis Reservoir flows south in the aqueduct, down the valley. Because the south valley is higher in elevation than the north, water has to be raised over a thousand feet by four pumping plants before reaching the foot of the Tehachapi Mountains.

In the southern San Joaquin Valley, the short Coastal Branch Aqueduct serves agricultural areas west of the California Aqueduct. Current plans call for the branch to be extended to serve Santa Barbara and San Luis Obispo Counties.

The California Aqueduct also supplies water to the southern San Joaquin Valley, as well areas to the south. In Kern County, at the base of the Tehachapis, the A. D. Edmonston Pumping Plant raises the water 1,962 feet into 8.5 miles of tunnels and siphons. It is the highest single-lift of any pumping plant in the world. At the other end is more of the California Aqueduct extending into the Antelope Valley.

The California Aqueduct divides into two branches, East and West, in the Antelope Valley. The East Branch carries water through the Antelope Valley into Silverwood Lake in the San Bernardino Mountains. Here it enters the San Bernardino Tunnel and drops 1,418 feet into Devil Canyon Power Plant, out-flowing to Lake Perris, the project's southernmost reservoir.

Water in the West Branch flows through the William E. Warne Power Plant into Pyramid Lake in Los Angeles County. From here it flows through the Angeles Tunnel, the Castaic Power Plant, and into Castaic Lake, which is the terminus of the West Branch.

Energy needed to operate the State Water Project comes from numerous project-owned and external sources, including hydroelectric, coal-fired, and wind-generated plants. There are eight hydroelectric power plants, with three pumping-generating plants, producing enough electricity to reduce the project's demand for energy significantly. More than six billion kilowatt-hours are produced in an average year, a volume adequate enough to serve the entire annual electrical needs of the City of San Francisco.

KERN'S DESERT,
MINES, AND AERONAUTICS

Somewhere there is a dividing line between early day mining efforts and those of the late nineteenth and early twentieth centuries. However, it is a tough line to draw, as the early mining areas of Kern continued to be mined well into the 1900s. The likely place to divide the discussion of mining in Kern County is the desert gold and silver found in Kern's eastern desert, the Rand Mining District. It is hard to believe that what appears to many as a vast wasteland could produce some of the richest mines in California.

Mining interests go far back into the mid-nineteenth century. Two stories exist about John Goler and the discovery of gold in Kern's desert. One finds him mentioned in William Manly's *The Jayhawker's Oath*, where Goler and a German companion were coming out of Death Valley and found gold along the trail at the springs, but apparently Goler was more interested in getting water than gold and never could find the location again.

Another story states that in 1867, when Goler crossed the southern corner of Kern County on the way to Los Angeles, he stopped at a spring to quench his thirst and found chunks of gold lying beneath the surface of the water. Leaving a rifle upright on a hilltop as a location beacon, he drew a map of the area and scooped up some of the nuggets. He then headed into Los Angeles hoping to interest investors in his find. The two parties later went back to find the prize, but it would not be until 1893 that the rush to the desert occurred.

Small-time mining was carried out in Kern's desert throughout the latter part of the nineteenth century. Even the boom at Goler Gulch in 1893 would pale in comparison to the finds of a couple

✧

Traversed by western immigrants as early as the 1840s, in 1968 Red Rock Canyon became the first site in Kern County to be established as a state park.

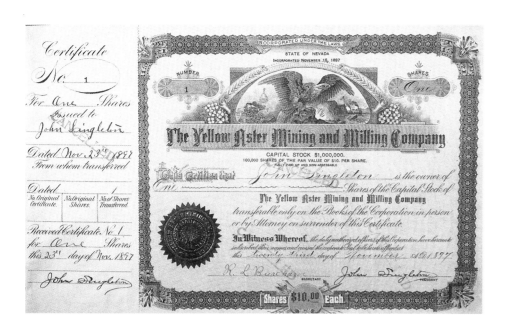

John Singleton, one of the founders and the president of the Yellow Aster Mining and Milling Company, built the Howell House that now resides at the Kern County Museum. The first stock certificate issued by the company is pictured in this photograph.

COURTESY OF GREG IGER.

of years later in what would become Randsburg. Over in Red Rock Canyon, Rudolf Hagen had found gold, stating that in the old days he and his partners washed over $2.5 million worth of gold from their surface workings. They spent it defending law suits to protect their claims. Hagen wanted to work into the bedrock beneath the worn out placer diggings. His theory was that an underground river washed ore out of the Sierras and into the Red Rock Canyon area, where the gold was different than the ore discovered elsewhere in Kern County. According to Hagen, the underground river is still there. For years he was the chief promoter of an idea in which modern machinery would be used to pump the water out onto the surface, so mining could take place in the shafts below.

By the spring of 1893, over $50,000 in ore was taken out in the Goler Mining District. The influx of miners at Cow Wells caused a small community to spring up, and, by 1894, Eugene Garlock had moved his stamp mill out of Tehachapi to the desert. Soon Cow Wells became Garlock, and most of the Goler Canyon (Gulch) population to the east was located there.

By 1895 men were scouring the hills for signs of gold, and F. M. Mooers was among them. Mooers had made a prospecting trip up onto Rand Mountain the year before and found his signs. Partnered with John Singleton, Mooers went to Charles Burcham, who had been in the area on the elusive hunt. Burcham

had a wagon, but he was ready to depart for home, discouraged with his findings.

Mooers and Singleton convinced Burcham to haul them to the untouched mountain. They left camp, putting out the word they were discouraged and going home. They headed north out of camp, but as soon as they were out of sight they turned toward Rand Mountain. Here they set up camp on the yet unspoiled, desolate hillside. On April 25, 1895, they found the elusive signs they were looking for.

Mooers and Singleton stayed and staked claims and Burcham went to San Bernardino seeking supplies and financing. His wife, Dr. Rose La Monte Burcham, had staked him before, and he thought she might take the risk again. He was right. He neglected to tell her about the deal his partners had made with O. B. Stanton of Bakersfield, to trade half interest in the mine for his erecting a stamp mill on the site. Rose Burcham had a keen sense of danger, and quickly traveled to the camp. Finding problems, she quickly took charge and was able to make progress in getting the operation going. Soon she would be hauling bars of gold to Mojave to cover the expenses of the mine, plus dividends.

The mine was always in legal trouble, with a number of parties filing suit for control, but by May 1897 most of the initial problems were solved, and it was incorporated as Yellow Aster Mining and Milling Company. Continual legal hassles plagued the mine until it closed. In 1969 the hundred-stamp mill building built in 1901 was burned by an arsonist, removing the last vestige of the huge mining operation. The Yellow Aster brought millions of dollars to Kern County's economy. It was one of hundreds of mines in the area that produced precious metals for their owners.

Tungsten was another major ore found in the mountains around Randsburg. Discovered in 1904, it wasn't until 1915, during World War I, that it became a critical mining operation. The Atolia Mining Company operated for a number of years, only to close in 1911, when the price of ore was too low to operate. It reopened in 1912 with a renewed interest in tungsten. By the time the First World War

was over, the mine had produced tens of millions of dollars worth of ore. With the end of the war came the end of tungsten mining until World War II, when interest renewed.

Another wild and amazing story out of the Rand Mining District is that of the "Big Silver" or California Rand Silver Mine Inc. Perhaps the story of the California Rand Silver Mine does not belong in this Kern County history volume because it is actually mostly in San Bernardino County. However, the players in the mine were Kern County residents, many of whose families are still in Bakersfield and Kern.

In 1917 J. J. Nosser, who had been operating a small tungsten mine, found out about some claims nearby that a friend, Patrick Byrne, wanted to relocate. Offered half ownership, Nosser was indeed interested. The two were to meet on November 6, but Byrne was hurt in an accident and died. Nosser remembered the location and took on J. W. Kelly as a partner. Nosser hoped Kelly would be able to get a grubstake to work it. Kelly went into Bakersfield and talked to a friend, Edith Coons. She provided the initial funds and they formed the K.C.N. Group.

Kelly got back to the site six weeks later and by this time had "Hamp" Williams with him. Edith Coons had sent him along to examine the property and to bring her ore samples. Samples of the outcrop assayed at $60 per ton in silver. Williams was given a

share in return for sinking a fifty-foot shaft. Nosser gave up his job on the tungsten property, joining Williams and Kelly in the new project. Williams took care of the windlass and sharpened tools, then he and Kelly would go off prospecting during the day, seeking to locate new claims, while Nosser stayed in the shaft and continued the drilling.

When they ran low on funds again, Kelly went back to Edith Coons, who was able to borrow from her employer, J. M. Jameson, Kern County assessor. For his loan, Jameson was also given an interest in the desert claims of the group.

Kelly received a letter from a friend in Los Angeles asking for a one-hundred-pound sample of red ochre from nearby Red Mountain. They also wanted Kelly to locate mining sites that were open on the mountain. Nosser and Williams agreed to handle his work while he was in Bakersfield seeking further funding. The day following Kelly's departure, his partners located six claims on Red Mountain. They started back to Randsburg, when Nosser again told Williams of a "blowout" like the one found on the K.C.N. claim. Since it was nearby, they stopped to look at it. Years before, someone had blasted a small hole about three feet in length and two feet wide with a depth of eight inches. These are Nosser's words regarding the discovery:

> I sat down in one end of the pit and in a couple of minutes Williams came up and took his seat in the other end. Both of us sat there fully five minutes, too tired to make much of an examination; too tired even to talk. Williams picked up several pieces of the rock and tossed them aside, and looked away toward town, as if the long walk was more on his mind than a new find. "Nosser," he said, "this is the biggest and richest thing I have ever seen. The ore from this little pit will assay one thousand dollars a ton or better."

They built the first monument and located the mine, then took three samples from where the gallows frame of the California Rand Silver shaft was placed.

Back at the spot early the next morning, the two prospectors came upon what was later

known as the Uranium Group of claims. Upon Kelly's return, his associates told him of the find, and that the only conflicting claim in the district was the Juanita, located years earlier by D. J. McCormack of Los Angeles, who had offered Kelly the land when the gold appeared to be played out. After some legal wrangling McCormack's son sold the property for $15,000.

Meanwhile, Williams sold a half of his quarter interest to a group of investors in Bakersfield, with E. T. Grady as their representative. Nosser, through the efforts of J. M. "Jack" Jameson, sold half of his quarter interest to Alfred Harrell, publisher of the *Bakersfield Californian*.

In June 1919, work began on the mine. The California Rand Silver Mine sent its first load of ore to the smelter one month later, gaining $16,000 for the efforts. The richest carload ever shipped out from this mine was $54,000. A one hundred-ton mill was built on site in December 1921, the mine having paid dividends of just more than $1 million up to that date. It was estimated that the ore on site would feed the mill for three more years, and as things turned out, it was a pretty good guess.

Meanwhile, B. H. Sill, of Bakersfield, bought an eighth interest, partly from Coons and Kelly, for $50,000. Another eighth

interest was later sold to another Bakersfield syndicate for $105,000. As of March 1924, the mine paid sizable dividends, but they were suspended at that point. The benefits of the Pittman Act, supporting silver prices, had ended. As of this time, the mine had paid its stockholders a total of just over $3 million.

The partners sought the advice of Edward T. Grady, who was a veteran of the mining industry. Grady was quite optimistic about the early assays and himself headed a syndicate of investors. The company leased Grady and his partner B. H. Sill land out on the flat east of the California Rand. No one wanted this land for mining, but Grady had a feeling there was a good vein of ore there. To the amazement of the local residents, the shaft yielded the partners over $1 million before the lease expired. So go the stories of the Rand Mining District.

Other mining booms in the county were significant in their own times. Kern's desert also hosted a borax rush in its dry lakes. In March, 1873, the *Los Angeles Star* reported H. I. Lent made a discovery of a vast deposit of borate of lime 120 miles from Los Angeles. The quality was compared with the English-imported borax in the drug stores and was thought to be an inexhaustible supply. Since $250 a ton was paid for import tariffs for the English borax, there was a call for a company to form and mine the material. This eventually became the Pacific Coast Borax Company, at Boron, now U.S. Borax.

Underground mining started north of Boron in 1926. The town of Amargo was founded in the same year by the company and named after the Santa Fe siding there; the name means "bitter water." By 1930 the small town was well in place, with a store and café. By 1938, people had been calling the town Boron for some time, but when the Post Office arrived the name changed. When the Santa Fe Railroad moved its depot from Kramer several miles to the east to Boron, the name was officially adopted.

Nearly half of the world's refined borax originates from the sodium borates mined at Boron. In 1957, the company began operating as an open pit mine. At one time it was known as the largest open pit mine in the world. U.S. Borax also mines borate minerals from other desert lakebeds and has deposits in the remote Argentine Andes. When the pit was started, extensive new facilities to process tincal ore were built. By 1980, the company added a plant to make boric acid from Kern's own mineral, Kernite. This gave the company a greater utilization of local kernite ore. In 1984, they developed a technology for converting kernite into borax, further utilizing the great resources at the site.

Today, the area is more of a high-tech community than one would imagine. Just around the corner at Edwards Air Force Base are the Phillips Laboratory Propulsion Directorate and the NASA Dryden Flight Research Center. Directly to the east is the Kramer Junction Company, which operates the world's largest solar power facility, producing enough electricity to power one hundred thousand homes.

Boron has finished a new plan to create a 1930s-era downtown to draw travelers from Highway 58 into town for shopping, antiques, museums, and meals. There are historic display signs along Twenty Mule Team Road into the community, and the Twenty Mule Team Museum draws many visitors. An aerospace museum and a train museum are in the works, and the visitors center at U.S. Borax offers a history of the mine. This is quite a change from yesteryear in Kern's easternmost community.

Salt deposits were also found on Kern's desert. The deposits at Saltdale, west of Randsburg on the flats, created a major salt-works with the recapturing operation still in service today. Consolidated Salt Company began the operation, and, just before World War I, the company was sold to Diamond Salt. Long Beach Salt Company bought the holdings of Diamond Salt Company in 1928, eventually to be bought out by Western Salt Company. A post office was in place at Saltdale in 1916 and lasted until it was moved in 1950 to Cantil.

One of the major mining operations still in business in Kern County is the old Monolith Cement Company's plant outside Tehachapi. This plant has produced huge quantities of limestone for Portland cement for the growing west. At one time the air and ground in the eastern Tehachapi Valley was full of the dust from the operation. Due to the air emission efforts of the company, the valley is once again clear. Monolith was founded in 1909 as a work camp for the construction of the Los Angeles Aqueduct. It was named by William Mulholland, with a post office established in 1910. Monolith Portland Cement Company purchased the town in 1919, continuing to use it as a company town into the 1960s. Now called California Portland Cement, the town is gone, but the plant continues as a vast resource for the growing west.

✧

Seen here are the inner workings of Randsburg's King Solomon Mine in 1939.

Without mining and transportation, Mojave would have failed to develop. It was founded by the Southern Pacific Railroad in 1876 as a construction camp on the eastern slope of the Tehachapi Mountains. Mojave is an unincorporated community located in the southeastern portion of Kern County at the junction of State Highways 14 and 58. Coincidentally, Mojave is 58 miles east of Bakersfield and less than 75 miles north of the Los Angeles city limits.

August 8, 1876, is celebrated as Mojave's birthday, as it is the date of the arrival of the first passenger train. The railroad line continued on to Needles on the Colorado River and reached the Arizona border in 1883. As part of a larger agreement, the Southern Pacific sold the rail line to the Santa Fe Railway in 1898, also allowing the use of the tracks over Tehachapi Pass. In 1994 the Santa Fe Railroad was merged into the Burlington Northern Santa Fe.

Another branch of the railroad that ran through Mojave is the old Southern Pacific Lone Pine Branch, built in 1910 as part of the Los Angeles Aqueduct project. It was used with the Carson and Colorado Narrow Gauge Railroad at Owenyo, allowing service to continue over Donner Summit. The branch is now limited to hauling coal and potash to the Trona Railway connection at Searles Station between Randsburg and Ridgecrest. The Oak Creek Branch, between Mojave and the California Portland Cement plant at Creal, hauls coal and cement.

Mojave is well known by old timers as the location of one of the great "Harvey Houses." Mojave's was located in its railroad depot and had the "works" including a host of "Harvey Girls" who served the famous great meals to travelers and miners.

Between 1884 and 1889, the town was the terminus for the famous twenty-mule team wagons that hauled borax between the mines in Death Valley and the railroad in Mojave. Huge wagons, still seen at Boron and Furnace Creek in Death Valley, were built in Mojave by J. W. S. Perry to haul the mineral. Like all communities, Mojave has had its share of disasters, including the fire of 1884, when ninety cases of blasting powder in the railroad depot exploded with a bang heard twenty-five miles away.

Gold was also a factor in Mojave's growth with its discovery on Soledad Mountain in 1894. At Mojave and nearby Rosamond, gold was and is still a factor in everyday life. Mines with colorful names as the Golden Queen, Yellow Dog, and Elephant Eagle are well known.

The Los Angeles Aqueduct provided a real economic boost for Mojave with local cement production in 1908. One plant is still in operation and run by the Calaveras Cement Company. California Portland Cement built a more modern plant west of Mojave at Creal in 1955.

Mojave is probably best known for its airport, now used as a facility for experimental and space age flight technology. There were several small airports built near

Mojave over the years, including Meyer Field along Barstow Road.

The Mojave Airport was originally a County facility, established in 1935 as part of the county system. Kern was known for its progressive system of airports in the 1920s and '30s. The airport is well suited for general aviation, having taxiways and minor support facilities. At the beginning of World War II, the airport was taken over by the U.S. Marine Corps as the Mojave Marine Corps Auxiliary Air Station. During the war, thousands of Navy and Marine pilots were trained for combat in SBD dive bombers and F4U Corsairs.

The airport was decommissioned after the war but recommissioned again as a training facility for Korean Conflict airmen. It was finally closed in 1959. In July 1961, the County of Kern received title to the airfield and reverted it into the county general aviation system. The Mojave Airport District, now the East Kern Airport District, was formed in February 1972 to oversee the operation of the airport. It is home of the National Test Pilots School. Burt Rutan developed *Voyager*, the first aircraft to circumnavigate the globe without refueling, at Mojave.

Rosamond is located south of Mojave in southeastern Kern County. It is a high desert community at an elevation of 2,330 feet, located in the Antelope Valley. Edwards Air Force Base is adjacent to the east side of Rosamond.

Rosamond was founded as a railroad station in 1876 and named after the daughter of a Southern Pacific Railroad official. It was already a mining, farming, and cattle town when, in the late 1890s, the Lida Mine (later the Tropico Mine) was discovered. A couple of years later, in the era of the Randsburg discoveries after prospectors found paydirt, the rush was on. Ore assays were as high as $100,000 per ton, with the Tropico Mine continuing to operate for decades. Eventually Glenn Settle turned it into a tourist attraction.

Today, Rosamond is still a mining and ranching community, with one major addition: aerospace. Edwards Air Force Base and Plant 42 at Palmdale are great providers of local aerospace employment. Highway 14 connects the area with Los Angeles, and the town serves as a bedroom community for the area.

Out in the middle of the desert, east of Mojave is a land forbidding and occupied by all kinds of desert creatures. It has a wealth of Joshua trees and creosote bushes. It is also the home of one of the United States' premier Air Force Bases, Edwards Air Force Base.

The Southern Pacific Railroad ran its line through the area in 1876, and in 1882, ran eastward rail from Mojave to Barstow. The railroad built a water stop at the edge of Rodriguez Dry Lake, twenty miles southeast of Mojave. It was commonly known at the time as "Rod." The lake, now called Rogers Dry Lake, was a Pleistocene body spreading out over forty-four square miles. It is said to be the largest formation of its type in the world.

The area was settled in 1910 by Ralph, Clifford, and Effie Corum. They grew alfalfa and turkeys, and made a practice of bringing other homesteaders into the area for a dollar per acre fee. It also happened that the Corum brothers got contracts for drilling their water wells and clearing their land. They eventually

✧

The Monolith Cement Company in the Tehachapi Valley is seen in this 1954 photograph.

also opened a general store. Requesting a post office under their name, they were denied because of another community with a similar name. Not to be daunted, they reversed the spelling and came up with Muroc. The name held for nearly forty years.

Today, the main concrete runway at Edwards Air Force Base is located next to Rogers Dry Lake. The combined runway and nine thousand-foot lakebed overrun gives pilots twenty-four thousand feet to land in case of in-flight emergency. It is one of the safest and longest runways in the world.

There are two dry lakes in the area, with Rogers Dry Lake being the largest of the two. Rosamond Dry Lake is the other, and both lakebeds are used for emergency and test landings of aircraft. The flat surfaces of the lakebeds have saved hundreds of aircrew lives and millions of dollars in aircraft because of their large long flat surfaces. Rogers Dry Lake has been declared a National Historic Landmark by the National Park Service because of its role in the development of the nation's space program and its use in the development of aerospace systems.

The reason for this is the combination of the two dry lakes, Rogers and Rosamond, which is several miles southwest of Rogers. Rogers Dry Lake has a surface area of about forty-four square miles. Seven runways crisscross the surface of Rogers, the longest being 7.5 miles. Rosamond Dry Lake has twenty-one square miles of smooth flat surface also used for routine flight test, research flight testing, and emergency landings. The lakebeds are among the lowest points in Antelope Valley and collect seasonal rain and snow runoff from nearby hills. Snow and rain are also collected off the San Gabriel Mountains to the south and the Tehachapi Mountains to the west, however in minuscule amounts. The lakebeds are exceptionally flat, with the Rosamond surface

measured with a curvature of less than eighteen inches over thirty thousand feet.

It was Lieutenant Colonel H. H. "Hap" Arnold who saw the area's potential in the early 1930s, stating that it was a one-of-a-kind "natural aerodrome" that could be utilized at an exceptionally low cost. The Muroc Bombing and Gunnery Range was the first such use of the lakes and was established as a remote bombing and strafing range for March Field squadrons in September 1933. This continued until July 1942, when it was activated as a separate post, Muroc Army Air Base. Training at Muroc was meant to provide final combat training for aircrews prior to overseas deployment.

In early 1942 the site was chosen because of its isolation to test a top-secret prototype with year-round flying. A location was selected along the north shore of Rogers Dry Lake about six miles away from the Muroc training base. America's first jet, the Bell XP-59A Airacomet, was the plane to be tested. On October 1, 1942, Bell test pilot Bob Stanley lifted the wheels of the jet off the lake bed's surface in a high-speed taxi. The next day it lifted off officially, and the age of the turbojet began in the United States. The Airacomet was terribly underpowered and required long rolling takeoffs. It also had the habit of flaming out, making the forty-four square mile lake bed an ideal location for the tests. Testing of the XP-59A took place at the small Materiel Division test site (now known as North Base). Data was reviewed over a year's time, but the formal preliminary military test and evaluation program did not begin until the fall of 1943. Formal operational suitability and accelerated service tests did not get underway until 1944, but the Army Air Force had already decided that the airplane was not suitable for combat operations.

These informal safety practices lasted several years and contributed to a fearsome accident rate. The year 1948 was a particularly tough one, with at least thirteen known fatalities recorded. One of them was Captain Glen W. Edwards, who was killed in a crash of a YB-49 flying wing. By December 1949, the base was renamed in his honor. On June 25, 1951, the area was officially designated as the U.S. Air Force Flight Test Center (AFFTC). The USAF Test Pilot School also moved to Edwards from Wright Field the same year.

Experimental rocket planes continued to fly faster and higher into the stratosphere. By the beginning of the decade, the first-generation X-1 flew at Mach 1.45 (957 mph) at a height of nearly seventy-two thousand feet. The D-588-II Douglas Skyrocket soon surpassed this in 1951, when Bill Bridgeman flew at Mach 1.88 (1,180 mph) at an altitude of close to seventy-five thousand feet. The records kept on growing with names like Lieutenant Colonel Marion Carl, Scott Crossfield, Chuck Yeager (who broke the sound barrier in 1947), and Arthur "Kit" Murray. Captain Iven Kincheloe became the first man to soar above one hundred thousand feet with the Bell X-2. Captain Mel Apt became the first man to exceed Mach 3, at Mach 3.2 (2,094 mph,) but the flight was tragically cut short as the plane tumbled violently out of control with Apt never able to recover it.

Meanwhile, the era of the turbojets was at hand with aircraft like the F-100 Super Sabre, F-102 Delta Dagger, the Mach 2 F-104 Starfighter, F-105 Thunderchief, and F-106 Delta Dart. With these planes, supersonic flight was almost routine.

The 1960s saw a new trend toward space flight, with the Test Pilot School redesignated as the Aerospace Research Pilot School. The X-15 was flying at many times the speed of sound and at altitudes well above the earth's atmosphere. Within eight months in 1961, it became the first aircraft to exceed Mach 4, 5, and 6, later becoming the first and, so far, only airplane to fly in near space at a peak altitude of more than sixty-seven miles.

Major William J. "Pete" Knight flew a modified X-15A-2 at a top speed of Mach 6.72, (4,520 mph) on October 3, 1967. This remains the highest speed ever attained in an airplane.

In the 1960s, NASA and the Air Force developed what was called the "High-Range," which was a four hundred-mile chain of radar and data acquisition sites. These can be seen throughout the east side desert. Test pilots continued to fly jet-powered aircraft like the XB-70 Valkyrie, and the YF-12, and SR-71 Blackbirds. The half million-pound Valkyrie could sustain Mach 3 flight operations at altitudes above seventy thousand feet, while the Blackbirds provided better performance in excess of Mach 3 and at altitudes well above eighty-thousand feet.

Edwards was also the site of the Vietnam-era aircraft with a new generation of increasingly complex aircraft. One such aircraft was the trouble-plagued F-111. By far the most sophisticated design of its time, the F-111 also demonstrated what problems could occur when a product was not fully tested. It was first flown in 1964, but its initial operational testing came during the highly publicized Combat Lancer deployment to Thailand in 1968. This clearly showed that the aircraft was far from combat ready, having been still undergoing Category I tests in 1972 and Category II tests in 1973. The Category III testing was finally skipped altogether.

By the early 1970s, military manned space missions were in decline, and the Aerospace Research Pilot School was redesignated as the USAF Test Pilot School. The school replaced the space-focused part of its curriculum with systems tests and test management programs.

✧

An aerial view of Edwards Air Force Base (South Base), c. WWII.

COURTESY OF DON THOMSON AND EDWARDS AIR FORCE BASE.

aeronautical challenges have been met since the early '80s as aircraft capabilities have been continuously refined and expanded.

The development of craft like the new F-15E dual-role fighter demonstrated remarkable combat effectiveness in the Persian Gulf conflict of the early 1990s. Low Altitude Navigation and Targeting Infrared for Night (or LANTIRN) helped revolutionize air-to-ground combat operations by denying adversaries the comfort of night flight. The late 1980s arrival of the first newly designed B-2 Bomber, or flying wing, saw a thin silhouette with compound curves and other low-observable characteristics flying overhead. This represented third-generation stealth technology (after the SR-71 and Have Blue/F-117) and it was, at that time, the most sophisticated airplane ever built.

In the early '90s, a pair of prototypes, the YF-22A and the YF-23A, squared off in a brief demonstration and validation (DEM/VAL) risk-reduction flight test program. These two craft blended stealth with agility and high-speed, supersonic cruise capability, contrasting with the F-117A and the B-2, both of which had been designed for stealth. The facility is testing the F-22A, selected to become the Air Force's next advanced tactical fighter. EMD airplanes incorporate a state-of-the-art, fully integrated avionics and sensor suite employing common hardware and software modules linked to a single computer with the capability of up to ten billion signal-processing operations per second. This allows fusing and analysis of diverse streams of data from each of the fighter's sensor systems into a synthesized and highly readable "glass cockpit" display.

All aircraft entering the Air Force's inventory have been put through a battery of tests at Edwards Air Force Base. It is a notable facility where undoubtedly more major milestones in flight have occurred than anywhere else in the world.

Another facility on Kern's desert deserving notice is the Naval Ordinance Test Station at China Lake in the Indian Wells Valley. It is a facility that is still somewhat cloistered in secrecy due to the nature of the testing that takes place. Historically, it is another base in a

The F-15, with advanced engine and fire-control systems; the B-1, with highly sophisticated offensive and defensive systems; and the F-16, with its "fly-by-wire" flight control system, were examples of crafts tested during this era. Tests at the center led to the development of a new subsonic attack aircraft designated the F-117A. The stealth revolution had begun.

By the 1980s, the base was once again part of aeronautical history with the April 14, 1981 first landing of the Space Shuttle *Columbia* on Rogers Dry Lake. Two astronauts, John Young and Robert Crippen, successfully landed the first orbiting space vehicle to leave the earth under rocket power and return on the wings of an airplane. Spectacular

secluded area where this kind of testing could take place.

China Lake is located at Ridgecrest, a bustling community, incorporated in 1963, and located in the northeast corner of Kern County. It is now a community of nearly thirty thousand residents. Before the Naval Ordinance Test Station (NOTS) arrived in 1943, Ridgecrest consisted of a few scattered farms and homesteads. The community touts its "vast uninhabited space, clean air, good water, highway accessibility, accessibility to multiple recreational sites, and proximity to Los Angeles and Southern California" as a primary reason to come live in Ridgecrest.

With the first mining discoveries around 1873 in the Panamints, northeast of China Lake, a few hundred people inhabited the general area until the 1890s. The rush to Randsburg in the 1890s brought people into the Ridgecrest area, where soon, at Haiwee Meadows, Bart Bellows had the "Goat Ranch," with eight thousand imported Angora goats. Junction Ranch was another operation in the area, and it is the only permanent ranch known to have been located on China Lake. It served as a station on the roads branching out to Darwin, Panamint Valley, and the ridge road of Renegade Canyon.

Most early settlement in Indian Wells Valley centered around Inyokern, which was first known as Siding Sixteen, a part of the railroad built during the construction of the Los Angeles Aqueduct. Later named Magnolia, it was renamed Inyokern in 1910.

The Robertson homestead was one of the early settlements in the area and was later purchased by John McNeil and his wife. They owned a store in Inyokern and started a dairy on the property. Robert and James Crum bought the McNeil Ranch and dairy after McNeil's death, and a small community soon sprung up. By late 1912 it was known as Crumville.

By 1914 a post office and name change came to the community. Ridgecrest was officially established. NOTS was established in November 1943 at the Inyokern Airport, then called Harvey Field by the Navy. Harvey Field was subsequently deactivated after the war and returned to the County of Kern. It had eight Quonset huts and a number of test ranges.

In 1943 facilities were needed to test rockets developed for the Navy by the California Institute of Technology. The Navy also needed a proving ground for aviation ordinance. The Naval Ordinance Test Station was described as "a station having for its primary function the research, development and testing of weapons, and having additional function of furnishing primary training in the use of such weapons."

By mid-1945 NOTS aviation operations were transferred to the new Armitage Field at the China Lake site, and testing began within less than a month. The area around China Lake and Inyokern, with near-perfect flying weather year-round and practically unlimited visibility, proved ideal for the needs of the facility. The Navy-CalTech partnership was indeed a winner, and the civilian scientists and experienced military personnel made it the preeminent testing, research, and development institution in the world.

In 1948 Michelson Laboratory was constructed. It was made up of sixteen huge concrete buildings, accommodating a staff of over six hundred when it opened. It was here at Michelson that the work was and still is undertaken on the Navy's weapons systems. The lab was named for Dr. Albert Abraham Michelson who, among other things, was a physics professor at the University of Chicago. He was the first American to be awarded the

✧

A large crowd and a worldwide audience witnessed the second landing of the Space Shuttle Columbia on November 14, 1981, at Rogers Dry Lake. Note the Space Shuttle Enterprise is in the background. The Enterprise was used solely in approach and landing tests and never flew to space.

Nobel Prize in Physics, winning in 1907 for conducting precision optical instrument and spectroscopic and meteorological investigations. In other words, he taught people how to measure. Michelson had been a Navy officer and developed many patented range finding and other devices.

Early on, NOTS personnel began research on fire-control systems that evolved into the concept of the Sidewinder guided missile. It was involved in the Manhattan Project as the location for "Project Camel," developing non-nuclear explosive bomb components. This continued into the 1950s. The Holy Moses, Tiny Tim, and other spin-stabilized barrage rockets were tested while the station was built. The station's Pasadena Annex was added to NOTS after World War II. Here development and testing of torpedoes and other underwater ordinance took place.

The Korean conflict brought more rockets, missiles, and torpedoes, with an array of guns and bombs, including a 6.5-inch tank-killing Ram rocket, which it delivered to the combat forces in Korea after only twenty-eight days in development and testing. The China Lake facility is responsible for the development of Weapon A, Mighty Mouse, and BOAR rockets; a series of torpedoes; new aircraft fire-control systems (now called "avionics"); and Sidewinder missiles. The station also played a significant part in the development and testing of the Polaris missile system, and weather modification and satellite-delivery systems.

By the mid 1960s, with the U.S. involvement in Southeast Asia, a new generation of smart bombs, cluster weapons, and night-attack systems was developed to meet the needs of the Navy. At this time, the Eye series of free-fall weapons first saw action. Snakeye and Rockeye bombs, the Zuni rocket, the ASROC antisubmarine system, the Shrike anti-radar missile, the TV-guided Walleye, and advanced Sidewinders were all a result of development at China Lake. It also developed Forward-Looking Infrared (FLIR) technology and systems, fuel-air explosive (FAE) devices, electronic warfare, and space and undersea research vehicles during the decade.

NOTS China Lake and the NOTS Pasadena Annex were separated in 1967. NOTS China Lake and the Naval Ordinance Laboratory, Corona, joined to form the Naval Weapons Center in 1971. During the 1970s, with the Navy shifting focus to advanced, computer-intensive systems, the center also changed direction. Now research focused on aircraft systems or avionics, which became a primary research area. The same applies to advanced electronic-warfare systems.

Weapon system support activities were developed for the AH-1, A-4, A-6, A-7, AV-8B, and F/A-18 combat aircraft, and the center began developing avionics software and hardware for systems like weapons integration and advanced self-protection. It continued to develop advanced versions of the Sidewinder, Walleye, Shrike (including the original HARM program), and FAE weapons. Programs were also conducted for Sparrow, Phoenix, Harpoon, and Maverick missiles. China Lake research extended the technology base in optical and laser systems, advanced propulsion technologies, and anti-radiation guidance. The National Parachute Test Range function was moved to China Lake in 1979, adding a new arena for research.

During the 1980s, NWC continued to expand with new projects, including the Advanced Common Intercept Missile Demonstration (ACIMD) program, developing and demonstrating technologies for the next-generation air-to-air missile. The Sidearm and HARM anti-radar-missile programs; the Skipper 2 laser-guided weapon, Tomahawk Cruise Missile, vertical-launch weapons, and others were all again combat-proven in the Middle East and in the Falklands. Parachute systems (including the Space Shuttle escape system) also were developed, as were full-scale aircraft targets, such as the QF-86 and QF-4.

NWC China Lake was de-established on January 22, 1992, and consolidated into the Naval Air Weapons Station, China Lake. They are clearly able to meet the challenges placed upon them. Today China Lake has about forty-four hundred civilian employees and about one thousand military personnel, with over fifteen hundred contractor employees. It continues the work started nearly fifty years ago as a rocket testing range for the Navy.

OIL, GAS, AND ENERGY

The history of petroleum in Kern County dates back farther than recorded history. The local natives used the seeps in the McKittrick and other areas of the upper San Joaquin Valley for construction of every-day materials, and aboriginal baskets and ornaments have been excavated demonstrating this. The Yokuts occupied the area, and it has been found that they traded deposits of tarry asphaltum for other goods they needed. Shamans used the substance for healing, and small lumps of it were also used to weigh down women's skirts. They would use the material as a waterproofing substance, putting it on their roofs, baskets, and pots. It also appears it was used in the fashioning of death masks.

When the Spanish came into the southern valley in the late 1700s, it appears they paid little attention to the asphaltum deposits. Few records are found documenting the tarry deposits.

Once the Americans arrived in the area in the 1850s, the deposits were still of little interest. Thomas Baker is said to have had knowledge of them, especially those around the Kern River north of Bakersfield. Yet Baker, had very little use for the petroleum. In the 1850s, the only use for it was to lubricate wagon wheels and machinery parts.

In 1861, Thomas Harvey began marketing some of the unrefined oil for farm machinery lubrication. Soon others were interested and in 1864, the Buena Vista Petroleum Company was

✧

Kern River Power Plant #1, several miles up Kern Canyon, is still functioning today. Built in 1906, it was part of Southern California Edison's experiment with hydroelectricity.

formed. It produced very little in the way of product and by 1867 was defunct.

During the period of 1870-1898, numerous wells were dug or drilled along Kern, Fresno, and Tulare Counties' western foothills. Oil was found but none of the wells amounted to a commercial quality venture. Asphalt recovery and refining was another story. From 1870 to 1877, the recovery of asphalt took place at McKittrick, with some success. Asphalt and exceptionally thick oil from seepages were undoubtedly the sole source of raw materials.

Later, around 1890-91, a second asphalt refinery was built around six miles southeast of Maricopa, in what is now the Midway-Sunset Field. Again, thick or heavy oil was taken from several wells as deep as thirteen hundred feet. This was used as a flux to assist the refining of asphalt mined from the nearby seepages. The refined asphalt was initially transported to Bakersfield by wagon. Lighter materials or fractions in the form of probably lubricating and fuel oil were stored for local use or sale. This plant closed in 1892, when the Sunset Railroad was extended to Asphalto, where the Standard Asphalt Company erected another refinery. This time heavy oil was used as a flux in refining, obtained from wells in what is now the McKittrick Field. The plant refined and marketed asphalt until 1900, when the development of the Kern River Field provided a more readily available supply.

In 1872 John Hambleton began the first commercial oil development in the county out of hand-dug pits. His claim lasted into the 1880s, when the Sunset Oil Company was formed. Early lands had to be claimed as mines, but as time went by, the government changed its mind and threw open all of the early oil mine claims. The Sunset Oil Field was opened, but the Sunset Oil Company had filed under the old rules. A frantic scuffle ensued, with some losing their initial right to the oil. Solomon Jewett and Hugh Blodget formed Jewett and Blodget and filed on the mines of the Sunset Oil Company. A negotiated settlement was made and the Barnard Lease was created. Jewett and Blodget operated in the Sunset Field up until they assigned the lease to Union Oil Company in 1908.

Heavy oil and a nominal amount of gas were recovered from wells drilled in the McKittrick,

Midway-Sunset, and Temblor Ranch areas prior to 1898. But nearly all of the oil and all of the gas were used locally or wasted. The first large-scale commercial development of an oil field in Kern County for the purpose of producing oil was at the McKittrick Field in 1898, where ten thousand barrels of oil were produced. This early development undoubtedly came about by the newly arrived Southern Pacific branch line, the McKittrick Sunset Railroad, from Bakersfield to McKittrick.

Other early oil discoveries led to an interest in claiming the substance, and although drilling and recovery of oil was taking place out at McKittrick, it wasn't until the spring of 1899 that something was brewing north of Bakersfield. Speculation around Bakersfield was that oil had been discovered up at the Kern River. James Munroe Elwood and Jonathan Elwood hand

Kern's Yokuts Indians used asphaltum as glue, ornamentation, and other practical applications. For ease of storage, they would roll warm asphaltum into balls that hardened as they cooled (above). The Yokuts made tools of various materials, including wood and stone. Asphaltum was used to glue together these tools (right).

COURTESY OF GREG IGER.

dug a seventy-five-foot hole on the banks of the Kern River, at the ranch of Tom Means. Means frequently gets credit for the discovery, but it was the Elwoods, father and son.

They first augured a hole beneath a cliff on the banks of the Kern River, but finding it too unstable, they moved to higher ground, where they sunk a shaft. According to Elwood, they moved to where the bank was worn off by the water and started digging three or four feet into the bluff. They then were able to put their auger down and after three or four hours hit oil sand. They went up onto the bluff, dug forty-three feet, and hit the oil sand again. Getting timber to support the sandy shaft, they dug to seventy-five feet, finding so much oil and gas they went for a steam rig. Eventually they dug the hole to 260 feet, fueling the steam rig with the oil from the shaft. It produced fifteen barrels a day.

Several weeks later, Angus Crites who worked for Jewett and Blodget told the newspaper the Kern River area was producing so much oil they were storing it in whiskey barrels, milk cans, kerosene cans, beer kegs, and other containers. Crites said he watched while workers took about four barrels of oil from a shaft with no appreciable difference in the level of oil.

Crites was pretty shrewd and well known as a good oilman. By Friday, June 2, 1899, the *Daily Californian* published the story on the oil discovery. It praised the quality of the oil and went on to tell of the exploits of the Elwoods. Almost overnight, the race was on to the Kern River oil boom!

Over two hundred oil companies were formed to develop the Kern River Field. The assessed valuation of the oil lease lands rose to $1,000 an acre, and the Southern Pacific Railroad promoted sightseeing trips from San Francisco so tourists could see for themselves the workings of a real oil field. Ten dollars and sixty cents got you a round-trip to visit the Kern River Oil Field.

Developing around the field were numerous communities, some long gone from the landscape. Oil Center was one such town, and it was located in the center of the ten-square-mile oil field. Most of the Kern River Field workers lived there, the community

The Kern River Discovery Well was dug in an area like this along the banks of the Kern River in May 1899.

reaching a population of over seven thousand. But by the 1940s, the Field had progressively produced less oil, with prices dropping to a point where it wasn't economical to produce. The town had around 160 homes, in addition to rooming houses, stores, and its own justice of the peace. Many Oil Center houses were moved into Oildale in the mid-1930s, due to the tax assessor's policy change, causing the oil companies to be assessed property taxes on them. Thus was the end of Oil Center.

Several generations of children were raised at the Kern River Field, necessitating the formation of three school districts for their education. The Aztec School District was the first and longest lasting, formed in 1901 and operating continuously until it was incorporated into the Standard School District in Oildale. The Oil Center schoolhouse was closed forever in 1966. Toltec and Petroleum School Districts were created in 1910 and 1911, but, with the diminishing oil production and prices, were merged into the Aztec School District in 1932. Although modified, Texaco still uses the last Aztec (1939) schoolhouse.

Oil in the Kern River Field was as often as not laced with water, and in those days the water was left to settle and separate in ponds or sumps. Some of these are still visible in the Kern River Field. Pumping stations called Jack Plants with jack lines and rotary heads sprung up all over the place, allowing the pumping of many shallow wells at once. It was a wondrous collection of Jack Plants and redwood troughs, known in the oilfields as flumes, leading into the storage tanks.

The production of the Kern River Oil Field peaked at sixteen million barrels a year in 1906, but showed a steady decline from that point on. Sections were shut down during the lean Depression years, to be reopened into full production during World War II. After the war, production again drastically fell.

During the years between 1925 until 1955, the Kern River Oil Field averaged a bit more than ten thousand barrels a day, with workers constantly fighting the water that flooded producing zones. In the late 1950s and '60s, production was increased to around twenty thousand barrels per day in an effort to bring more out of the ground.

The early 1960s saw the introduction of steam into the operation. Kern River crude was thicker than molasses and resisted the pumping efforts of the producers. Steam injection allowed them to thin the oil's viscosity, thus making it easier to pump it out of the well. Shell Oil Company was the first to bring steam into the Field. Tidewater Oil Company was heating the oil in its wells at Kern River. It soon changed to steam, and so did the other producers. By 1968, production had increased 40,000 barrels to nearly 69,000. This extended the life of not only the Kern River Field, but many others like Midway-Sunset.

Getty Oil owned two-thirds of the 166 steam generators in the field, but it seems they also used up a tremendous amount of oil in their operation. This, of course, caused air pollution and water pollution, as excess water was being allowed to flow back into the Kern River. With expensive water treatment plants and air pollution controls on the generators, the overhead was rising too fast.

Oil prices collapsed in the early 1980s causing operators to look for better and more efficient methods of producing the oil. Here entered the concept of the cogeneration plant, which in this case is a power plant producing two types of power, steam and electricity. They use natural gas, which is clean burning and generally readily available. They provide electricity that can be sold to an outside market. They provide steam for the field to enable producers to maximize production. There are a number of cogeneration plants north of Bakersfield providing service to the Kern River and other northern fields.

The Kern River Field was a ten-square-mile, nearly four-billion-barrel reservoir of crude oil. For Bakersfield, the Elwood discovery meant a transformation. There are four such fields and dozens of smaller reservoirs in Kern, providing nearly ten thousand workers with employment. The county provides more than two-thirds of the state's oil production and millions of dollars in property taxes to local governments.

Oil exploration among the many oil seeps on the west side continued from that point resulting in the discovery of oil on the Temblor Ranch in 1900 and at the Midway-Sunset Field in 1901. As remote as they were, development of their resources was delayed until adequate transportation routes could be put into place. Once this occurred, the Midway-Sunset Field was to become the largest field in the state of California. During the development of this field in 1910, one of the world's greatest gushers, the famous Lakeview No.1 blew out, spewing oil which flowed out of control for five hundred and forty-four days. During this time, in 1910 and 1911, the well gushed out a total

of eight million barrels of oil over the surrounding terrain. Over half of this was saved by constructing ponding dams around it.

At the turn of the century, all of the oil fields discovered and most exploratory wells drilled were located near petroleum seeps. But as the development of the petroleum industry progressed, so did its science.

Geologic technology was accepted as an effective tool of petroleum exploration with many oil discoveries made by determining the surface and subsurface geologic features. This was called "prospecting of anticlinal and fault structures with surface expressions" and it soon led to led to the discovery of such productive fields as Buena Vista (1909), Lost Hills (1910), South Belridge (1911), Elk Hills (1911), Cymric (1916), Mount Poso (1923), Kern Front (1925), Fruitvale (1928), Edison (1934), and others.

The 1930s ushered in more than the Great Depression. Reflection seismography was to be the new method of oil exploration. This allowed exploration companies to determine the position of concealed anticlines beneath the floor of the San Joaquin Valley. The first success of the reflection seismograph in Kern County was in 1934 when the Buena Vista Lake gas field was discovered. It is now a gas zone of the Paloma Oil Field. Further and deeper drilling into the anticlinal structure also led to the discovery of the oil and condensate of the Paloma Field in 1939. In 1936, the work of a reflection seismograph party led to the discovery of the Ten Section Field, leading to the conclusion that large anticlines and thick Miocene oil sands are hidden beneath the valley floor. From this activity came the discovery between 1936 and 1939, of the Greeley (1936), Canal (1937) Rio Bravo (1937), North Coles Levee (1938), South Coles Levee (1939), and Strand (1939) Oil Fields. The Trico, Semitropic, and

Bowerbank Gas Fields were also found with this method of oil exploration.

At the beginning of the Second World War, it appeared the major fields had been discovered and most of the important anticlines had been explored. In other words, easy oil had been located, and now it was time to get down to business. A new geologic approach to oil exploration came about as a result of knowing much of the already found oil was in stratigraphic traps associated with folds and faults. Stratigraphic studies, seismic and other geologic procedures have spurred the discovery of many new small fields like Antelope Hills in 1941, as well as numerous new pools and areas analogous with known fields.

An example of this was the Belgian Anticline Field, discovered in 1946 and felt to be the most important of this type of field. It has yielded tens of millions barrels of oil. The 1948 discoveries of oil on the East Gosford area of the Canfield Ranch Field and the Tejon Hills Field were also significant finds. The Tejon Hills Field has also yielded millions of barrels of oil from wells ranging in depth from 539 to 1,904 feet. The North Tejon Oil Field was also an important discovery in the area, with the March 1957 completion of its discovery well and oil pumped at a depth of about twelve thousand feet for 245 barrels of oil daily.

Ten miles west of the North Tejon Field is the San Emigdio Nose Field, where Richfield Oil Corporation completed its discovery well in July 1958 with twenty-five hundred barrels of oil a day. The problem here is the great depth of the oil and expense of its recovery.

It was about 1910 when an Associated Oil Company geologist described Elk Hills as only: "An occurrence of organic material, probably plant remains, and the Elk Hills might have

Tidewater Oil Company
WELL NO. 204
SEC. 30-31/23

small scattered deposits of oil, but that they would not be important in an economic sense."

In 1918 Standard Oil Company began exploration of the school section it purchased nine years before in Elk Hills. Potentially there was an oil shortage ahead, and World War I clearly demonstrated oil's importance to the United States. It was increasingly becoming more apparent that oil was not as abundantly available as might be preferred, and Standard Oil wanted to ensure that availability.

Many disagreed that Elk Hills was the place to drill as shallow wildcat drilling in various parts of the Elk Hills came up short, with around three and a half million dollars wasted in the attempt. By the fall of 1918, Standard had a wooden derrick and rotary drilling tools at Elk Hills and were ready to drill the first well, named Hay No. 1. On January 11, 1919, Standard Oil struck oil at Elk Hills with a wildcat well producing two hundred barrels a day of high gravity oil from twenty-four hundred and eighty feet.

Of course, a two hundred barrel-day well wasn't nearly as interesting to people as many other wells nearby that had ten times and even as much as forty times the volume. In fact, the Honolulu Consolidated Oil Company's No. 19 well at Buena Vista Hills reverberated with oil few days after Standard completed the Elk Hills discovery well with an estimated seven thousand-barrel flow over the derrick.

The news of the Elk Hills well was also diminished in its stature by news of the passage of the prohibition amendment. While the United States was going dry, Elk Hills had its first well. Drilling continued at Elk Hills with a second four hundred-barrel well and a third eight hundred

and fifty-barrel well. Clearly there was something positive to be said about the field. By 1992 the Elk Hills Field became the fifth California oil field to exceed one billion barrels of cumulative oil production, behind Kern's Midway-Sunset, and the Kern River Fields.

The significance of Elk Hills is the location of Naval Petroleum Reserve No. 1 and Naval Petroleum Reserve No. 2. These areas were set aside by President William Howard Taft in an executive order in 1912. Both were set aside as reserve fuel for the United States Navy, to avoid potential shortages during national crises.

The Elk Hills Field is located near Bakersfield. The property encompasses more than forty-seven thousand acres and includes significant oil and gas reserves, more than one thousand producing wells, a forty-seven-megawatt electricity-generating facility, and two large gas plants. By 1997, daily production from the field was approximately sixty thousand barrels of oil and almost four hundred million cubic feet of natural gas. Elk Hills has been in commercial production since Congress authorized its development in 1976. It reached peak production of 181,000 barrels of oil per day in 1981.

In 1998 the Department of Energy sold U.S. interest in the reserve for $3.65 billion to Occidental Petroleum Company, making it the largest privatization in the history of the federal government. Time will tell whether this was a wise strategy.

West Side communities include Taft, which got a slow start as Siding No. 2. This name was given as a result of the construction of the Sunset Railroad line to the Midway Oil Field in 1908. The Sunset Railroad was operated by the Santa Fe and Southern Pacific Railroads. A converted boxcar served as the first depot for the town in 1909 with building occurring around it. The town was near the center of the Midway District, and the railroad designated it as Moro in January 1909. Confusion ensued about the name, confusing it with Morro Bay in San Luis Obispo County. So someone from the Southern Pacific added an "N" to the name and changed "Moro" to "Moron" in March 1909. The name was a stretch for local residents who when the time came to establish a post office, changed it to Taft, after President William Howard Taft.

Taft is a bustling city with the appearance of a community with a future. It is the commercial center of Kern's west side. Taft is the home of Taft Community College, a seventy-five-year-old institution of higher learning. As part of the West Side Community College District, the college serves a role in teaching not only general education, but vocational education to the community and the West Side. The West Side Oil Museum, in Taft, depicts the area's early oil history.

Maricopa was originally laid out as an exploration camp of the Maricopa Oil Company of Arizona. The company was incorporated in Arizona and began the process of drilling for oil on forty acres it owned at the site in early 1901. The company's first well reached oil sand as early as the beginning of February 1901, and oil was flowing by early April. A post office was established near the camp in December 1901, and the Sunset Railroad, owned by Southern Pacific, extended its rail line south to the company town in March 1904. Maricopa was used as the siding's name until 1907, when the Southern Pacific changed it to Monarch in an attempt to avoid confusion with Maricopa, Arizona. However the post office never changed, and local pressure caused the restoration of the name Maricopa as the railroad's official designation.

Maricopa is not only an oil community, but serves the agricultural needs of southern Kern County. With thousands of acres of citrus and stone fruit planted in the Maricopa and San Emigdio areas, Maricopa is the nearest community to serve those needs. It was incorporated in 1911 and is at the crossroads of Highways 33 and 166.

Fellows is still a working oil community on Kern's west side. Originally Siding No. 4 of the Sunset Railroad, it was established in 1910 and named after Charles Fellows, the railroad contractor who built the railroad line into the west side. The line was extended to Fellows in the Midway Oil Field after the 1908 blow out of the Midway Gusher. In 1910, the Lakeview Gusher No. 1 blew south of Taft, dwarfing the Midway Gusher. The Fellows Hotel, built in 1910 and owned by Martha "Ma" Randall, is now at the Kern County Museum. Fellows is on Highway 33, north of Taft.

McKittrick is another of the west side's once booming communities with its roots steeped in the lore of oil. A camp nearby, named Asphalto, was laid out in the late 1860s with the work done by the Buena Vista Petroleum Company. Three early exploration camps contemporary with the McKittrick Field, were named Asphalto, each built in consecutive years, starting in 1891. By 1893, the third Asphalto camp was laid out on the present location of the town of McKittrick. The community was renamed in 1900 after Captain William McKittrick, who owned property nearby.

The McKittrick Field is well known for its vast deposits of oil and asphaltum. A large surface seepage of asphaltum, known as the McKittrick Tar Pit is located about a half-mile northwest of the community. It has been widely excavated for fossil remains, many of which are in the Los Angeles Museum of Natural History and the Smithsonian Museum. The Kern County Museum also explored the site and has examples of the material.

Over one hundred years ago, several visionary men of Kern County set forth on a venture that would eventually become part of Pacific Gas & Electric Company's vast network of electrical power systems. Today's electrical use in Kern County ranges from that of the simple agricultural pump to the

✧

Hundreds of small speculative oil companies were created as a result of the 1899 Kern River Oil Field. One of these was Lone Star Oil Company, as seen in this stock certificate from the collection of the Kern County Museum.

COURTESY OF GREG IGER.

Photographer Frank G. Aston took this photograph of McKittrick in 1900. McKittrick came about as a result of the vast amount of oil that was being discovered in western Kern County. The Oil Exchange Building (far right) was operated by Eyraud, Gay, and Blondeau.

megawatt usage of some of Kern's large industrial firms. But in the early days, nothing seemed more important than bringing electricity to Kern County and Bakersfield.

The first real efforts toward bringing early power and light in Kern County began in 1888, when the county of Kern awarded a franchise to two Bakersfield men, L. P. St. Clair, Sr., and O. O. Mattson, to build a gas plant in Bakersfield. Bakersfield was an unincorporated town at the time, and such actions on the part of the Board of Supervisors were routine. They constructed a crude plant with eight retorts for making gas from naphtha. St. Clair, Blodget, and Henry Jastro bought out Mattson and had their share of trouble operating a new plant.

A wood-burning steam engine powered it. Numerous minor incidents marred the plant's early service, and because of a high carbon content of the manufactured gas, a bellows had to be installed to produce gas that would not smoke. Some blame the gas plant for the Great Fire of July 7, 1889 that burned down all of downtown Bakersfield, but others insist it started in a residence behind the Southern Hotel. Whatever started it, the fire devastated not only the town, but St. Clair's plant as well. He later reported that, with only three or four customers left, not much gas was made until the town was built up again. By 1890 the plant was operational, with a forty-light dynamo supplying electricity for a few downtown customers.

Soon coal was substituted for the naphtha to make the gas and the plant was blown up in another explosion. St. Clair purchased an arc lamp plant from the California Electric Light Company in San Francisco and placed it into production in October 1890. The California Electric Light Company was the earliest electric predecessor of today's Pacific Gas & Electric (PG&E), and St Clair's purchase brought that company's presence into Kern.

The new incandescent electric lights invented in 1879 by Thomas Edison were being manufactured, and St. Clair was eyeing Kern River Canyon as a location for a hydroelectric powerhouse. But the Power Development Company's formation and plan to build on the Kern River thwarted his efforts. Once the power plant was constructed and operational on the Kern, St. Clair contracted to distribute electrical power in Bakersfield once transmission lines were built. But St. Clair's health failed, and he left the operation of the electrical business to his son. Meanwhile, by 1896, crude oil was being used for the first time to manufacture gas.

It was H. A. Blodget, S. W Fergusson, W .S. Tevis, H. A. Jastro, and C. N. Beal, who were the driving forces who approached Lloyd Tevis of the Kern County Land Company for the funds necessary to create the power system that would survive to this day. With the Tevis and Kern County Land Company money behind them, they soon began construction on a wooden flume to carry water out of the Kern River and into what became known as the Kern River Powerhouse (located at the mouth of the canyon). On December 13, 1894, construction was started on a wooden flume. The plant began operation in 1897. The Power Transit & Light Company ran its lines into Bakersfield, delivering small quantities of electricity in 1898.

One of the major elements of the Power Transit & Light Company was the streetcar system in Bakersfield. It was also one of the largest users of electricity in Bakersfield. The Bakersfield and Kern Electric Railway, which began operating on February 17, 1901, ran not only through the community of Bakersfield, but also between the Southern Pacific Railroad Depot in Kern City and the Santa Fe Railroad Depot in Bakersfield. Meanwhile, Southern California Edison had built a power plant up the Kern River, generating power for the Southland.

Another company was organized in Los Angeles that would shape Kern County's industrial, agricultural, and oil field economy. The San Joaquin Light and Power Company was incorporated on May 13, 1905, with an authorized capital of $3 million by William G. Kerckoff, with A. G. Wishon as its manager. Wishon was the key to the success of the company. It took several years to expand its operations in Fresno, Tulare, and Merced Counties, and once completed, the company turned its attention to Bakersfield and Kern County. The company incorporated on July 19, 1910, to became San Joaquin Light and Power Corporation with a capitalization of $25 million.

In 1909 the Buena Vista Field natural gas wells were discovered, making it possible to use natural gas on a large scale. Pipeline plans were made, and by early 1910 Standard Oil was using gas to power its west side plants. The California Natural Company, a subsidiary of Standard Oil, was organized later in 1910 and ran a gas pipe line to Bakersfield, where it was connected to the distribution system of the Bakersfield Gas & Electric Company.

The West Side Gas Company was then formed to serve the oil field towns of Maricopa, Taft, and Fellows. In 1913 a pipeline was built across the Tehachapi Mountains to supply Los Angeles with as much as twenty-four million

cubic feet of gas. It was built by the Midway Gas Company, founded by William G. Kerckhoff, president and a founder of the San Joaquin Light and Power Company, predecessor to PG&E.

On August 10, 1910, San Joaquin Light and Power acquired control of the Power Transit & Light Company in Bakersfield. PT&L owned the Kern River hydroelectric plant, transmission lines to Bakersfield, distribution lines within the city, the Bakersfield and Kern Electric Railway System, and the Gas Works. A. Emory Wishon became manager in Bakersfield and later succeeded his father in Fresno, eventually becoming vice president and general manager of PG&E in San Francisco. Wishon was responsible for convincing San Joaquin Light and Power to spread its lines into rural Kern County.

On the day before the take-over of the assets of Power Transit and Light, the load on the generators at the Kern River power plant became too great, and the hydroelectric plant failed. The area was without power, and even a 750-kilowatt steam generator that replaced it was consumed in a fire a short time later. Wishon oversaw the installation of a new steam generation plant at Espee and Union Avenues in Bakersfield, with a five thousand-kilowatt generator. One million dollars later and with a total of fourteen thousand kilowatts, the company had an up-to-date plant with enough electricity to meet the area's needs.

✧

Derrick Avenue, as seen before 1912. It was a well-known feature of Kern's Sunset Oil Field.

✧

At the turn of the century, in Kern County's oil fields, flumes served as pipelines for oil and water. This photo was taken at the Reed Oil Company lease in the Kern River Oil Field.

By 1913 a drought had hit Kern, and the Kern River Plant could not operate without enough water to run its turbines. The plant was shut down and again the area suffered a power shortage. However, the company quickly ran a transmission line from its Kern River powerhouse to connect to the Southern California Edison plant in Kern Canyon. Power was restored, and this became one of the first interchanges of power between two power companies in the United States and a forerunner to the current interchange system.

San Joaquin Light and Power now increased its transmission lines to sixty thousand volts, constructing a 225-mile segment connecting Kern to its hydroelectric plants at the San Joaquin River. Now the company now had

enough electricity to help provide energy for pumping water to irrigate Kern County's farms. New communities like Wasco, Shafter, and McFarland could be served with adequate and reliable power supplies. By 1914, the company had substations at Bakersfield, Famoso, McKittrick, and Midway at a cost of nearly $2.25 million. They built a twenty-five thousand-kilowatt steam plant near Buttonwillow in 1921, extending lines to serve the surrounding area.

At the start of the 1920s, three major utility systems were located in Northern and Central California: Great Western, San Joaquin Light and Power, and PG&E. The end of 1930 would see them all combined into one vast network of electrical power.

As early as 1922, PG&E was offered a chance to buy the stock of Western Power Corporation, the eastern holding company which controlled Great Western. PG&E declined, but it was just a question of time. But Western Power wasn't waiting for PG&E to decide what it wanted to do. Meanwhile, Western Power offered to buy San Joaquin Light and Power.

The combined territories would unite a vast area of California north of the Tehachapi Mountains. The mostly agricultural San Joaquin Valley load complemented the heavily metropolitan Great Western load. Negotiations began in 1924 and James B. Black, who had worked for Great Western since 1912, became the principal architect of the PG&E system of today.

In November 1924 Western Power agreed to buy a controlling interest in the San Joaquin system. The two were interconnected by a 103-mile line from the Brighton Substation to the Wilson Substation near Merced. Around the same time, the North American Company, a larger New York investment firm, obtained stock control of Western Power Corporation including Great Western and San Joaquin Light and Power. But the North American Company board was convinced by Black that it could not acquire the bigger, stronger PG&E, so North American offered to exchange its holdings in Great Western and San Joaquin for PG&E stock.

On March 29, 1930, PG&E agreed to deliver $114 million worth of shares of its common

stock. In return PG&E got stock representing control of Great Western Power, San Joaquin Light and Power and a smaller utility, Midland Counties Public Service. PG&E now served most of Northern and Central California. The actual merger took a bit longer. Great Western was made a direct part of PG&E in 1935. San Joaquin Light and Power stayed under its existing management and in 1938 was merged into the PG&E system as San Joaquin Power, now called the San Joaquin Division.

During World War II, the state's natural gas resource reserves were being drained, and PG&E contracted with El Paso Natural Gas to run a $62 million, thirty-four-inch natural gas pipeline from the company's terminus in Arizona to Milpitas. This gas line ran through Kern County. Afterwards, PG&E put in another pipeline from Canadian gas fields.

In the 1960s the company invested over four million dollars to construct a larger facility at Buttonwillow, constructing the southern anchor of its one thousand-mile, half million-volt transmission system. The Midway Substation is tied to the Los Banos Substation by a 145-mile, half million-volt line. PG&E and Southern California Edison Company, both members of the California Power Pool, were interconnected at Midway Substation. In May 1964, PG&E opened its nearly $1.5 million Kern District service center on a twenty-acre site at Wible Road and White Lane.

PG&E continues to build new transmission lines and facilities to support the growing population of Kern County. It is in the process of shutting down its nuclear facility at Diablo Canyon and others of its facilities are being sold, due to deregulation. The company is building a co-generation plant on the west side to boost its power output in Kern.

PG&E is one of nation's largest investor-owned electric and gas utilities, serving nearly thirteen million people in Northern and Central California. It has widely diversified renewable technologies such as wind power, solar power and biomass. Its natural gas comes from Canada, the U.S. Southwest, and California. The company's seventy-thousand-square-mile service area stretches from Eureka to Bakersfield in the south and from the Pacific Ocean to the Sierra Nevada.

Another important energy resource of Kern County is wind power. The Tehachapi Wind Resource Area is the largest wind energy producer in the world, producing as much energy as the rest of the nation's wind farms. More than forty-six hundred wind turbines are located in the Tehachapi Wind Resource Area, with many visible from Highway 58 east of Tehachapi. Collectively, they generate nearly 1.4 billion kilowatt-hours of electricity per year.

Automatic controls on each machine sense wind direction and speed. With low wind speed, they are disconnected from the power grid. With winds higher than safe operation permits, the use of brakes on the turbines helps to eliminate stress on the machines. The areas newer turbines adjust blade angles to allow the generation of more power over a wider range of wind speeds.

Three types of propellers are in use in the Tehachapi Wind Resource Area. Most unusual is the eggbeater-like Darrieus propeller, operated by FloWind. Early types of turbines used two-blade propellers, while the current designs have three blades. Capacities of the turbines as well as their physical size have increased over the years. The early turbines from the

✧

This was a typical tenthouse from the early 1900s, photographed at Reward on Kern's west side.

mid-1980s had a maximum output of only ten kilowatts and the later Enron Wind Corporation turbines can generate 1.5 megawatts and have many automatic performance optimizing controls for the various wind speeds. The various companies operating at Tehachapi include Zond, CalWind, SeaWest, Mogul Energy, FloWind, Cannon, Coram, and AWT.

This wind turbine area should be seen as a gigantic power plant that feeds the nation's power grid. Its energy production should allow the reduction of pollution created by coal and other fossil-fuel generators. The latest estimates show that Tehachapi's wind plants can reduce the emission of greenhouse gasses by over one billion pounds annually and that of sulfur oxides, nitrogen oxides, and related particulate matter by seven million pounds annually.

Thousands of people from around the world visit Tehachapi's wind power plants. Hikers can enjoy visiting several wind energy farms which are situated on the Pacific Crest Trail, accessible at the intersection of Highway 58 and Cameron Road, about seven miles east of Tehachapi. Especially dramatic is the view offered north of Oak Creek Road.

Tehachapi itself is an old community, first settled by Americans in the 1860s. Old Town, as the first settlement was known after the town moved, was located west of the present city of Tehachapi. The population declined, and most moved over to a new settlement named Greenwich, named for its first postmaster, Peter Green, in 1875. Greenwich was a mile west of present-day Tehachapi, which was first settled when the Southern Pacific Railroad laid out the community along its line in 1876, first calling it Summit Station.

The town was incorporated in 1909. By 1912 a forty-acre commercial pear orchard was in the area, beginning the fruit tree industry in Tehachapi. Tehachapi is well-known for its apples and other tree fruits that are sold worldwide.

The community was stricken at 4:52 AM on July 21, 1952, when a shattering earthquake demolished much of the community. Measuring at 7.6 on the Richter scale, it lasted for forty-five seconds and was responsible for the deaths of eleven people. The earthquake also damaged much of the southern San Joaquin Valley, where a further aftershock in August damaged much of Arvin and Bakersfield.

VALLEY DEVELOPMENT: BOOM AND BUST IN THE EARLY TWENTIETH CENTURY (1898-1945)

After the arrival of the Santa Fe Railroad (San Francisco-San Joaquin Valley Railroad) in 1898, things seemed to change in Kern County. Transportation was easily available up the valley and down to Los Angeles. Although the Southern Pacific Railroad had more than adequate passenger service prior to the arrival of the Santa Fe, shippers of produce now had two major railroads to compete for their business and the railroads knew it.

The age of the automobile was upon us, and the horseless carriage was about to come to Kern. It is said that a Locomobile was the first such vehicle in Bakersfield, owned by William S. Tevis, president of the Kern County Land Company. Tevis would later have a number of big automobiles, including a White Steamer. Roads around the county were unpaved, but this did not stop booming automobile sales by the middle of the first decade of the century. By 1912, there were over four thousand automobiles in the county.

A number of automobile clubs were started at the time but it wasn't until 1915 that the Board of Supervisors authorized the mapping and posting of signs on Kern's important roads and highways.

The state recognized the need of a state-wide road system as early as 1896, when a map and a report were submitted by the three members of the newly formed State Bureau of Highways. They prepared a sketch map showing a general outline of a possible state highway network. In Kern County, the north-south roads, Highway 99 and Interstate 5 are exceptionally close to the report's proposals. East and west aren't as close, but the general idea was nevertheless there. Not until 1902 would the State Highway System be established, and it took an amendment to the state constitution to give the legislature power to do so.

It wouldn't be until 1909 that the legislature would authorize the state's first bond issue of $18,000. The voters narrowly passed it in 1910. By 1923 a gasoline tax was first put on the books and is still there. Its purpose was solely to finance the state's highways.

One of California's and Kern County's first foray with highways was the north-south Highway 99. The original route, the Midway Route to Los Angeles, ran through Tehachapi and Mojave. But the new

✧

Kern General Hospital, in East Bakersfield, as seen in 1937. The hospital replaced the old county hospital located at Nineteenth and Oak.

1915 road would cut the distance by fifty-eight miles by going south. Between Gorman and Castaic in Los Angeles County, there were 697 turns. The road was covered or hard-surfaced with oiled rock or bituminous macadam when it opened in 1915 but was paved four years later with four inches of reinforced concrete. This was called the Ridge Route.

A straighter thirty-six-mile, three-lane road was built between 1931 and 1934 and was known as the Alternate Ridge Route. This was good for driving but bad for the rest stops along the old road, most of which closed. Once in the valley, the highway ran north, extending into Union Avenue south of Bakersfield. It took a number of turns through town, generally up Chester Avenue to Robert's Lane. At different times, it went down Brundage Lane, California Avenue, and Nineteenth Street in Bakersfield. Before World War II, an alternate route, Golden State Avenue, was cut through the east side of Bakersfield, diagonally running parallel with the Southern Pacific tracks from Twenty-fourth Street. In the mid-1960s, a larger-scale highway was opened west of Bakersfield, parallel with Oak Street and Wible Road. Though significantly widened, this is today's Highway 99.

Construction of Interstate 5 started in 1960 making old Highway 99 look like a toy road. But it wasn't until 1970 that the first stretch of freeway in Kern County, between Taft Highway and Lerdo Highway, would open. It was constructed as an all-weather highway but hasn't quite lived up to that title. It runs into Kern's west side and up the valley, paralleling the California Aqueduct.

Other highways in Kern were soon to change. State Route 58 over Tehachapi Pass and

through Mojave was the old road, winding up Caliente Creek. By the 1960s it was moved to its present course, making the climb up the grade much easier. Over the years it has been widened to its present state. Highway 178 through Kern Canyon has pretty much the same historical pattern, having been first constructed at the turn of the century. Part of it above Miracle Hot Springs was widened into a four lane highway in the 1970s. Bakersfield is a hub for all these highways in Kern County.

Bakersfield has a somewhat checkered past when it comes to the organization of government. It has been incorporated twice, once from 1873 to 1876 and again in 1898. Residents of Bakersfield petitioned to incorporate, thus establishing a government of their own. The Kern County Board of Supervisors declared that Bakersfield was an incorporated town and called for an election on May 24, 1873.

In 1874, the county seat was moved to Bakersfield, but it would be years before the town grew into what could be reasonably called a city. From the late 1860s on, residents assumed the Southern Pacific Railroad would come into Bakersfield. To aid in this, residents of the county squeaked through a vote to move the seat of government from the declining Havilah to Bakersfield. The vote was contested and probably rightly so, but it wasn't until January 1874 that the victory for Bakersfield was made official. The railroad didn't come to town, however. Instead, it ran to the north of Bakersfield into its own community named Sumner, now East Bakersfield.

Both newspapers in town openly criticized the city trustees who had piled up debt with no means of paying it back. Town services were not being performed. In addition to problems with the town marshal, the powers of the incorporation did not allow the city fathers to gain the finances for any type of city improvements. The water system consisted of ditches flowing along the streets. The sanitation system was stagnant and ridden with disease. Outhouses were left unattended and created a health hazard. Streets were either filled with alkaline dust or bogged down in mud.

By mid-1874 the townspeople had enough and began circulating petitions to disincorporate Bakersfield. In July the Board of

Supervisors, perhaps out of touch with the residents of Bakersfield, decided to table the issue until the next legislative session, hoping the state would remedy the town's power structure. They felt that most of the people who signed the petitions really wanted only to bring the matter to the attention of the board. But it was all in vain as by January 3, 1876 the board had enough of the problem. The legislature had failed to act upon the problem while in session, so the only recourse was to accept the petition of the citizenry and disincorporate the town.

Over the next twenty years, residents of Bakersfield were continually dissatisfied with the lack of services the county had been providing the community. On Tuesday, January 4, 1898, voters decided to try again. The vote for incorporation won by a two-to-one margin, and once again Bakersfield was an incorporated city. The first trustees were to be Paul (Pablo) Galtes, Leonard P. St. Clair, W. MacMurdo, H. H. Fish, and Jacob Walters.

The city operated under the management of individual department heads appointed by the board of trustees. The city clerk, assessor, treasurer, auditor, attorney, street superintendent, fire chief, marshal, and police magistrate all worked directly for the trustees. This presented some interesting problems with special interests on the board of trustees. In the early days of the city of Bakersfield, after the 1898 incorporation, City Hall was located at 1523 Wall Street.

Further changes were on the horizon for Bakersfield with the 1909 vote and 1910 merger with the town of Kern (formerly known as Sumner), now known as East Bakersfield. In 1914, Bakersfield became the twenty-ninth city in the United States to adopt the city manager form of government, as a charter city. This segregated the city management by department heads.

By this time Bakersfield was known as having more ready money per capita than any other city on the West Coast. The same is said to have applied to automobiles. The city had an opera house and four theaters. It also had over twenty saloons in the two blocks of Nineteenth Street, between K and M Streets. But the city also had the County Board of Trade, a

Merchant's Association, and a Realty Board. Things were looking up for Bakersfield.

The area north of the Santa Fe Railroad tracks and west of F Street was also developed after the arrival of the railroad in 1898, and after the oil boom of the 1900s. This land was part of the vast Kern County Land Company property and had been held back for years, partly due to its proximity to town but also due to the lack of need on the part of the Land Company to increase revenues and the poor building potential of the land. The land had been part of the old middle fork of the Kern River with Panama Slough and Reeder Lake running right through the middle of it. Reeder Lake was a body of shallow water formed by low lands which backed up water of the old slough. It was full in the winter and marshy in the summer. Reeder Lake was located in the area approximately where present-day Jastro Park is located.

In 1896 the County built its hospital and "Pest House" at the end of Nineteenth Street near Oak Street. The hospital provided indigent care and was a beautiful facility. Once the county built it, the hospital opened the door for further development in the area. The Land Company, by coincidence, was also divesting itself of land at the time. This allowed the development of the area from Twenty-second Street to the Santa Fe tracks. Earlier, in 1891, the Kern County Land Company opened a small tract roughly between

✧

The Bakersfield Opera House, seen here in 1908, later became the Nile Theater.

F Street and A Street, and California Avenue and Seventeenth Street. Part of this area is now Bakersfield High School, and another part is the Mercy Hospital complex.

Another very small tract, the Brower Tract, opened up in 1889. This was located between D and F Streets and Seventeenth and Nineteenth Streets. It was designed specifically for the large Celsus Brower House, which has been gone for many years.

With the growth came other problems. Bakersfield was well known as an "open town" where anything goes. The city police under Marshal James McKamy seemed to allow houses of ill repute, gambling houses, opium dens, and other activities of less than stellar behavior. Although McKamy was ousted by court order in 1914, it would still be years before things got better in Bakersfield.

Bakersfield had its second major fire in 1919, when the northeast side of Chester Avenue and Nineteenth Street burned. Hochheimer's bakery and grocery warehouse, between Nineteenth and Twentieth Streets, caught fire in the evening of August 21. The fire was so intense it damaged or destroyed nearly the entire block and the Grand Hotel on the northeast corner of Chester Avenue and Twentieth Street. Water pressure, or lack of it, was a key factor in the immense blaze. After the fire, a better water system was installed. Hochheimer and Company, the Hopkins Building, American Jewelers, the Grand Hotel, Weill's Warehouse, the Monte Carlo, and Exchange Bars were all destroyed. The apartments above Weill's Department Store were also damaged.

Fires were a constant worry in the city with so many wood frame buildings and houses. The great fire of 1889 eliminated all of the old wood frame buildings in downtown Bakersfield, but outside the commercial area they still exist. The Bakersfield City Fire Department has come a long way from the days of a call man on duty at night in the station. Although Bakersfield still has large fires, their damage is usually limited due to fire plans and a well organized fire department.

Kern County has been known as a leader in innovation. In 1891, twelve years before the Wright brothers flew at Kitty Hawk, Charles Howard ascended a hot air balloon one thousand feet up and successfully jumped with his parachute. He took home a sizable purse paid by curious onlookers. Lighter-than-air flights were made every year during the Kern County Fair season since the 1891 jump. In 1910 the Kern County Board of Trade arranged for Glenn Curtiss to bring airplanes to Kern. Charles K. Hamilton piloted the craft twice; it was Kern's first airplane flight.

A major landmark of note in the Oildale area is the old Terminal Building at the Kern County Airport, Meadows Field. Constructed in 1927, the building represents the world's first county-owned airport, then known as Kern County Airport No. 1.

Originally established in 1926 at a location approximately one mile west of its present location, the airport was relocated in 1927. It is now known as Meadows Field, named after Cecil Meadows, long-time superintendent of Kern County airports beginning in 1935.

Before the airport facility north of the river was established, another landing field was located north of the corner of Sacramento and Monterey Streets in the Alta Vista Tracts, a large vacant area. This facility was known as Bernard Field and was operated by the Pacific Aero Club. It was the landing strip for the U.S. Airmail service later (1923-1926) known as the Alta Vista Tracts One and Two. Yet another field was located on the bluffs, approximately where Greenlawn Cemetery is located.

Since then, the Kern County Airport System has expanded into many other areas of the county, from the west side to the desert. At Meadows Field, fantastic new facilities blend in with the old, creating a collage of varying architecture. The Army Air Corps had a flight training school at the airport during the Second World War. A new school, the International Flight Training Academy, operates today, training pilots and flight crews from around the world. Meadows Field is Kern's answer to up-to-date flying. It is continually expanding to accommodate ever-increasing business.

As the economy prospered, Kern grew and expanded its industrial base. Through the 1920s the economy soared, even with prohibition at hand. But as fate would have it, the good times soon turned to bad. The stock market had been acting erratically in 1929, so much so that funds were being infused by bankers in the hope of riding through the storm. But by October there was clearly an overwhelming problem, and soon the nation would be in the grips of the Great Depression.

The issue of public relief was now a real one with thousands of people out of work. Jobs were needed to supply wages for survival, and the several hundred jobs working at the county parks, on road crews, and in fire prevention provided by the citizens relief programs didn't seem enough. But they did help to ease at least some of the problem. Transient camps were set up in the southern valley, with an early one between Bakersfield and Oildale near the old fairgrounds. Another early camp was set up near Taft. These were the predecessors to the larger migrant camps of the mid to late 1930s.

The Civilian Conservation Corps came to the county in 1933 with laborers working on Kern's roads, planting trees, cutting under-brush, and other laborious work. Camps were set up in Isabella, Glennville, Havilah, and Tehachapi. Later, classes were set up in the camps, enabling workers to gain their high school diplomas or training in other fields. Other government programs provided food and other commodities for those in need. The Civil Works Administration provided jobs landscaping Kern River Park, now Hart Park.

The WPA was responsible for the construction of some of Kern's most notable public buildings, including the Fort in Taft, and the now gone Welfare and Agricultural buildings, later known as the Golden State Complex, on Golden State Avenue in Bakersfield. It also brought art projects to Kern, including the Garces Statue on Chester Avenue in Bakersfield.

By the mid-1930s, Kern was at least surviving, but another blow from afar was to fall on its shoulders. By 1934 the Dust Bowl of the mid-west was becoming a factor in western migration. Migrants were coming into the county by the hundreds, and locals were becoming alarmed that the migrants were taking local jobs, leaving Kern's residents dependent on relief programs. By 1935, George D. Nickel, county administrator for the State Emergency Relief

✧

The Shafter Migratory Farm Labor Camp, seen here in 1939, was an expansive facility for migrant workers.

By 1939 the area was ripe for criticism in literature and photographs with writers such as John Steinbeck working in the area. Steinbeck's *The Grapes of Wrath* caused such a furor in Kern County that the Board of Supervisors banned the book from the libraries. Pickets gathered at the courthouse demonstrating for the cause of free speech, giving the downtown area of Bakersfield a circus appearance.

Shafter, named after Spanish-American War General William Shafter, was founded as a potential agricultural colony by the Kern County Land Company in 1912. It was located along the Santa Fe Railroad line that was built through the area in 1898. The townsite was surveyed beginning in late 1912 and given the name because Shafter was a friend of Kern County Land Company President Henry Jastro. Formal colonizing efforts never materialized, but the community did thrive. Its two most famous landmarks, the Santa Fe Depot and the Green Hotel date from near the beginning of the community and have both been restored and placed on the National Register of Historic Places. Shafter was incorporated in 1938 and became a charter city in 1995. It is in Kern's farm belt and is rich in agricultural products, known especially for its potatoes and cotton.

Wasco is another Kern County community whose name originated with the Spanish-American War. When the Santa Fe Railroad (SF-SJV) established a depot along its new line in 1897, it named it Dewey, after war hero Admiral George Dewey. The name was soon changed to Deweyville.

In June 1900 the name was changed to Wasco after it was discovered by early settler William Bonham that there was a town already named Deweyville. His foster child Jimmy was a Wasco Indian from Arizona, and he proposed the area be renamed Wasco.

A number of settlers eventually came to the area, but it would not be until 1907, when Marshall V. Hartranft bought 640 acres from the Kern County Land Company and began to resell it. This initial settlement area was called the Fourth Home Extension Colony, and from it emerged the community of Wasco.

Early on the community had the railroad depot, a hotel, a general store, post office, two saloons, and a blacksmith shop. By 1911, the

Administration, told the Board of Supervisors that the conditions of the migrant camps were deplorable and recommended that labor camps be built near Arvin with SERA funds.

The Federal Migratory Camp was opened in December 1936 by the Farm Security Administration. For a token charge, the campers were given a platform with camp amenities. The county's camp near Shafter was closed and reopened as a FSA camp in 1937. Families flocked to the camps. Many locals were opposed to the camps and the federal aid given to the Okies and Arkies who came from the east. An informal tiered class system began and lasted into the 1960s.

Public facilities such as schools and hospitals were overwhelmed for the next several years.

Communities such as Shafter, Wasco, McFarland, Delano, Buttonwillow, Arvin, Taft, and Bakersfield were affected by the influx of unemployed poor migrants.

San Joaquin Light and Power Company had run power to Wasco, and local residents were installing much needed irrigation pumps. This aided in the eventual development of local cotton and the famous Wasco potato, with large enterprises like Maple Leaf Enterprises having potato sheds, cotton gins, and, later, even a radio station. The Wasco Creamery was built by the Kern County Dairyman's Cooperative Association, which organized in 1915. The creamery was known throughout the county and operated until the end of the Second World War.

The Biofirm was another well-known business in Wasco, taking over some of the old Wasco Creamery property. It served the agricultural community with a wide variety of developmental projects before closing in the late 1960s.

Lately the focus from Wasco has been roses, acres of them. Wasco is now known as the rose capital of the world. There are hundreds of varieties of roses growing in fields that once grew cotton and potatoes.

Incorporated in 1945, Wasco has always been an agricultural community. However, like many communities, changes had to be made to survive. The city of Wasco chose to be a location for a state prison in which there are currently close to six thousand inmates. The city plans to add another four thousand inmates with a new private prison.

McFarland is an agricultural community located along Highway 99. The town was founded in 1908 by real estate developers William F. Laird and James B. McFarland. It was placed beside the Southern Pacific Railroad tracks to ensure the availability of adequate shipping facilities. The community

was incorporated in 1957, after forty years of failed proposals. Mount Whitney Power Company was the first supplier of power in 1910, but others in the area were later supplied by San Joaquin Light and Power in 1912.

The State Department of Corrections has contracted the Wakenhut Corporation to build and operate three community correctional facilities in McFarland. For McFarland it was undoubtedly a boon, at least to the tax and revenue base. McFarland is a small community consisting mostly of workers from Kern's agricultural industry. The community continues to work with the difficulties of most rural communities.

McFarland's neighbor to the north, Delano, was founded in July 1873 and was the temporary terminus of the Southern Pacific Railroad. The railroad was in the process of laying its tracks south to Sumner, near Bakersfield, where it would turn east into the Tehachapi Mountains. The town was named in honor of then U.S. Secretary of the Interior Columbus Delano.

Delano became an important shipping point for sheep and cattle, and the community prospered. Soon the area became a focal point for dry farmers, growing wheat, which they also shipped from there. Mount Whitney Power Company finally reached Delano with its lines in 1908, allowing for great improvement of agricultural irrigation.

The community grew steadily, becoming incorporated on April 13, 1915. By 1920, the community had a Masonic Lodge, a Woman's Club, an Odd Fellows Lodge, and other organizations to support its population. Today, Delano is well known for its table grapes, almonds, and other agricultural products.

❖

This 1917 photograph of Main Street in Wasco shows how it looked at the end of the second decade of the twentieth century.

The soil is fertile, water appears to be abundant, and growing conditions allow for the cultivation of premier vineyards. It has a state prison and is developing a strong industrial complex. Being on Freeway 99, Delano is positioned for growth in the near future.

Like McFarland, Delano serves a large agricultural labor community and is an important trade community for northern Kern and southern Tulare Counties. In the 1960s and '70s, a growing disdain for working conditions of local farm laborers caused Delano to be the center of activities by the United Farm Workers Union. Delano suffered from unrest for a period of time, but community, farm, and labor leaders were able to mutually work out their individual concerns and allow the community to resettle. Although the unemployment rate in Delano has been over twenty-five percent for a number of years, continual efforts are being made to reemploy the population. Delano has over thirty-four thousand residents and has become a community with great ethnic diversity.

Buttonwillow is the home to what was called one of the "greatest real estate transfers in the history of Kern County." This involved the huge holdings of Miller & Lux when they were sold off in 1927. On the block was the multi-thousand acre Buttonwillow Ranch, one of the key holdings of the company. Miller & Lux actually held the town as a company town, with its post office opening in 1895.

The town was named Buttonwillow after a native tree, one of which still stands behind a state historical landmark monument. At the turn of the century, Miller & Lux began to import Italian colonists to farm its land, including the Torrigianni, Romanini, and Pierucci families. Later, Miller & Lux sold them property, and many

became prosperous Kern County residents. It wouldn't be until 1954 that curbs and gutters were in place in Buttonwillow, but the town has now grown into a cozy farming community. Its proximity to the off ramp at Interstate 5 and State Highway 58 made it ideal for expansion.

The Arvin area was first settled by dry farmers growing wheat in the 1880s, but nothing permanent was developed until the founding of the Foothill Citrus Farms Company colony in 1907. The colony was plagued with problems from the beginning, including silting of its well and frozen citrus trees. But they persevered, and by 1914 the townsite had been surveyed and a post office established. The town was named Arvin after a well-respected resident, Arvin Richardson.

By 1920, the community was doing well, with a long growing season for their potatoes, grapes, and cotton. By 1923, the Southern Pacific laid in a rail line to the area, after which the Santa Fe Railroad obtained a half interest. Land sales were brisk, with buyers like Thomas Derby, John Kovacevich, brothers Forrest, Lester, and Lloyd Frick, and Elza Mitchell. Joseph DiGiorgio had purchased the Earl Fruit Company and, with holdings north of Arvin, became a major grower, packer, and shipper in the area. DiGiorgio Corporation is still a major grower, packer, and shipper of fruit in Kern County.

Arvin was incorporated in 1960 and is well known for its Arvin Lions Club and Arvin Boosters Club. The *Arvin Tiller*, its newspaper, has been a fixture in the community since 1939 and is still in operation.

Lamont, Arvin's neighbor to the northwest, was founded in 1923, by Arthur J. McFadden, and named Lamont after his Scottish family clan, LaMont. Early settlers in the area were the Cattani, Clendenen, Thompson, and Thornburgh families. By 1939 the community was occupied by migrants from the Midwest and workers from the then-closing DiGiorgio worker camps. This led to the increased need for various services and businesses.

Soon clubs and churches were arriving, and the town was more like a small developed community. Lamont has been a community with a high farm labor population for the last fifty years and struggles perennially to keep up with health care, education, housing, and various other social-related services. It is located on Weedpatch Highway between Panama Lane and Bear Mountain Boulevard.

The United States was not the only country to suffer from the economic slowdown of the Depression. In Europe and the Far East, material shortages and restless populations were hotbeds for change, and change it did. By the late 1930s, Germany had openly been aggressive in Europe and the Mediterranean, and Japan had begun its spread into the Pacific on the quest for oil, rubber, and other supplies. The war clouds in Europe overshadowed the Japanese Army's brutal expansion into China.

Kern County has had a large Chinese population since the days of the Southern Pacific Railroad, when Chinese workers came into the area to build the line. Several of the community's favorite residents were Chinese-Americans with ties to the old country, and local people wanted to help. A number of Bowl of Rice days were held in 1939 to raise funds for Chinese relief for the hungry, ill, and suffering. Bakersfield and Kern County raised the third largest amount of funds, second only to New York and San Francisco.

Meanwhile the National Guard was gearing up to be prepared for any possible outbreak of hostilities in the United States. A Kern County battalion of the 144th Field Artillery out of Santa Barbara began training in October 1940 and went on active duty in February 1941. This coincided with the beginning of conscription and the formation of five draft boards in Kern County. The first draftees left for Los Angeles in November 1940. A quota system was created and quotas filled as needed. By June 1941, even the National Guard was called to active duty.

By December 1941, an air squadron from Moffett Field near Sunnyvale was moved to Kern County Airport in Bakersfield to train. The airport was taken over by the military as a training school for five weeks until the weather at Moffett Field was better. By July 1942, the airport was designated a sub-base of Hammer Field near Fresno. Named Bakersfield Airdrome and known as the "bomber base," it had five hundred officers and men training with bomber, fighter, and later, new jet-propelled craft.

Shafter's Minter Field was named for Lieutenant Hugh C. Minter, a Kern County High School graduate and Army Air Corps career officer who was killed in a midair collision in 1932. The field served as a training base for a diverse number of pilots, including an all-black aviation squadron from Louisiana. It was later used to train cadets from China for preflight and basic training.

At Minter Field are the remains of the U.S. Army's Defense Landing Area Program Flight Training Center, which was opened in 1941. The field was constructed for the Army and was like a small city. In all, there were seven thousand personnel stationed at the airfield during World War II. Much is now gone, but built there were a chapel, swimming pool, theater, post office, infirmary, barracks, and many support buildings.

Minter Field was operated by the U.S. Army from 1941 to 1946, when it was deactivated.

✧

The late nineteenth century Delano Grammar School was believed to have been damaged in the 1906 earthquake, after which it was strengthened with iron braces. The building was torn down in 1915.

The United States Army Air Corps training base of Minter Field as seen at its dedication ceremonies on February 7, 1942.

By 1949, it was turned over to the County of Kern. The county operated and managed the airport until 1985, when it was turned over to the Minter Field Airport District. Local residents and tenants of the facility who were willing to take over the ownership and operation of the airport from the County formed the district.

In more recent history, Minter Field was the site of the first flight of the Gossamer Condor, the first sustained man-powered flight. A state-registered historical landmark marks the field near its entrance. Several operators of air racing planes are located at Minter Field. Other former military planes frequent the field, and an annual air show, Warbirds in Action, was presented there for a number of years. The Minter Field Air Museum is also located there.

Another Kern County airfield was Gardner Field, located about eight miles southwest of Taft. Gardner Field was constructed between April and October 1941 and named after native Californian Major John H. Gardner, who was killed by a whirling propeller in 1938. Initial training took place in June 1941 at Taft, with flight training at an auxiliary field until Gardner Field could be finished. Operations were to the field in July, Gardner Field was dedicated in October 1941. As the U.S. became more entangled in World War II, several hundred mechanics were recruited to keep the planes in the air. A Women's Army Auxiliary Corps unit was billeted at Gardner Field in June 1943 to deal with numerous jobs.

Gardner Field served four years as a basic training school, graduating its last class in February 1945. Eventually all structures were sold off and moved, leaving the field site abandoned.

A number of volunteer State Guard units were formed in Kern County, first in Bakersfield, then in Taft. Sheriff John E. Loustalot organized an air raid detection corps with volunteers stationed strategically throughout the county. Over one hundred spotter posts were located throughout the county by December 1942.

The order to secure Japanese Americans hit Kern County pretty hard, as over eight hundred lived in the county. The fear that they could include saboteurs of Kern's oil and power plants caused their evacuation to relocation centers. Most of Kern's Japanese Americans were relocated to Poston, Arizona, where they sat out the war. Many young Japanese-American men served in the armed forces during the war.

Agriculture suffered from lack of labor during the war years. Many crops were simply abandoned and plowed under because of this. An interesting planting of guayule rubber plants was made on nine thousand acres, supervised by the U.S. Forest Service. The first harvest was in April 1945, when forty-five hundred pounds were harvested for shipment. Once the war was over, plantings ceased, and most of the land went back to other uses.

During the war, there were several prisoner-of-war camps for German and Japanese captives in Kern County, including Arvin and Shafter. Farmers were able to use the POWs by contracting with the government, which paid them prevailing wages. Once the German POWs were removed in October 1945, a couple of thousand Japanese POWs were moved into the Lamont camp. They were released in 1946.

By the end of the war in 1945, there were around fourteen thousand Kern County men serving in the armed forces. Nearly five hundred Kern County men lost their lives in the war. As the war ended, local residents celebrated the return of their soldiers, sailors, airmen, and marines, and looked forward to recovering their pre-war lifestyles.

SHAKY START TO A NEW ERA: POST-WAR KERN COUNTY

Less than fifty years have passed since the devastation of the 1952 earthquake and aftershocks. Bakersfield has grown several-fold in that period of time, developing onto the old Kern County Land Company lands and Miller & Lux properties to the west. Although the Kern County Land Company began releasing blocks of land before the war, it was not until the purchase of the company, first by Tenneco West, and then by Castle and Cooke, that an immense growth of housing and commercial development took place. Urban sprawl toward the mountains continues and is swallowing up the old historic communities that started it all. Perhaps the old predictions of a sprawling southern valley, full of houses and commercial buildings, are not so far off after all.

Not coincidentally, the discoveries of recoverable oil in the Kern River Fields in 1899 also stimulated a boom in construction in Bakersfield which was unparalleled. Thousands flocked into the area, again causing an upsurge in the building trades. More houses and commercial buildings were constructed in Bakersfield between 1905 and 1915 than in the city's first forty years.

Further west on Truxtun Avenue, the area north of the Santa Fe Railroad tracks and west of F Street was also developed after the arrival of the railroad in 1898 and after the oil boom of the 1900s. This land was part of the vast Kern County Land Company property and had been held back for years, partly

✧

This photograph, taken by Jack Knight on General Beale Loop at Highway 58, shows the severity of the 1977 dust storm that caused millions of dollars of damage in Kern County.

due to its proximity to town. The Kern County Land Company, later to become Tenneco West, first developed southwest Bakersfield. Areas such as Old Stockdale, which were sold off in the 1920s and 1930s, were part of the old Kern County Land Company ranches.

Old Stockdale is part of the Stockdale Ranch, which dates from the 1880s. This ranch was a local base for the Tevis family of the Kern County Land Company. Further west, in the area where Cal State University Bakersfield is located, is where the old Bellevue Ranch covered many acres. This was an extensive cattle ranch with its own slaughterhouse and packing plant. The ranch survived in one form or another until the early 1980s, when its last remaining vestiges were removed for development.

Another of the Kern County Land Company's early ranch properties was the Greenfields Ranch, in the approximate location of present-day community of Greenfield. This ranch was once one of the land company's colony ventures, but, as with the Rosedale Colony, the effort failed. The original ranch dates from the 1870s.

Many of Bakersfield's earlier developments were parts of or entire parcels of property once held by Kern's pioneers. With the encroachment of new development, these parcels were either sold to developers, or developed by the owners,

thus adding housing or commercial property to the landscape. Much of the prime early ranch land in the Bakersfield area has been developed for more than one hundred years.

From the time of Colonel Thomas Baker to the beginning of the twentieth century, Bakersfield had grown into a thriving community, with fine brick buildings and wonderful homes. During the first fifteen years of the twentieth century the city prospered from the great oil discoveries all around it in Kern County. It also benefited from the mining discoveries in Kern's Desert, where many investors in Bakersfield made their fortunes.

From early in the twentieth century through the Second World War, Bakersfield was experiencing a slow but steady growth, and housing subdivision expansion in the northeast, with areas like Alta Vista and La Cresta Tracts opening up for home building.

After World War II ended, veterans flocked to California to settle down, and housing was, for a while, at a premium. Hundreds of veterans made their way to Kern County and Bakersfield, where the shortage was so severe that the Southern Pacific Railroad opened fifty portable units for the most desperate families. Many more than a hundred sought shelter with the Bakersfield Service Center during

December 1945 alone. Housing startups began in Bakersfield and other parts of the county, but it was quite a while until supply caught up with demand.

By 1952 Bakersfield was a thriving community with much to be proud of in the way of architectural style. However, nature would soon change forever the way the city looked. July 21, 1952, brought an early morning wake-up call in the form of an earthquake in the magnitude of 7.6 on the Richter scale to the communities of Tehachapi and Arvin. At 4:52 AM, it also pounded Bakersfield. During the thirty-one-day period afterward, Cal Tech Pasadena seismologists recorded one hundred and eighty aftershocks having a magnitude of 4 or higher. The counting of those below 4 in magnitude stopped when they exceeded three hundred in number. The earthquake registered on the 1 through 12 Modified Mercalli intensity scale at 10 to 11, indicating near total destruction close to the epicenter.

The quake occurred along the White Wolf Fault and caused extensive surface ruptures near Bear Mountain. Many aftershocks occurred, including two of magnitude 6.3 before the end of the month, contributing to the widespread damage. The July earthquake nearly leveled Tehachapi and did severe damage to Arvin at the base of the Tehachapi Mountains.

The 1952 earthquake was the largest earthquake in Southern California since the Fort Tejon earthquake of 1857 and the Owens Valley earthquake of 1872, both of which left heavy damage in those areas and were felt throughout Kern County. It was felt as far away as Reno, Nevada, and construction workers in Las Vegas were required to realign structural steel in their buildings. In San Francisco, people on the upper floors of tall buildings felt it. Los Angeles suffered from power disruption as well as minor building damage. Communities as far south as San Diego suffered structural damage.

The Tehachapi earthquake claimed twelve lives and was responsible for at least eighteen injuries. It directly caused more than $50 million in property damage, mostly to Tehachapi, Arvin, and surrounding areas. However, many buildings and structures in Bakersfield were also severely damaged, causing their eventual demolition. In Bakersfield, the

Beale Memorial Clock Tower suffered the loss of all four clock faces. The Paloma Oil Refinery caught fire and exploded in a huge ball of flame, causing some World War II veterans to believe the Russians had just dropped the bomb. And no wonder, as the U.S. Coast and Geodetic Survey estimated the earth had released the equivalent of 2,000 1952-era atomic bombs.

For Bakersfield, the Tehachapi earthquake was only the beginning of a month of terror, capped off with a jolt that would end Bakersfield's cosmopolitan appearance and usher in the so-called modern era. An aftershock of 5.7 on the Richter scale, not even close to the strongest of the aftershocks of the July 21 earthquake, made the brick and mortar of Bakersfield's proud downtown buildings crumble into dust. The earthquake aftershock had a high frequency which targeted the short, rigid buildings of Bakersfield. It was described as a sickening, rolling wave of terror that lasted for fifteen seconds, but for many, it felt more like a lifetime. There were at least eighteen other aftershocks of magnitude 5.0 or greater that had shaken the area.

Two people were killed and thirty-five injuries were reported as a result of this temblor. It had caused an additional $25 million worth of property damage, mostly confined to buildings in the sixty-four-block area of downtown Bakersfield.

It was the loss of the great architecture of Bakersfield that had the most impact on the

✧

Several casualties from the 1952 Tehachapi earthquake occurred in Hotel Juanita near the epicenter of the quake.

community's residents. The Beale Memorial Clock Tower, which had stood in the middle of the intersection of Seventeenth Street and Chester Avenue since 1904, was so severely damaged the city fathers had it torn down. The west spire of St. Francis Church, another turn of the century landmark, collapsed into rubble, causing the demolition of the entire structure. The same applied to many other churches, commercial, and governmental buildings. Bakersfield City Hall, built in 1876 as a county courthouse, had cracks large enough to put an arm through, and the same applied to the 1912 Kern County Courthouse. Today Bakersfield has large modern buildings, both private and public. It continues to grow, both in the original downtown and surrounding areas.

In 1960 Bakersfield's population was fifty-seven thousand and the city had nearly seventeen square miles. In the year 2000, the city had a population of over 237,000 with over ninety-eight square miles of city limits. It is still surrounded by fields of cotton, potatoes, grapes, citrus, pistachios, almonds, carrots, and other crops.

By the mid 1960s, the city was bustling with activity, with a metropolitan population of about 165,000. It had half the population of the county and was about to begin a growth trend unprecedented in its history. The two railroads still had their huge shops and passenger and freight stations in Bakersfield. The Southern Pacific was located on Sumner Street in East Bakersfield, and the Santa Fe station and freight house was on F Street, in the heart of the city. Both the Santa Fe and the Southern Pacific were transcontinental rail lines, connecting Bakersfield with the state and nation.

Augmenting the railroads in passenger and freight service were the Greyhound and Trailways bus lines that operated on regular schedules. By the year 2000, neither railroad had shops in Bakersfield, nor did they operate much in the line of freight, as most operations had been

Above: The Beale Memorial Clock Tower was a local landmark until damaged in the 1952 earthquake and aftershocks. A shorter recreation was built at the Kern County Museum and dedicated in 1964. The original clock tower was erected by the children of Mary Edwards Beale in her honor in 1903-04.

Right: Extensive damage is seen after the 1952 earthquake in Lerner's Dress Shop on Nineteenth Street in Bakersfield. One person was killed and several others were injured at the location.

consolidated into other yards either up the valley or in rail facilities like Barstow, where automatic switching takes place. Bus lines have consolidated and severely cut back on their schedules. Another connection to Los Angeles, Airport Bus, operates to fill the void of connecting flights into LAX that used to leave Bakersfield's Meadows Field, located in Oildale.

Oildale is just north of the Kern River, with its center running up North Chester Avenue. It has its own post office; in fact, the main Bakersfield postal center is at the west side of Oildale. Oildale has its own identity, initially established with the Kern River oil boom at the turn of the century, when it was called Waits. Though the boom is over, the area was heavily settled in the 1930s and 1940s by migrants from the Dust Bowl, sometimes giving it the nickname of "Little Okie."

But the community has outlived the name and offers a laid back lifestyle. Some see Oildale as just part of Bakersfield, but many residents of Oildale proudly claim their separate distinction.

The Standard School District is in Oildale and is considered to be one of the best in the state. The same applies to the Beardsley School District.

Oildale was for years the home of Buck Owens' KUZZ radio and recording studios, in the old River Theater on North Chester Avenue. The station had been the love of another country music legend, Herb Henson. Anyone who listened to KERO TV Channel 10 in the 1950s and early 1960s knows the name Kuzzin' Herb Henson, whose show ran five days a week for ten years. It was a staple of the station's programming and an afternoon must for many in Kern County. All watched as Billy Mize played his steel guitar,

✧

Kuzzin' Herb Henson (far right, seated) is seen here with Lewis Talley, Fuzzy Owen, Bonnie Owens, Roy Nichols, and Al Brumley. Henson hosted the popular Trading Post Show on KERO Channel 10 for ten years, solidifying Bakersfield as the country music capital of the West Coast.

Jelly Sanders fiddled away, and Henson slammed his open hand down on the used car hoods he was peddling during the advertising. In 1963 Henson died of a heart attack before reaching age forty. He was a genuine entrepreneur to whom many country musicians owe their start.

Buck Owens isn't a native Californian; in fact, he was born Alvin Edgar Owens, Jr., outside Sherman, Texas on August 12, 1929. His parents were sharecroppers whose house had dirt floors and no electricity. Owens got his nickname from the family mule named Buck, announcing at age three he was going to be called Buck, too. In 1937 they headed west, out of the Dust Bowl, breaking down in Phoenix and finding a place in nearby Mesa. Here he learned to play musical instruments and by age sixteen ended up playing on the radio and working for Mac's Skillet Lickers and meeting his future wife, Bonnie Campbell.

Owens began driving produce from the San Joaquin Valley and liked Bakersfield so much he moved from Arizona at age twenty, first working at the Roundup, then the Blackboard at 3601 Chester Avenue. The Blackboard and other establishments kicked off the careers of numerous country and western musicians, the most famous of which are Buck Owens and Merle Haggard. It was the foundation for what is now called the Bakersfield Sound.

Live radio performances were hosted by guitarist Bill Woods. With their Fender Telecasters and locally built Moserite guitars, the band set the tone for contemporary country music at the time. It was different from that of Nashville, and people liked it. Buck left the Blackboard, which continued on well into the 1970s, when it was finally closed.

Buck met his future song co-writer Harlan Howard at the Blackboard in 1956, and it was their songs that spelled stardom for Owens. He is still the owner of KUZZ AM/FM and KCWR AM/FM Radio in Bakersfield. He has owned several radio stations and still owns *Camera Ads* and *Home Preview* in Bakersfield. Most of all, Owens is the owner of Buck Owens' Crystal Palace, the Academy of County Music's "Nightclub of the Year" for 1998. It is here that Owens performs with his friends and band, The Buckaroos, bringing entertainment to Bakersfield. Owens has had twelve number one albums. He was ranked number ten on Billboard's All-time Country Music list, and local boy Merle Haggard coming in at number three. In 1969 he was named the co-host of *Hee-Haw*, the highest rated syndicated television show in history. He was elected to the Country Music Hall of Fame in 1996.

In 1998, amidst some controversy, Bakersfield renamed Pierce Road as Buck Owens Boulevard in his honor. In 1999, Owens finally bought the old BAKERSFIELD sign over Union Avenue. He built a new sign and placed the old letters on it, over Sillect Avenue, in front of his Crystal Palace, thus completing the saga of the *Streets of Bakersfield* (a popular Owens' song).

Kern County and Bakersfield have tremendous educational systems. In Bakersfield, there were four high schools in 1960. Now the Kern Union High School District has twenty-five school sites and is the largest school district in the county, with over twenty seven thousand students. Incidentally, Blake Elementary is the smallest, with nine students in 1999.

The Kern County Superintendent of Schools offices have broadly expanded into downtown Bakersfield with multi-story buildings and school sites the likes of which no one could have imagined. But retired Superintendent Kelly Blanton had a way of making things happen during his tenure. He was able to mold the office into one of the more dynamic educational offices in the state and country. In fact, it was during his last years in office that the Kern County Museum and the California Living Museum (CALM) came under the administration of the superintendent's office, ever strengthening its commitment to the youth of our community.

The Bakersfield City School District is the largest K-8 elementary school district in the state of California. The district comprises of 42 schools, with 33 elementary schools and nine junior high, or middle, schools. The district also has a program to work with parents in teaching

their children through a home study program. The district continues to provide quality education for the children of Bakersfield. Many of its schools are named after prominent local residents like Millie Munsey, Myra Noble, Dr. Juliet Thorner, Bessie Owens, and Henry Eissler. All that is missing is a school named after the founder of Bakersfield, Thomas Baker.

Kern County is home of Bakersfield College, founded in 1913, one of the nation's oldest continually operating community colleges. It is part of the Kern Community College District which includes Cerro Coso Community College and Porterville Community College.

Bakersfield College serves thirteen thousand students on a 153-acre main campus in northeast Bakersfield. A separate learning center is located at the Weill Institute in downtown Bakersfield and another at the Delano Center. There are also satellite campuses throughout the county.

✧

Merle Haggard (right) and Buck Owens (center) are seen here with Andy Griffith. They garnered top ten status in Billboard's Country Artists of the Century. Haggard was number three and Owens was number ten.

✧

The new Bakersfield College campus as seen in this February 18, 1960, photograph.

Cerro Coso Community College provides education for the desert and mountain communities, serving a twelve-thousand-square-mile, four-county area of eastern California. The college opened in the fall of 1973 and quickly expanded its service area. The Indian Wells Valley campus in Ridgecrest serves the second largest population base in Kern County. The South Kern campus at Edwards Air Force Base serves the base, Mojave, Boron, California City, and areas of San Bernardino County. The campus at Kern River Valley serves the mountain communities. There is also an Eastern Sierra College Center serving the northern desert area.

Taft College is another of Kern's fine secondary education facilities, having established itself on the west side of the San Joaquin Valley in 1922. It principally serves the west side, but also offers courses for "distance learning" over the Internet and through videos and compact discs. Taft College opened in 1922 on the campus of Taft Union High School and took on the responsibility of providing upper-level education for local residents. It has continued to serve in that role, separating from the high school campus in 1955. Taft College is well known for its courses in criminal justice

and its dental hygiene programs. The college gained some notoriety when featured in the 1986 film *The Best of Times* with Robin Williams and Kurt Russell. The college's sports teams are among the top teams in their league.

Taft College offers a great opportunity for west side residents to gain a good basic college education without all the distractions of a larger school. Its six thousand-plus annual student population benefits from a faculty with years of experience. Taft College offers personal attention not often seen at a school of its kind.

California State University, Bakersfield was created out of the Donahoe Higher Education Act of 1960. Dorothy Donahoe was a true friend of Kern County, representing the area in the California State Assembly for years. During that time she worked with community leaders to bring higher education to Bakersfield and Kern County. In 1970 the effort paid off when the school opened out on the dry plain of what used to be part of the old Kern County Land Company's Bellevue Ranch west of Stockdale.

The university first opened as a four-year college, and was finally approved as a state university in the late 1980s. It is the only four-year institution within a one hundred-mile radius. Cal State Bakersfield strives for excellence in three academic schools: the School of Arts and Sciences, the School of Business and Public Administration, and the School of Education.

It was clear early on when the college was importing faculty that Bakersfield would change. Faculty members became involved in local activities and politics, raising the bar for community standards. Currently, more than ninety percent of the tenured faculty hold doctorate degrees in their fields of study. The university has about fifty-five hundred students and a faculty of nearly three hundred. It is located on a 375-acre site donated by Tenneco West, successor of the old Kern County Land Company. There are over thirty buildings on campus with classroom, laboratory, administrative, and technical support facilities.

One of the more spectacular facilities at Cal State University, Bakersfield is the Walter W. Stiern Library, which was completed in 1994. It is a facility with state-of-the-art information technology, housing a collection of more than six hundred thousand books and periodicals, a media center, and most of the university's computer laboratories. It is the first building on campus that was planned from the beginning to provide state-of-the-art information retrieval and storage.

The university has a vast richness of resources, including several centers and institutes. These include the Applied Research Center, Archaeological Information Center, California Well Sample Repository, Facility for Animal Care and Treatment, Center for Economic Education and Research, the Kegley Institute of Ethics, and the Small Business and Public Service Institutes. California State University, Bakersfield will help lead Kern County into the twenty-first century with its diverse programs and educational leaders. The University also boasts one of the top Division II athletic programs in the country, having won the Sear's Cup for athletic excellence in 1997-1998.

Kern's healthcare boom began in the 1960s with the expansion of several local hospitals. Kern County has a health care system that probably can be rated as one of the best in the state, if not the country. Bakersfield is home to a number of hospitals, including Bakersfield Memorial Hospital, Kern Medical Center, Mercy Hospital, San Joaquin Community Hospital, Mercy's new Southwest Hospital, and Good Samaritan Hospital, which was the old Physicians Hospital in Oildale. Of these hospitals, the first four were in service in the 1950s, with the first three around as early as the 1920s. Most have specialty areas and with changes in federal funding it is a necessity. Health care expansion efforts continued into the late 1990s with the construction of the new Mercy Southwest, the HealthSouth Bakersfield Southwest Rehabilitation Center, and the Bakersfield Heart Hospital.

Healthcare in Kern County has developed to meet the changing needs of the population. Family and internal medicine, pediatrics, and obstetric services are available throughout the county, supported by specialty hospital services and physicians in Bakersfield. Clinics provide care to residents of rural areas who have difficulty accessing traditional healthcare resources due to lack of transportation or funds.

Hospitals in Kern County have a long history of service, today providing an array of specialty services easily equal services found in major metropolitan areas. Bakersfield hospitals include Bakersfield Memorial Hospital, Mercy Southwest Hospital, and San Joaquin Community Hospital. Mercy Hospital, which has been in downtown Bakersfield since just after the turn of the twentieth century, will be closing its doors. However, things are not as they appear. Mercy will be moving or consolidating its services to the Mercy Southwest Memorial Hospital facilities. Bakersfield Heart Hospital is the county's newest hospital, serving the county with top-notch heart-wellness care.

The sixty-four-bed Good Samaritan Hospital furnishes service to the Oildale and north-of-the-river residents. Other facilities in the Bakersfield area include the sixty-bed Health South rehabilitation facility, Bakersfield Family Medical Center, and Kaiser Permanente, both in the southwest area of Bakersfield.

Delano Regional Medical Center makes healthcare available for residents in the northern part of the county, providing a full range of facilities for that region. On the desert is the Ridgecrest Regional Hospital with its eighty beds. Ridgecrest takes care of the ever-growing population of Kern's desert. In Tehachapi is the smaller Tehachapi Hospital, which takes care of the population of the southeast mountain area of Kern County. Kern River Valley Hospital has more than twenty beds in its facility and cares for the residents of the Lake Isabella area.

California has enacted strong seismic safety laws that will impact all hospitals in the state.

✧

Dignitaries like then Governor and future President Ronald Reagan attended the groundbreaking of California State College, Bakersfield on April 11, 1969.

BOBBY. NINA. DOTTIE. EARL. JR. VIRGINIA. JIM. MRS. WARREN. EARL WARREN

Two major and six minor reasons why Earl Warren will be elected Governor on November 3rd, 1942. A Blessing to California and a true prophesy.

❖

California Governor Earl Warren and family are pictured in this photograph in 1942. Warren, who was raised in East Bakersfield, later served as chief justice of the United States Supreme Court.

Because of the stringent engineering safety requirements of the law, many of the county's smaller healthcare facilities will have to close or be rebuilt. This is not just an issue for Kern County, but for the whole state. Time will tell whether this issue was resolved.

Bakersfield also has the services of Kaiser Permanente and the Bakersfield Family Medical Center. Both of these facilities serve an ever-growing population of health-conscience residents. Many healthcare professionals serve the Kern County community with quality care.

Ridgecrest Regional Hospital is the only hospital in eastern Kern County and has eighty beds. The hospital operates twenty-four-hour emergency care, X-ray, MRI, CAT scan and other laboratory services, intensive and coronary care, home health, obstetrics, pediatrics, nuclear medicine, and respiratory and physical therapies. Mercy Westside Hospital is the old Westside Hospital at Taft, which used to be operated by the County of Kern. Once taken over by Catholic Healthcare West, the hospital was able to serve Taft with twenty-four-hour emergency medicine, X-ray and other laboratory services, a wellness clinic and long-term skilled nursing care.

The Kern Valley Hospital is an acute care facility with three-bed intensive care unit, twenty-four-bed acute care unit and skilled nursing care. It has around the-clock emergency

room, an in-house rural health clinic, and its own pharmacy. Tehachapi Hospital operates a twenty-eight-bed facility with an emergency room, lab and X-ray department, and surgery department, and it runs two rural health clinics. The Delano Regional Medical Center is Kern County's largest hospital outside Bakersfield and has 156 beds. It offers a full range of general acute care services including inpatient and out-patient surgeries and cardiology, an emergency room, and a special care unit. The hospital also runs Wasco Medical Plaza in that city.

During the post-World War II era, rural communities of the San Joaquin, Salinas, and Coachella Valleys suffered from an increasing influx of non-resident aliens as a result of rapidly growing corporate agribusiness. This growth was fueled by the application of war-related technology to farm production, the arrival of the state and federal water projects, and the state's utilization of the emergency Bracero Program. At least five million Mexican *braceros*, commonly called guest workers, were contracted under the auspices of the federal government to provide farm labor in the United States. Wages stagnated for years throughout the post-war boom era.

With Kern's agricultural might, it was natural that many workers would seek employment and housing in the county. By the time the Bracero Program ended in 1964, the state had helped growers work with thousands of the former *braceros* and their families, allowing them to settle in California so as to maintain an adequate labor force. These workers brought others from Mexico and provided short-term shelter, food, and job leads to them. They also sought to improve their working conditions and were the foundation of the most powerful farm worker movements in rural America.

Enter Cesar Chavez, union organizer. Chavez was the champion of the farm worker, fighting for better working and living conditions. A Yuma, Arizona, native, Chavez formed the National Farm Workers Association in 1962, merging it in 1966 with the Agricultural Workers Organization of the AFL-CIO. The merger was the beginning of the United Farm Workers.

By 1965 Chavez organized a boycott of table grapes in the Delano area that would reach worldwide notoriety. The Union demanded wages of $1.40 per hour plus twenty-five cents a box for workers. They then staged a walkout against the grape growers. Packing sheds in Kern and Tulare Counties were picketed by approximately one thousand people, mostly of Filipino descent. Growers replaced workers from out of state and ran advertising for their cause on local radio stations. It was a tense time, and occasional confrontations occurred, with some violence and arrests, including the arrest of Chavez.

By 1969 Chavez was on *Time Magazine*'s cover and had the support of many in the Democratic Party. Several agreements were signed but ultimately always failed. The UFW has been able to help workers gain higher wages and other benefits. It ran two radio stations for farm workers and constructed a housing development in Delano for elderly American-Filipino laborers.

By the late 1970s, Chavez was working in the political arena and had gained the support of Bishop Roger Mahoney of Stockton (later the archbishop of Los Angeles), Governor Jerry Brown, and state agriculture official Rose Bird to create the Agriculture Labor Relations Act, which, among other things, banned the use of the short-handled hoe and created health care rights for farm workers.

Chavez died April 22, 1993, at age sixty-six. A reported 30,000 people attended his funeral in Delano. He was buried at La Paz, the UFW's headquarters near Keene. Along with the AFL-CIO, the UFW continues to fight for equitable work conditions and benefits for its many members.

With all the agriculture around Bakersfield and in Kern County, the county vies with Monterey County each year as the number three agriculture county in the United States, behind Fresno and Tulare Counties. Grapes, citrus, almonds, cotton, and carrots are the big crops grown on Kern's 840,000 acres of farmland. Grapes top the list with over $400 million worth of crops. An additional 2.2 million acres are rangeland.

Kern is number one in the state as a producer of almonds, pistachios, carrots, potatoes, apples, watermelons, sheep, and wool. Kern County has been one of the leading farm counties in the country for the last fifty years, with farm revenues having risen from nearly $187 million dollars in 1950 to just under $2 billion in 1990. The fruit and nut, vegetable, and nursery industries as a whole comprise about sixty-six percent of total farm revenues.

As of April 1999 there were approximately 225,000 employed in Kern County. The unemployment rate was just over thirteen percent. Agriculture comprised more than 37,000 of that labor force, with government at just under 51,000. Industries providing service such as trucking, utilities, communications, and warehousing overwhelmingly employ the most people with a workforce of nearly 160,000.

Four of the top ten employers in Kern County are agriculturally based. They are Giumarra Farms with forty-two hundred employees, Grimmway Enterprises with 2,500 employees, Dole Bakersfield, Inc. with nearly 2,400 employees, and William Bolthouse Farms with 2,000 employees.

The residents of Kern County need to be entertained, and Kern County has many opportunities for those who like to get out and party. Bakersfield especially has great opportunities for this in its Convention Center on Truxtun Avenue, where there is fifty-one thousand square feet of exhibit space. Many musical programs are held there, including the Bakersfield Symphony Orchestra.

✧

Cesar Chavez brought worldwide attention to Kern County at several points in his life. Dignitaries such as Robert Kennedy and Jesse Jackson (shown here) paid visits to Chavez while he was in the Golden Empire.
COURTESY OF THE CITY OF BAKERSFIELD, CALIFORNIA.

The newly built Centennial Garden is in the same complex and has twenty-thousand square feet of event space, a ten-thousand-seat arena for concerts, theater productions, and sporting and other events. It is a full-time entertainment center with state of the art equipment. The future will surely bring a new baseball diamond to replace the historic but aging Sam Lynn Ball Park at the recreation park area on Chester Avenue. Bakersfield's Fox Theater has been refurbished and is functioning to bring a renaissance of cultural arts to Kern County. The theater's ambiance is second to none in the south valley.

By the beginning of the last two decades of the twentieth century, Kern County had a population of four hundred thousand, with the new construction of homes at a record pace. The southwest end of Bakersfield was the particular target of the construction efforts because of the initial decision of Tenneco West, then Castle and Cooke, to open up its prime agricultural land to development. This was not a random decision on the part of Tenneco, but was the result of a careful master planning effort in conjunction with the city.

Castle and Cooke was fairly quick to move on selling its developments and sold over twenty-one hundred homesites southwest of Bakersfield in the first five years. This equaled about thirty-five percent of the city's building permits. It is said that by 1991, one-quarter of the available residential property was controlled by Castle and Cooke, as well as nearly sixty percent of the area's commercial land.

Kern's economy is solidly based in oil and agriculture, but Bakersfield and other valley communities have attempted to make themselves more attractive to outside companies. Kern County is not only an economically reasonable place to live and work, it is a hub of transportation for the west. The cost of living in Kern County is among the lowest in the state.

Many of Kern's farms are larger scale operations, well-equipped to handle economic downturns. The same applies to the petroleum industry. Many of Kern's products are exported, and, as has been seen in the citrus and tree fruit industries, a lopsided import-export ratio can be devastating to farming. The same applies to the oil industry.

As the last recession hit bottom in early 1992, unemployment was nearly eighteen percent. With the upturn in the economic climate, it quickly dropped. By the end of the following summer, the jobless rate had fallen back to less than thirteen percent. Both the oil and farming industries suffered greatly from the downturn and still do today, even with oil prices climbing. Although dollar numbers appear to be constantly increasing, farming seems to be in a perennial state of downturn with higher labor and production costs and lower crop returns. Water supplies are in an ever-tightening noose from state and federal water policy changes. Where at one time water was abundantly supplied to farmers, now it is a fight to see if there is any water at all.

The Arvin-Edison Water District continues to fight to preserve the water it has at the end of the Friant-Kern project. It seems likely that with the cross-valley canal, water will surely soon be transferred to Los Angeles for domestic use. Because of the proposed disastrously high water prices from the federal government, there may be no choice but to sell it. Many water districts up and down the state are looking at the possibility of these transfers simply to save their own water supplies.

As for Kern County, it will continue to diversify its economic base with manufacturing assuming a greater role in the basic economic structure. It seems inevitable that agriculture will give way to industrial growth in the upcoming century

Because of the influx of new industry into Kern County, more and more people are finding the relaxed lifestyle of both the southern valley and the Tehachapis in close proximity to both their old and new workplaces. Retirees from Southern California are moving up into Kern's mountains and desert areas. Although once a very young population, Kern's residents are, as everywhere, getting older. It is clear that services for an older population are necessary, and the county and private health service providers are meeting these needs.

Around the south valley there are areas of older residential neighborhoods that still have the rich charm and ambiance that attract newcomers into the area. But is seems the newer developments, closer to the highways and nearer Los Angeles, are at a premium. After all, it is no less than a half hour closer to the Southland to live out in the area south of Bakersfield than to drive all the way into town, or the northeast.

Kern County is exploding with cultural enterprises, including Bakersfield's downtown convention center projects, the proposed new baseball park, Mesa Marin Speedway, the Kern County Museum, the Fox Theater, Bakersfield College, Cal State Bakersfield, and other exceptional cultural resources. There are wonderful golf courses, water recreation areas, desert and mountain recreation, and more.

Kern's mineral wealth and rich alluvial soil still attract industry and people alike, and with Bakersfield and Kern County at the hub of transportation in California, it seems likely that development of the county's resources will continue. With oil and agriculture suffering from lowered economic expectations, the development of other industry and business opportunities is crucial to bolster Kern's economic might. With agencies like the Kern Economic Development Corporation and KernCOG, the county continues to plan and grow to meet the upcoming needs.

Besides just finishing up the Bakersfield Amtrak Station project, with the city of Bakersfield and the railroad, KernCOG is working on many transportation projects. These include the proposed High Speed Rail Project connecting the county with both Northern and Southern California via high-speed train. The South Beltway Project in Bakersfield is designed to carry east-west traffic around the Metropolitan Bakersfield area, relieving urban congestion and connecting State Route 58 to State Route 99 and Interstate 5. Other projects include expansion and major improvements on Routes 46, 58, and the Kern Commuter Connection, among others. Many community and county leaders see the county becoming a major distribution center for the Southland, with regulated freight and passenger traffic.

Kern County's Meadows Field continues to expand and is seen as a major resource for the distribution of industrial and commercial goods. With the expansion of its runways in the early 1990s, Meadows Field is now able to handle any aircraft made. Plans call for a new

terminal and other facilities to handle international flights. Kern County continues to focus on international trade and is creating the infrastructure to handle the job.

With the climate of good political relations between the Kern County Board of Supervisors and the Bakersfield City Council, further development of local resources will continue, with the emphasis on bringing resources to Kern. Both local governments are committed to lower unemployment and more jobs for local residents. Large-scale companies are scouting the area for potential new locations, and it is imperative that the county continue to maintain the appearance of a wholesome lifestyle.

Good schools, parks, commercial centers, clean communities, and inexpensive locales are essential to attracting new industry. With the cost of living in Kern County considerably lower than elsewhere in the Southland, it is only natural that the county will soon reap the rewards of its efforts.

✧

By 1963 Highway 99 had been constructed around Bakersfield, bypassing downtown. This spelled doom for the dozens of hotels and hospitality businesses that were located on the old Golden State Highway.

✧

*This painting of the Jewett Ranch was
painted by American landscape artist
Thaddeus Welch in 1893. The painting
represents early agricultural life in Kern
County. The painting is in the collection of
the Kern County Museum.*

SHARING THE HERITAGE

*historic profiles of
businesses, organizations, and
families that have contributed to
the development and economic base of
Bakersfield and Kern County*

✧

*This 1914 Dorman Brothers photograph
depicts a deserted and dilapidated Fort
Tejon. Built in the 1850s, it was once used
to protect the horse and cattle trade, as well
as local Indians. Fort Tejon is now a
California State Park.*

QUALITY OF LIFE

healthcare companies, educational institutions,

families, historical, and civic organizations

contribute to the quality of life in

Bakersfield and Kern County

SPECIAL THANKS TO

Dr. Larry E. Reider and the Office of the Kern County Superintendent of Schools

Greenfield School District

Wasco Union School District

KERN MEDICAL CENTER

Kern Medical Center traces its beginnings to the rough and ready days of gold prospecting at Stoney Creek and "Havilah" nearly a century and a half ago. Although the gold-seeking frontiersmen could "tough out" wounds from Indian fights and injuries from their toils, an epidemic of fever led the local population to purchase a small, one-room adobe hut for treating the afflicted. This $200 outlay in 1867 marks the beginning of a county health service that has grown into the modern Kern Medical Center, Kern County's best provider of comprehensive medical care to more than two hundred thousand patients per year.

The early adobe hospital remained in the gold area of the county until 1875 when the gold was all but played out and the county seat had moved from the hills down into Bakersfield. The new hospital opened in a one-story wood-frame county building on G Street, which is today the site of Bakersfield High School. Private companies who leased their services to the county provided hospital services. Contracts went to the lowest bidder who in turn made their profits by keeping healthcare costs down. Hot competition for the contracts prompted bidding wars among the healthcare providers, which cut into their profits that led to practices that denied indigent patients good care.

While care may have suffered as a result of the leased care system, the facility improved with a move in 1895 onto six acres located at Nineteenth and Oak Streets. The new county hospital was a two-story structure with a gabled roof that provided forty beds served by five doctors and eight nurses. The building also offered surgical facilities, offices and a well-appointed kitchen that made it a gleaming contrast to the G Street hospital. This newer location served well as the century changed and brought with it new ideas on county medical care.

A new concept based on the premise that health is as important to the average citizen as education, that failure to meet the health needs of the individual is failure to meet the needs of a modern civilization, was the brainchild of County Supervisor Stanley Abel, Dr. Joe Smith, and Dr. R. G. Broderick. In 1917 these men began working together for a hospital that would meet this new concept. Kern General Hospital was to be situated "on a hill on the northeast outskirts of Bakersfield, where the clean country air and perfect drainage give assurance of a healthy atmosphere for all time." The vision became reality on September 27, 1925 when the first unit of Kern General Hospital opened its doors at 1830 Flower Street, where Kern Medical Center remains today.

By 1939 the county-administered Kern General Hospital had 761 beds, admitted

❖

Above: In 1898, the Kern County Hospital was located on Oak Street.

Below: An aerial view of Kern Medical Center.

10,460 patients per year, delivered 1,253 babies, performed 12,000 x-rays, dispensed 250,000 prescriptions and 100,000 aspirin tablets, washed more than 1,000,000 pounds of laundry, and prepared 840,000 meals for patients and staff. Patients were cared for by 33 doctors and 142 nurses. A new era of hospital care for Kern County was well on its way, but Kern General was to have a major test of its resilience.

The earth first shook before dawn on July 21, 1952. The second quake, a month later, devastated seventy-five percent of the hospital and left only a single building, the "A" wing, safe for occupancy. Offices and other services operated from tents as the county resolved to rebuild the great hospital on the same spot. Dedications for new buildings were held in 1956 and Kern General Hospital began its transition into the institution it is today.

The name changed to Kern Medical Center (KMC) in 1975 to reflect the hospital's broadening capabilities and its ongoing mission, to serve people with the most extensive medical care in Kern County regardless of their ability to pay. Comprehensive care comes in many forms. The Emergency Care Center offers full-service emergency care in Kern County and handles thirty to forty ambulances per day. Minor Surgery, laproscopy, and major surgeries are performed in the vast Center for Surgical Services opened in 1998, offering state-of-the-art care for patients with thoughtful provisions for waiting families. KMC's progressive Maternity Services Center delivers the very best mother and infant care with family-focused birthing rooms, a highest-level Neonatal ICU, educational programs, and even free car seats for newborns. Furthermore, KMC is the county's only "teaching" hospital in affiliation with the UCLA, UC San Diego, and UC Irvine Schools of Medicine.

Annually KMC cares for over 16,000 inpatients in it 222 bed hospital and over 100,000 people through its clinics. KMC's Sagebrush Medical Plaza at 1111 Columbus offers a full range of medical services and is home to a service specifically for the elderly. The Elder Life Adult Day Health Care Center provides health, therapeutic and social service programs that enable functionally impaired seniors to maximize their independence and remain at home. Even with all of these services, KMC is always looking for new ways to serve patients and remain the hospital of choice for Kern County.

✧

Kern Medical Center as it appears today.

NATIONAL HEALTH SERVICES, INC.

✧

Above: Wagih H. Michael, Ph.D., executive director and the board of directors for NHSI stand outside the Buttonwillow Medical/Dental Center.

Below: The staff of the Wasco Medical Center.

Opposite, from top to bottom: Shafter Community Health Center, Delano Family Medical Center, Taft Community Medical Center, and Lost Hills Community Health Center.

"Health for all," is the motto and mission of National Health Services, Inc. (NHSI), which has been providing healthcare for the western reaches of Kern County for nearly a quarter of a century. NHSI began as Buttonwillow Health Center in 1978 and has grown to include six locations offering a wide range of medical, dental, and health educational services to communities and individuals previously without local care. These services are offered in an environment that is bilingual and multicultural.

NHSI, a non-profit corporation, serves an area roughly sixty miles in diameter. In addition to the original clinic in Buttonwillow, NHSI has opened health centers in Lost Hills, Wasco, Taft, Delano, and Shafter. The expansion of NHSI was prompted by demand for services in areas with limited access to healthcare providers. In these predominantly agricultural communities, most of

the health centers' patients are farm workers who depend on federally funded community/migrant centers for primary medical care. Although NHSI receives state and federal funding to help primarily low-income patients, the doors of the health centers are open to everyone and they will accept any type of medical plan or insurance. More than twenty-two thousand patients are served by NHSI each year.

At the beginning, Buttonwillow Health Center opened with the goal of providing a full range of primary and preventative care and supportive services to an area whose remoteness had previously made such services unavailable. The Lost Hills Community Health Center opened in December of 1980 to meet the increased demand for primary care services in the northwestern portions of Kern County. Supported by self-pay, private insurance, Medi-Cal, workers' compensation, a state primary care grant, and the California family planning program, the center provides about two-thirds the annual number of services as the Buttonwillow operation. The largest among all the sites, Wasco Medical Center, opened in 1990 and began offering dental services in 1993.

Southwest Kern County is served by Taft Community Medical Center, which opened for one day a week in March 1991 offering family planning services to teenagers with the support of the State Office of Family Planning and Taft Westside District Hospital. Full medical services have been offered at the Taft facility since August 18, 1992. The following year, the Delano Family Medical Center, for awhile known as the Rodrigo Terronez Memorial Clinic, opened to serve the large numbers of farm workers in the Delano area without adequate medical services. The sixth center, Shafter Community Health Center opened July 22, 1998 in an area that had been served by the Buttonwillow and Wasco clinics. The new center was opened in response to the demands of managed care.

NHSI is a family-oriented center and, as such, their medical services begin with a family practice physician. Patients are urged to choose a member of the medical staff as a family doctor who can help them decide on any specialized care they might need. Such a consistent relationship with a single doctor personalizes the care process and leads to a more sensible and

balanced course of healthcare. Specialists offer expertise in a full range of medical services covering patients from childbirth to old age. Health services offered at the NHSI centers include general medicine, obstetrics & gynecology, family planning, pediatrics, chiropractics, podiatry, internal medicine, behavioral care, immunizations, urgent care, and physicals for school, sports, and the DMV.

Three of the centers—Buttonwillow, Lost Hills, and Wasco—offer a full range of general dental services. The exam rooms offer the latest in dental care equipment and are staffed by experienced, skilled dentists and dental assistants. Patients can have their teeth cleaned, cavities filled, crowns and bridges made, root canal work performed or dentures made. Limited oral surgery is also available and no extensive dental work is done without the patient first receiving a written appraisal on the cost.

Educational programs are a very important element of what NHSI offers its communities. As in medical services, the educational programs cover a broad spectrum. Family planning classes providing counseling, examinations and supplies for men and women have long been offered at the centers. Pre-natal education classes prepare parents for birth, postpartum, and infant care. HIV/AIDS programs offer confidential education and testing. NHSI's dedication to preventive healthcare is further evidenced by classes designed to help people with tobacco addiction and programs offering nutritional counseling, both individual and group, to help head off or control high blood pressure and control body weight.

Individuals and families who never before had access to medical services have had their lives improved in small and large ways thanks to the creation and growth of NHSI. The kind of work the centers do is very satisfying to the doctors, nurses, assistants and staff who work in them. Executive Director of NHSI Dr. Wagih Michael, PhD, believes in the long-term benefits of spreading medical care and education to those whom have been without it. "The public benefits from these services," he says. "If people are healthy, then their community will be healthy and that will lead to a healthier economy and so forth." There can be no doubt that Kern County is healthier thanks to NHSI.

RIO BRAVO RESORT

✧

Below: Rio Bravo resort features 19 lighted tennis courts.

Bottom: A typical Rio Bravo Resort suite with a fireplace.

Beautiful Rio Bravo Resort, nestled in the foothills of the Southern Sierras just east of Bakersfield, is the realization of the dreams of two area natives. "I've always loved the beauty here and what the resort offers," says Konny Boyd, owner and CEO of Rio Bravo Resort. Boyd bought the resort in 1996. Original owner and founder George Nickel built the resort along the Kern River back in 1975. Rio Bravo Resort was a success from the start and soon became the most attractive destination spot in the area.

The beautifully landscaped Rio Bravo Resort offers a tree-shaded complex of tennis courts, swimming pools, spas, and a gym with a splendid view of the golden mountains rising majestically away to the east. For Boyd, the resort as it is today represents the "completion of a dream" not only for her, but also Nickel who is one of her strongest supporters.

The resort on the Kern River closely resembles the Rio Bravo that opened in 1975. The only major addition is the open air pavilion Boyd dedicated to her father, John Boyd, which has become the premier spot in Kern County to conduct weddings. Hundreds of couples have taken their vows on the hill above the sparkling river in sight of the rising mountains. The scenic location also draws honeymooners and couples for romantic retreats. There is something special about the dry breezes that blow from the mountains to rustle the branches of the eucalyptus, pine, and native pepper trees that stirs the heart and transports the soul.

To really get the heart going, Rio Bravo offers nineteen lighted tennis courts for organized and casual play. Richard Gonzales, after playing the courts with his father, Wimbledon Champion Pancho Gonzales, fell in love with the resort and returned to become the tennis pro at Rio Bravo. And tennis is only the beginning. Rio Bravo's main courtyard surrounds an Olympic size swimming pool just steps from a first-rate weight training and aerobic gym. Visitors can enjoy volleyball, hiking, whitewater rafting, windsurfing, power boating, kayaking, and fishing on the Kern River and Lake Ming. Public and private golf courses are just minutes from Rio Bravo Resort. To relax, there is a spa and on-site massage therapist to help work the kinks out of the muscles.

Two restaurants at the resort offer a variety of eating pleasures. Coming off the tennis court or just after a swim, Club Rio Bar & Grille offers guests a fun, casual atmosphere with seating inside or outside on the breezy deck with a view of the courts. The Restaurant at Rio Bravo is the place to go for elegant dining. In the magnificent open-vista dining room or on the patio, dinner guests enjoy a wide variety of cuisines in an unforgettable setting. The restaurant is a popular site for private banquets and other special events. The

excellent Rio Bravo blend of coffee is roasted right on the premises.

Before obtaining Rio Bravo Resort, Konny Boyd opened the state's first home for Alzheimer's clients in 1988 and, before long, found herself running a growing business that had sprung from her affinity for the senior members of the community. After twenty years in healthcare, Boyd was attracted to the possibilities and tradition of Rio Bravo Resort. A pleasing continuum from the previous career is the number of people of retirement age who belong to the tennis club and the close proximity of a retirement community. "I like it very much that this is a place where people from a lot of different generations come together," Boyd said. There are days when school children are learning about kayaking from visiting Olympians, a gray-haired couple plays mixed doubles against their grandchildren, and honeymooners are swimming in one of the pools.

Rio Bravo Resort employs seventy-seven workers year-round and up to 121 during the busy months from February to July. A number of Boyd's family members work with her at the resort including her mother, Sally Boyd, who oversees quality control, and Boyd's sister, Karen Smith, general manager. The family has helped in solidifying

and building Rio Bravo Resort's standing as the first choice of many Fortune 500 companies for business conferences. The family connection to the community is reflected in Rio Bravo Resort's consistent participation in charitable fundraisers and local programs.

Rio Bravo Resort is a place very distinctly tied to the land and people of Kern County. Developed by one local family and now owned by another, the resort has established itself as a unique and beautiful destination for nearby couples to marry or far-off corporations to meet for business. After more than three decades, Rio Bravo Resort stands as a dream fulfilled with the promise of continuing to be the gem of the Kern River.

Above: The open-air pavilion offers a sweeping view of the Kern River and the rising mountains. It is a favorite location for weddings.

Bottom: Rio Bravo Resort's main Olympic-size pool offers a cool break from the tennis courts and exercise rooms located nearby.

HENRIETTA WEILL MEMORIAL CHILD GUIDANCE CLINIC

✧

Above: An early location of the Henrietta Weill Memorial Child Guidance Clinic in the 1300 block of K Street.

Bottom: Henrietta Weill with children Irma, Blanche, Adele, and Lawrence, c. 1901.

"A child guidance clinic must be part of its community and can be successful only when there is a constant flow to and from it to the community." These words appeared in the first annual report of the Henrietta Weill Memorial Child Guidance Clinic, which was founded in 1946. After more than fifty years, the clinic has proved the truth in that early statement. Thousands of children a year benefit from the Clinic whose mission is to improve the fabric of the community which created it and which it serves.

The remarkable sisters, Blanche and Irma Weill, worked with the Mental Hygiene Committee of 1945 to bring Bakersfield its first psychiatrist and child guidance clinic. The Weill sisters, each highly educated and devoted to child education, established a foundation that began the Clinic and named it for their mother, Henrietta, who opened the first kindergarten in Bakersfield. The first year, the Clinic operated with a budget $13,085.93, a staff of two, and served 133 children. By the century's end, the budget had risen to $6 million, the staff numbered 114, and more than 3,000 children were served per year.

The five offices of the Clinic offer a number of programs for children of all ages starting with the Early Intervention Program that helps parents develop the skills that create strong family bonds that are critical to the future mental health of a child. In coordination with the Bakersfield City School District and the Kern County Superintendent of Schools Office, the Clinic's Intensive Outpatient Program takes students unable to participate in standard education because of severe emotional and behavioral problems and places them in a classroom environment within the Clinic with immediately available psychological counseling. This program aims to help these children and their families assist the student in returning effectively to a regular public school environment. Families are always included as an integral element in treating the mental health of children.

The Clinic also works with local government in programs addressing chemical dependency, juvenile incarceration and sexual abuse. The funding for the private, non-profit clinic comes primarily from government contracts but a significant element comes from private donations, among them Guild House which has provided $1.8 million since its founding in 1958. The "flow to and from" the community since 1946 has made the Henrietta Weill Memorial Child Guidance Clinic a vital part of a better Kern County and a fulfillment of the Weill sisters' vision.

Prominent among the blue-collar businesses on South Union Avenue is the twenty-acre BARC Industries site where more than three hundred workers go every day to do a variety of jobs from packaging products in the assembly area to fashioning crates and pallets in the Wood Products Division. The employees are diligent, motivated, and known for doing first-rate work. They also happen to be developmentally challenged.

The Bakersfield Association for Retarded Citizens (BARC) is a Kern County endeavor that dates back more than fifty years to the concerns and determination of a handful of local families to educate and improve the lives of challenged children. Thirteen families joined to become the Parent Study Group for Mongoloid Children in 1949 forming a strident advocacy for children with mental retardation. Their efforts helped establish a local classroom and pass a state bill addressing the rights of persons with mental retardation to a public education. By 1951, the group, under the name Bakersfield Association for Retarded Children, had opened the first city school special education classes at BARC's location on Fourth Street on property donated by the Kern County Land Company and built with local help.

This beginning established a pattern of community cooperation to further the cause of helping people who are developmentally challenged to reach their full potential. As the focus of the organization broadened from children to include adults, BARC sought out work appropriate for their clients and a workshop was built on site in 1954. By 2000, BARC has grown to offer services to five hundred adults with developmental disabilities through a staff of more than 175 at locations in Bakersfield, Lake Isabella, and Tehachapi with an annual budget of $12 million.

BARC Industries at 2240 South Union offers therapeutic programs and an industrial campus with various occupations at different skill levels to accommodate the differing capabilities of the clients who work there. From the simple sorting of recyclables, the skills applied by workers extend to packaging and wood product manufacturing. Work is procured by contract with businesses and industries across the nation. A computer lab offers training with opportunities to explore the Graphic Arts Division. Hundreds of client-employees have gone through the site and moved on to work on service crews at workplaces in the community where their reputation for dedication and performance are exceptional. BARC trains workers, provides or organizes transportation to different work sites, and provides therapy and education for clients who continue at the BARC site.

The goal of BARC has always been to enable people within their potential to be self-sufficient, hold jobs in the community and become independent. The success of the association is a reflection of the community it serves and relies upon.

BAKERSFIELD ARC

✧

Below: Bakersfield ARC at its original location on Fourth Street.

Bottom: Bakersfield ARC at its present location.

THE THOMSON-FRICK FAMILY

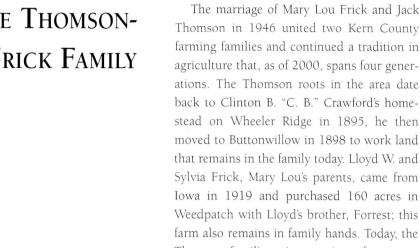

The marriage of Mary Lou Frick and Jack Thomson in 1946 united two Kern County farming families and continued a tradition in agriculture that, as of 2000, spans four generations. The Thomson roots in the area date back to Clinton B. "C. B." Crawford's homestead on Wheeler Ridge in 1895, he then moved to Buttonwillow in 1898 to work land that remains in the family today. Lloyd W. and Sylvia Frick, Mary Lou's parents, came from Iowa in 1919 and purchased 160 acres in Weedpatch with Lloyd's brother, Forrest; this farm also remains in family hands. Today, the Thomson families raise a variety of crops on three thousand acres divided between the Buttonwillow and the Lamont areas.

C. B. Crawford drilled an artesian well on the Buttonwillow acreage and opened a dairy farm. The farmhouse he built in 1910 is still used to house workers. Crawford's daughter, Naomi, married a Scotsman from Dundee named John Thomson who had come to Buttonwillow from San Francisco in 1908 to be paymaster for Miller and Lux. Meanwhile, the Fricks were raising alfalfa, grapes, and cotton in Weedpatch. Lloyd Frick served as chairman of the board of the California Cotton Cooperative Association (now Calcot) for twenty-four years.

Although they knew one another in high school, Jack Thomson and Mary Lou Frick did not begin dating until after World War II where both served in the Navy; Jack as a pilot and Mary Lou as an air traffic controller. Married in 1946, the Thomson family began farming 250 acres of leased family land in 1948 and steadily increased their acreage through purchase and reclamation. The expansion in Buttonwillow involved applying gypsum to neutralize the alkali in the soil so that crops could grow. The U.S. Junior Chamber of Commerce named Jack one of Four Outstanding Young Farmers in 1955 recognizing his innovative farming methods, family and community service. He has served the farming community in numerous capacities including President of the Kern County Farm Bureau, Kern County Water Agency member, and California Water Commission appointee.

Jack and Mary Lou have four children—Jeff, Sylvia, Winifred, and Tim—and welcomed Stacy, Jason, and Julie Peltier to their family in 1967. The Buttonwillow property originally purchased by C. B. Crawford has grown to fifteen hundred acres and is being farmed by Tim producing cotton, garlic, vegetables, melons, and onions. He is involved in the building of a tomato cannery as a board member of the Rio Bravo Tomato Company. Jeff farms cotton, grapes and vegetables on the original Frick Lamont property, grown to fifteen hundred acres as well, where he has also built garlic packing and peeling plants as well as a cold storage facility from which garlic is shipped year-round all over the U.S. and Canada. The farming tradition of two families lives on.

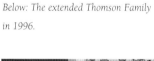

Top: Mary Lou (Frick) and Jack Thomson in 1999. Their marriage in 1946 united two Kern County farm families.

Below: The extended Thomson Family in 1996.

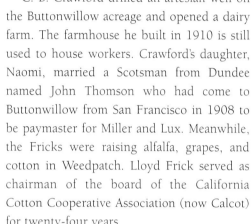

The Lamont School District began as a simple, one-room schoolhouse on March 5, 1894. Mrs. May Stark opened the first Mountain View School class that year and taught a daily average of seventeen students; H. D. West was the sole administrator. Annual reports from the teachers at Mountain View through those early years reveal that rattlesnakes were a constant worry, trees had a hard life on the school grounds, and classes were often canceled due to severe dust storms. For more than a hundred years, the teachers, administrators, and citizens of the Lamont area have met the many challenges of educating local students. And many challenges remain.

Mountain View School moved to its present location in 1917. In fact, the front of the current school is part of the original structure. By the mid-twenties, the district was using its first school bus and had graduating classes of fewer than ten students. Enrollment ballooned from 154 to 552 in the ten years from 1935 to 1945 as economic upheaval caused farmers to move west from the Great Plains. The Sunset Camp in John Steinbeck's *The Grapes of Wrath* was located just a few miles from Lamont. By 1955, attendance had more than doubled to 1,273 prompting the construction of the Myrtle Avenue School to relieve the necessity of holding double sessions at the Lamont School. Alicante, the fourth school that comprises the Lamont School District, was built in 1967.

At the beginning of a new century, the main priority of the district and people of the Lamont School District is improving the quality of education. Posted in the district office and prominently in every school is a story from the *Lamont Reporter* dated January 26, 2000, whose headline reads, "Lamont Schools Score Poorly on Test." "We posted that story so we can do a comparison over the coming years," says Superintendent Bruce Auld. "We're expecting to see a transformation beginning in August of 2000." The district has volunteered for a state program implementing new techniques in education. The people of the district demonstrated their commitment to the students by passing a $4.2 million general obligation bond to modernize the four schools with an overwhelming 86.4 percent approval rate. Superintendent Auld succinctly expresses the overall attitude of the community: "We're building a culture of performance."

LAMONT SCHOOL DISTRICT

❖

Top: Mountain View School as it looked in 1955.

Left: The Mountain View School Band of 1951.

PACIFIC HEALTH EDUCATION CENTER

✧

Below: A ceremony for a Cuban delegation attending sessions at the Center. CEO Gladys Hollingshead holds the microphone.

Bottom: A Pacific Health Education Center graduation ceremony that includes Korean and Romanian student professionals and members of the Center's staff and board.

It is particularly gratifying when an effort is begun locally to improve people's lives and its effect spreads over the horizons and across borders. "It always saddens me to see people dying young due to wrong choices made early in life," says Gladys Hollingsead, the current CEO of Pacific Health Education Center and chairperson of the board of directors. Hollingsead was vice chairman of the San Joaquin Community Hospital in 1987 when she and other board members were instrumental in establishing Pacific Health Education Center. Pacific Health Education Center is an organization "dedicated to helping people live healthier, happier, more successful lives" through health education focusing on healthy lifestyles.

One of the first classes offered at the original 27th Street facility was a Smoke-Cessation Seminar. The classes were packed with a variety of local citizens in attendance. Cooking classes were the next stage, which taught clients how to control their weight and keep dangerous cholesterol levels low. The courses offered by Pacific Health Education Center have continued to broaden and include instruction in stress management, diabetes education, nutrition, exercise, cancer awareness, and a variety of other topics to make life healthier for participants. The House of Manna is under the umbrella of the organization and this store offers health foods, Christian books, music, and gifts. The House of Manna Deli is Bakersfield's first vegetarian restaurant, which is open everyday from Monday to Friday.

In 1993, Pacific Health Education Center offered its first training program for health professionals from around the world through classes and workshops combined with live demonstrations of health education offered to the community. That first session had three people in attendance; by 2000, there were twenty-seven people from fifteen countries enrolled in the January session with fifty-five on the waiting list for the second session that begins in August. Two curio cases in the lobby of Pacific Health Education Center display gifts from former students including carvings from Mozambique, dolls from Korea and Russia, a Greek vase, a Mongolian hat and other items from Cuba, Peru, Mexico, Tanzania, and other countries around the world.

"We get letters from our health professionals, and the tears flow," says Hollingsead about the gratifying results and the impact that the Center's programs have around the world. Pacific Health Education Center moved into its current location at 5300 California Avenue in 1992 to accommodate its growing programs. The organization is very much a part of the Kern County fabric. In 1994, the Central California Heart Institute awarded the Center the Crystal Heart Award; the same year the Center received the Public Health Partnership Award for the Healthy Kern 2000, presented by the Kern County Department of Public Health. There have been several nominations by the Bakersfield Chamber of Commerce for the health category in the televised Beautiful Bakersfield event.

Both at home and abroad, the Pacific Health Education Center is making lives healthier and better.

From the days of the first settlers, Bakersfield has been an education-minded community. The first tax-supported school appeared in the form of a crude, windowless cabin in the 1860s and offered only a few months of schooling for local children. Evolution and growth saw the building of a brick schoolhouse in 1869 where the three teachers and 100 students officially became the Bakersfield City School District in 1882. The District survived the fire of 1889 and the devastating earthquake of 1952 to become California's largest elementary school district with a current enrollment of more that 27,000 students attending 42 schools.

Today's Bakersfield City School District answers the challenges of a growing and diverse community with curriculum and programs never imagined by the farm boys and girls learning the "three Rs" a hundred years ago. Twenty-five percent of district students need language assistance and the number of different languages spoken in Bakersfield schools—thirty three, including Spanish, Cambodian, and Punjab—is staggering. The multi-cultural environment of the schools is viewed by the District as an educational advantage that gives students a chance to learn about other cultures and how to get along with someone who looks and sounds different from oneself. Bakersfield City School District is all inclusive—every child of appropriate age is welcomed and accommodated in district schools regardless of culture, physical ability, or learning ability.

The District offers a multitude of courses beyond core disciplines in English, mathematics, and history in traditional school programs and through magnet schools specializing in fields from computers to performing arts to agriculture and environmental studies. The impact of the Bakersfield City School District on the community goes beyond educating children in the classroom. The District sponsors programs that promote community health, as well as assisting parents with children from birth through age four. At the hospital, parents of newborns are given packets to help with developing their children. Bakersfield City School District has made itself a vital component of a better Bakersfield.

The challenges faced by the district have not always been educational ones. The earthquake of 1952 destroyed sixty percent of the classrooms in the Bakersfield City School District. With the bond approval of a community concerned about the welfare and future of its children, the district undertook a rigorous and large scale rebuilding process that put the district back on its feet. Whether rebuilding after a natural disaster or finding a way to improve education and the educational environment, the Bakersfield City School District has evolved and continues to evolve to meet the challenges of its community.

BAKERSFIELD CITY SCHOOL DISTRICT

✧

Below: Washington Junior High School, 1891.

Bottom: Dr. Juliet Thorner Creative & Performing Arts Magnet School, 1990.

MOJAVE UNIFIED SCHOOL DISTRICT

Life in the desert intensifies the need for individual self-reliance and the importance of community in a hard environment. From their first arrival and establishment of the town of Mojave in 1876, pioneers to the part of Kern County now defined by the Mojave Unified School District cared deeply about education for their children. That spirit of the high desert's earliest settlers is still very evident in the community's school system today.

Encompassing one thousand square miles and the communities of Cantil, Mojave, Red Rock, and California City, the Mojave Unified School District is the second largest in the State of California. The present district, established in 1953, has its roots in the Mojave School District that was formed on June 7, 1884 and the Red Rock, Soledad, and Landers School Districts, all created in the early 1900s. Attendance at the far-flung schools in the early districts was seldom more than a handful, and classes were sometimes held in tents or the Miner's Union Hall. Today, students of the district attend school in modern buildings using increasingly up-to-date technology.

"We use technology with a plan, we want kids to have access to the best tools possible," says assistant superintendent Penny Swenson. In order to increase the sense of community within the district, towers are going up to connect the campuses via broad spectrum technology capable of transmitting audio, video, and data. Students are connected to the broader worlds beyond the district through computers wired to the Internet. By developing ways to access distant databases, take virtual field trips or allow students to share lessons across the desert, the Mojave Unified School District has led the region in employing new technologies to enhance instructional improvement and student progress. But education involves much more than equipment and facilities.

The Mojave Unified School District is a remarkably diverse organization of students, teachers, administrators, and parents working together. Students are encouraged to take responsibility for their education, and parent involvement is a long-standing tradition for the area. As well as staying abreast of improvements and innovations within their field, teachers are active in determining district policies and approaches. "This is not a talk-down administration," says Swenson. "We have a great core of teacher-leaders who are key to developing standards and assessment."

The computers, telecommunication capability, and modern buildings would confound the early pioneers if they could see the schools of their community today. However, they would easily recognize the local determination to find the best ways to educate children of Mojave Unified School District: it is an ongoing legacy.

Members of the Bakersfield Country Club have enjoyed a challenging golf course, elegant dining, and other club activities for more than fifty years. One of only two private, member-owned, equity clubs in the area, Bakersfield Country Club traces its history back to a list of names inscribed on Noriega Hotel stationery in 1949. This association of founders started a tradition of excellence and friendliness that are hallmarks of the club today.

The men who met at the Noriega were farmers and oilmen who had been turned away by the Stockdale Club and were determined to open a club of their own. John Kovacevich, Dominick Corsaro, and Babe Lazane were the primary instigators among the seventy-five founding members who signed the document and pledged a contribution. Land was acquired east of the city and a premier golf course architect, Billy Bell, was hired to design a course making use of the gentle, hilly terrain. The course opened that same year with Babe Lazane as its first golf professional and was an instant success. Great care has been taken over the years to maintain Bell's original design and preserve the course's unique challenges and beauty.

The Bakersfield Country Club was selected as the inaugural site of the Ben Hogan/Nike Tour in 1990 and has hosted the California State Open and other tournaments. In addition to golf, the Club offers tennis on four lighted courts, fitness training equipment, a sauna, and locker rooms finished in mahogany with private showers and adjacent card rooms and lounges. The Clubhouse that accommodates these facilities is a beautiful early California-style building constructed and opened in 1993. The new Clubhouse takes advantage of its hilltop location offering panoramic views of the course and hills to the east and the twinkling lights of Bakersfield to the west. Members and their guests can enjoy these views from the second-story Grill Room and Dining Room, which offer fine foods and serve brilliantly for special occasions like weddings or banquets.

Many of the original names found on those sheets of hotel stationery are still active in the Club in their third and fourth generations. New members have joined them over the years and a variety of membership options keep the Club open for even newer members to join. The Bakersfield Country Club has lived up to the vision of its founders in becoming an exclusive yet friendly club offering outstanding facilities for sports and leisure.

✧

Top: The elegant Bakersfield Country Club Clubhouse, built in 1993, viewed from the Billy Bell-designed golf course.

Below: The grand staircase leads upstairs where diners enjoy spectacular views of Bakersfield and the golf course.

TAFT UNION HIGH SCHOOL DISTRICT

✧

Taft Union High School as it looks today.

The Taft Union High School District was formally organized in 1920, but the history of local high school extends back to the fall of 1911. Conley High opened that year as a branch of Kern County High School and was located in a classroom of the Conley Elementary School in south Taft. The high school's first two graduates received diplomas in 1915, the same year the school was accredited and granted separate status from KCHS. Enrollment grew enough for the high school to occupy the current building site, dedicated on February 22, 1918. In June 1918, eleven students graduated from the new campus' 162-student body.

The formation of the Taft Union High School District united the Conley, Elk Hills, Midway, McKittrick, and Olig School Districts offering a facility with thirty-nine classes, a library, study hall, gymnasium, auditorium, model apartment, and well equipped shops. The new district's valuation was set at over $60 million, and by 1925, the student enrollment of 610 high school students and thirty-nine in the "junior college" program was instructed by forty-two teachers. The District operated an extensive transportation system with eight buses and one touring car transporting 280 students approximately 510 miles per day. Steady growth in the community peaked in 1966 when approximately 1,350 were registered in school. The 1980s saw enrollment decline.

At the turn of the century, Taft High had an enrollment of 950 students in regular education, special education, continuation high school, and independent study programs offered to high school age students. Additional programs include adult education, adult independent study, and the regional occupational program operated through a joint powers agreement with the Maricopa Unified School District. Presently, the district boundaries include Belridge, Elk Hills, Midway, McKittrick, and Taft City Elementary School Districts. Valuation of the District was last set at $6.3 billion that supports a plant valued at over $23 million.

Taft High School today is a modern educational institution offering excellent facilities and instruction conducted in classes that average just twenty-three students each. Taft High has been a pioneer in multimedia and video technology and is a Digital High School. The student to computer ratio is a very good three to one. Over eighty-five percent of regular students have seven classes, and the instructional day exceeds the state's requirements for longer-day, longer-year incentives, as do the school's graduation requirements. The Taft Union High School District's commitment to providing the community's students with the best possible education in a safe and secure environment is evidenced by eighty years of graduates, or by a walk through Taft High School today.

As the quilt work of small farms spread over the area now known as Oildale replacing the huge sheep holdings begun at the time of the Civil War, the new community had a need for child education. The Beardsley School, established on May 3, 1882, takes its name from Louis A. Beardsley who donated an acre of land for the one-room schoolhouse and was, accompanied by C. M. Chadwick, one of the two original teachers at the school. Beardsley School was off to a promising start, and Beardsley School District has kept the promise.

The first year, 41 of the 51 children were between the ages of five and seventeen attended Beardsley with an average daily attendance of twenty-five. In 1913 burgeoning attendance prompted the passing of a $20,000 bond issue to build a two-story schoolhouse comprised of four classrooms downstairs and an auditorium on the second floor. A hot lunch program began in 1914 where students paid a nickel for a meal prepared in class by their teacher who often used vegetables grown on the school grounds. As a result of this resourcefulness, the school won a prize at a 1915 international exhibition in San Francisco for their fine garden products.

Community interest and participation has always been strong at Beardsley. PTA meetings in the early days were community affairs where skits and music were added to discussions of educational matters. In the 1920s the school district ran out of funds before the end of the year, and the PTA held its first school carnival to raise money. The initial carnival featured Vaudeville jugglers and booths offering food and souvenirs. Enough money was raised to finish the school year, and a Beardsley tradition was born. During World War II the school was the site of "victory gardens," and students helped farmers in the fields.

Beardsley was among the first districts to initiate industrial arts and home economics programs in 1923. As attendance ballooned from 743 to 1,900 between 1936 and 1958, North Beardsley School was added, and Beardsley began its renowned instrumental music program. Today, Beardsley has earned state recognition for its gifted and talented education program, comprehensive school program, and state-of-the-art computer and communication technology. The community and schools in the district continue to provide a rich tradition of educational excellence and support of its children.

❖

Above: This photo was taken in the late 1880s. This building was in service until 1914, when a new school building was erected.

Left: School records show this two-story structure was open for students in the 1914-15 school year.

KERN COUNTY MUSEUM FOUNDATION

❖

*Above: Holiday Lamplight Tours is one
of the many museum activities the Kern
County Museum Foundation hosts or
supports in an effort to entertain and
educate a broad public.*

*Below: Kern County Museum Foundation
trustees recognize members of the
Clock Tower Society at the 1999
International Museum Day Celebration.
Clock Tower Society members make
significant contributions to the Museum's
Endowment Fund.*

The Kern County Museum Foundation
was founded in 1991 to support the Kern
County Museum. Trustee representatives of
the community govern it. Other nonprofits
affiliated with the museum, the Kern County
Museum Alliance and the Lori Brock Children's
Museum Board, merged into the Foundation in
1993. It received the Regional Award of Merit
from the Kern Council of Governments for its
dedication to improving the quality of life in
Kern County through innovative, cooperative
regional planning efforts.

In 1993 the Foundation brought the exciting
exhibit, Dinosaur Invasion! to Kern County and
in 1995 Backyard Monsters II. In the area of

collection enhancement the Foundation has
funded the restoration of Fellows Hotel,
conservation of paintings and maps, and
provided funds to ensure better storage
conditions for the museum collections. The
Foundation hosts exhibit openings throughout
each year, as well as two annual special events:
Safe Halloween in October and Wine Fest in
April. Other major museum events such as
What a Cowboy Knows in the spring and
Holiday Lamplight Tours the first Saturday in
December are supported by foundation trustees
who work with staff in coordinating
sponsorships for advertising, refreshments,
entertainment and similar components of these
fun filled family events. Foundation members
also present their museum membership
program to the public at these events.

The Foundation produces publications
such as an award-winning cookbook, *Nuggets,
Nibbles and Nostalgia*, and *Historic Kern
County: An Illustrated History of Bakersfield and
Kern County*. In 1995 the Foundation started
an endowment fund to provide long term
operating dollars for the museum. Individuals
supporting the fund at levels of $1,000 and
above become members of the Clock Tower
Society and receive special recognition for
their investment in the museum's future.

The largest project undertaken by the
Foundation is the updating of the museum's oil
exhibits. Beginning in 1995, a citizens group
made up of representatives of various oil
industry organizations began to meet, and
became a standing committee of the
Foundation. Through its efforts a wonderful
plan for developing the oil industry exhibits into
the premier educational exhibit of its type in the
state was developed. Thanks to the efforts of
State Senator Chuck Poochigian, funding to
make this project a reality was obtained in 2000
through Proposition 12. Work has begun and
should be completed in 2002.

In 1999 the Foundation partnered with other
interested community members to generate a
plan for the museum's development in the
twenty-first century. This organization's top
priority is establishing a broader base of fiscal
support. With additional community investment, the Foundation will be able to accomplish
more of its goals for the museum.

get from the administrators, staff, and faculty. Students from out of state and from other countries appreciate the combination of personal attention, affordability, and the availability of residence halls. Of the 6,000 people who will attend a class at Taft in the course of a year, approximately 1,300 per semester are full-time students.

Always small, Taft College was established in 1922 and did not separate from the facilities of Taft Union High School until 1956 when the permanent campus was established on Emmons Park Drive. Among the variety of educational opportunities Taft offers is a great Liberal Arts program, a Dental Hygiene program ranked among the nation's top ten and a Criminal Justice Administration associate degree. The college has embraced technology to offer distance learning via the Internet, videos, CDs, and other electronic means. Taft College, the best-kept educational secret in Kern County, is reaching out to the world.

"There is no better place in the world to go to work or go to school than a small college," says Taft College Dean of Student Services, Patricia Bench. "It's a community where everybody knows everyone else, and that makes a big difference." Bench refers to the students drawn to Taft College for the personal attention they will

✧

The First National Bank and Farmers Hardware Company in Delano as seen about 1924. The truck door reads "Mt. Whitney P & E Co." Mount Whitney Power and Electric Company had a plant outside of Delano.

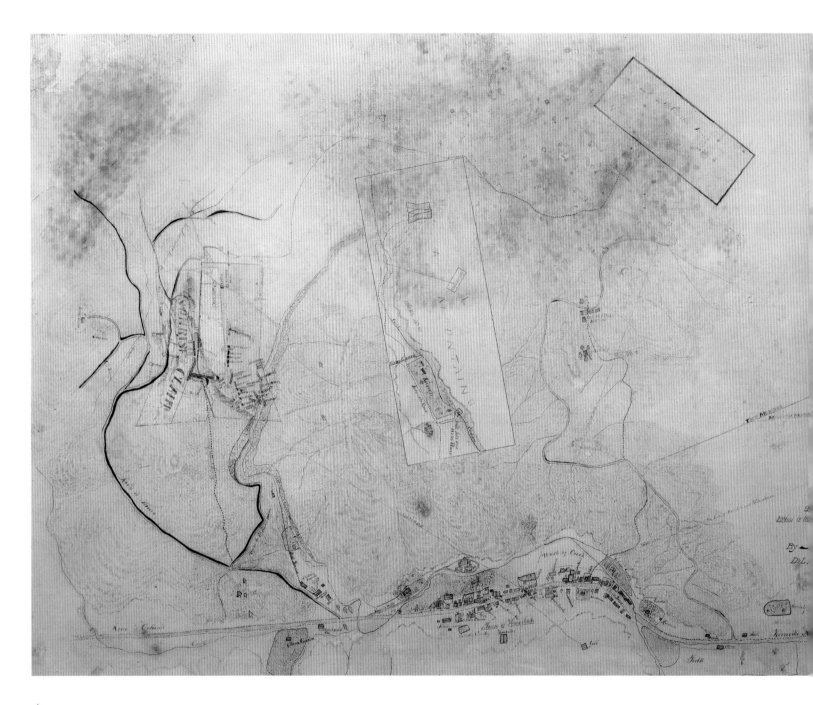

✧

D. L. Reese created this hand-drawn map of
Havilah in 1871. Havilah was Kern
County's original county seat from 1866-
1874. The map is in the collection of the
Kern County Museum.

THE MARKETPLACE

Kern County's retail and commercial

establishments offer an impressive variety of

choices to the people of Kern County

SPECIAL THANKS TO

Abate-A-Weed, Inc.

CONTINENTAL LABOR RESOURCES, INC.

✧

Above: Continental Labor Resources, Inc. Co-Owners Shannon Smith and Karen Cain.

Below: Vice President of Health & Safety Paul Smith and Ron Jordan, Risk Management.

Continental Labor Resources, Kern County's largest independently owned temporary labor service, began as a reluctantly opened office on a dirt road off of Fruitville Avenue. Today, Continental operates out of nine offices statewide and employs over four thousand workers in various industries including oil, agriculture, and construction work. Co-owners Shannon Smith and Karen Cain are emphatic about the source of the business's success: "God. And treating people right." They are quick to add, "And we have lots of fun!"

In 1993, Smith was working in marketing for another temporary agency when she mused aloud about starting a business of her own. When her brother, Tony Cain, and good friend, Jeff Flenniken, offered to put up money to get her started, Smith resisted the idea; she was apprehensive about leaving a secure job to undertake such a risky venture. With further prodding and persuasion from her friend and sister-in-law, Karen Cain, Smith decided to take up the challenge and opened an office in the building Flenniken was using as a welding shop. They chose the name Continental Labor because the welding company was named Continental Build-Up; that way they could answer the joint phone "Continental" and figure out which business the caller wanted by who they asked for.

Karen and Shannon poured great effort and prayer into the start-up company. There were nights in the first year when, short-handed, they themselves joined crews to work loading grapes until near dawn and showed up in the office after a shower to keep the business going. Karen, who had worked in the clay "kitty-litter" mine at Maricopa, learned the business from the ground up. She took accounting courses at night so she could assume administration duties as the business grew. It grew fast. After a year, Continental moved to a new office on Pierce Road. The start-up loans were soon paid off, and before the company was two years old, the women had reached their first goal: to be the largest independently owned temp service in Bakersfield.

By the year 2000, Continental had far exceeded its second goal, which was to become the largest independently owned temp service in Kern County and is now one of the largest in the State of California. "We go the extra mile for customers and employees to find a good match. Our good reputation is based on good relationships both with the businesses that use us and the people we employ." Customers know that they are going to be visited by an employee well versed in safety and drug free. Employees are encouraged to excel and their excellence is rewarded with bonuses, gifts, and certificates. Karen, Shannon, and their staff of forty-five at the nine offices really care about what they do and who they work with.

From the beginning, Continental has made safety a high priority. Employees take an eight-hour safety course before being sent out. The ten-person safety team on permanent staff trains individual employees on the requirements of specific jobs. Furthermore, the safety techs inspect job sites before employees are sent and then inspect them to be sure the employee is following the safest procedures. Employees who score high on a safety checklist are awarded bicycles or other prizes. Continental goes beyond government-required standards to be sure their valued employees are placed in the right environment with the right training.

The offices of Continental are very professional and efficient as would be expected, but what is perhaps unexpected is the lively atmosphere of people very happy to be doing what they do. At the main office on Mohawk Street, Shannon and Karen keep photo albums of their staff that they refer to like extended family. The staff tends to stay aboard. There is also a sense of responsibility toward the communities that Continental serves. The company is proud of their involvement with Cal State Bakersfield, Kern Hospice Foundation, and Teen Challenge, which is a Bible-based program to help young people with substance abuse problems.

When asked the trade secret behind their average annual growth of 150 percent, Shannon and Karen will answer in unison.

"God." The company's mission statement affirms this. "Acknowledgment that God is the provider of this business…The mission of Continental Labor Resources, Inc. is to provide our communities and its businesses with superior customer service and quality employees in a manner that will give honor and glory to Him." Both women tithe to Brimhall Road Assembly of God Church and pray over business decisions and locations, gladly accepting whatever God may choose for them. They feel particularly blessed with the customers they work with and the tremendous fun they have enjoyed creating their business.

✧

Continental Labor Resources employs over four thousand workers and is capable of meeting a wide variety of needs.

BAKERSFIELD VAN AND TRUCKIN' SUPPLIES

❖

Above: The Bakersfield Van and Truckin' Supplies storefront at 2814 Chester.

Below: The shop at Bakersfield Van and Truckin' Supplies can accommodate the needs of both walk-in customers and corporate vehicle fleets.

Bakersfield Van and Truckin' Supplies at Twenty-ninth and Chester is Kern County's pioneer auto accessories outlet and remains dedicated to the principles of customer service and competitive pricing that led Mike Barton to open the shop in 1979. Back then, when the industry of customizing vans and providing accessories was just beginning to take off, Bakersfield had only a single accessory dealer monopolizing the business. "They had a poor attitude and I didn't like dealing with them," says Barton. He opened his own shop with his own approach, "attitude is everything."

Barton is a native of Kern County. His father, Melvin, was a farm worker who moved to Arvin from Oklahoma in the 1930s; his mother, Nettie, was from Illinois and worked as a librarian at the Arvin Library. Like a lot of boys in high school, Barton loved cars and made them his hobby when he left school. He began his own drapery service, but by the late seventies he was looking to start an additional business that could become an ongoing source of income. Seeing the market for custom accessory business growing and not thinking much of the competition at the time, Barton and a partner each put up $5,000 to open a shop.

The original store was a little place on the corner of Mt. Vernon and Niles Road. After four months, Barton bought his partner out, and, in early 1980, he moved the shop to its present location at 2814 Chester. As is common in start-up businesses, the first year was tough. Barton's then wife (now good friend), Juanita, worked the counter, and Barton split time between the new venture and the drapery business. That first year, the store offered five hundred parts. By 1982 Bakersfield Van and Truckin' Supplies had hired its first employee and experienced an average and consistent annual growth of ten to fifteen percent. By 2000, Bakersfield Van and Truckin' Supplies offers more than two million parts on its computers, employs a qualified staff of fifteen, and offers a wide variety of parts and customizing service to a diverse clientele.

The business is extremely competitive; in fact, the shop that monopolized the industry in 1979 is long gone. Bakersfield Van and Truckin' Supplies has diversified to serve both the retail, walk-in customer with great service and prices that cannot be beat, and the wholesale customer looking for specialized customizing for industrial, agricultural, and public sector fleets. Local SWAT Teams have come to Bakersfield Van and Truckin' Supplies for configuration of surveillance vans equipped with periscopes and electronic gear. Haliburton Oil Field Services, Time Warner Cable, Bolthouse Farms, Grimmway Farms, Paramount Farms, and Giumarra Farms are prominent customers with varying fleet vehicle customization needs.

Retail customers are sure of getting expert service from a sales staff that averages

seven to ten years of experience in the business and an installation staff that is GM-certified. Furthermore, in addition to offering great bargains, Bakersfield Van and Truckin' Supplies will meet any price of any competitor whether it's a shop, a catalog, or a dot.com. Barton has embraced the Internet; his company has opened a site at www.customautoacc.com where customers can more easily access his shop's resources. Twenty years of adjusting to the market and the customers has earned Bakersfield Van and Truckin' Supplies a strong reputation.

A native of Kern County, Barton is very attached to the Bakersfield area, and he is glad that the success of his businesses has allowed him to "give back" to the community that he feels has done so much for him. "I totally love Kern County and Bakersfield." He is a member of the Elks Club and is regularly involved in charity barbecues for the Special Olympics, contributes to the San Clemente Mission Golf Tournament and St. Jude's Hospital. "My goal is to be able to do even more charity work." Another aspect of Barton's affection for Bakersfield is his purchase and restoration of the Lawrence and Helen Weill estate at 3020 Twenty-first Street.

Finding the home in fair condition when he acquired it from the Weill estate, Barton has taken great pleasure in indulging his passions for antiques and gardening while restoring this gem of a home. When adding a pool, great care was taken to replant all of the rare flowers and trees displaced. The gardens started by the Weills include exotic camellias, which have won prizes from the local Camellia Society and a blooming orchid tree. Barton is refurbishing a vintage pick-up to place under the carport that was part of the original, 1935 structure. In speaking of his home, his businesses, or his diverse interests, Mike Barton always conveys an enthused happiness. It's a homegrown happiness unique to Kern County and Bakersfield.

ALTAONE FEDERAL CREDIT UNION

FORMERLY NWC COMMUNITY FEDERAL CREDIT UNION

✧

Above: Old Dorm 1 in China Lake was one of the original homes of the Naval Ordnance Test Station Employees Federal Credit Union, predecessor of AltaOne Federal Credit Union.

Below: AltaOne Federal Credit Union China Lake Base Branch.

Upon returning from a shopping trip in 1947, China Lake resident Lorraine McClung reported to her husband, Rod, that there was a new enterprise on Halsey Street (today Inyokern Road). "They have a desk, a type-writer and a waste basket, and they call themselves a credit union." She was referring to the newly formed Naval Ordnance Test Station (NOTS) Employees Federal Credit Union, which had just opened with 9 founding members and $300 in total assets. The first loan was a small advance to help tide over a member until payday. By the year 2000, operating under the new name of AltaOne, that early organization has grown to include more than thirty-two thousand members across eastern Kern County with total assets in excess of a quarter of a billion dollars.

The original NOTS Employees Federal Credit Union, which was a project of the Employee Welfare Association of NOTS, had a field of membership limited to only Navy, government, and contracted employees of the China Lake Naval Station and their family members. The first office was Room 1 of a Quonset hut known as the "Old Training Building." Unsecured loans to members could not exceed $50, secured loans were limited to $2,000, and for the first year volunteers ran the operation. Carl Sandidge, one of the nine original members, was the credit union's first president of the board of directors. Growth came fast. After a year, the credit union had 616 members with assets of $37,160. After ten years, there were 3,269 members and assets were approaching $1 million.

As more people moved to the area and formed a community beyond the gates of the naval station, the membership was broadened to include other federal employees and retirees living in the area as well as credit union employees. This pattern of inclusion and community has been the hallmark of AltaOne for more than fifty years. Including more members made the credit union grow from building to building on the base. It moved from the original office to a succession of buildings called "Old Byrnes Street School" located at 90 Halsey Street, "The Housing Building" and "Old Dorm 1" on Blandy Avenue before moving into a permanent home specifically built for the credit union on land leased from the Navy at Richmond Road and King Street in China Lake.

The name changed from NOTSEFCU to Naval Weapons Center Federal Credit Union in 1968 and to simply NWC Community Federal Credit in 1989. The changes in name reflect the credit union's transition from an employee-based membership to one that is community-based. The new name, AltaOne, represents the culmination of efforts to include the broad community of Eastern Kern County into the field of members who can join the credit union and enjoy the broad array of services offered by AltaOne. Anyone who lives, works, owns a business, worships, or attends school in the communities of Bodfish, Boron, Cantil, California City, China Lake, Darwin, Grant, Inyokern, Johannesburg, Kernville, Kramer's Junction, Lake Isabella, Little Lake, Mojave, Mt. Mesa, North Edwards, Olancha, Onyx, Panamint Springs, Randsburg, Red Mountain, Ridgecrest, South Lake, Trona, Weldon, or Wofford Heights is eligible to join AltaOne as are their immediate family members.

"As the provider of choice for financial services in its communities, AltaOne Federal Credit Union is dedicated to the Credit Union Spirit of neighbor helping neighbor," states AltaOne's vision statement. The original sense of neighborly responsibility that initiated the credit union at China Lake has joined to a professional organization capable of meeting the variety of needs facing their

membership. Beyond China Lake/Ridgecrest, AltaOne has branches in Boron, California City, Kernville and Lake Isabella. Phone-A-Loan service, ATMs, and electronic banking make AltaOne the number one choice in their communities for financial services.

When deregulation of financial institutions in the 1980s changed the rules governing credit unions, NWC Community Federal Credit Union was swift to broaden opportunities for its members. Today, AltaOne offers savings, checking, IRA, and term share accounts, direct deposit and youth accounts. Financial services include credit cards; home equity lines of credit; real estate loans; signature loans; boat, car, truck, and RV loans. Beyond these general services, AltaOne is always ready to work with members on individual, personal needs.

AltaOne's professional, neighborly service has another dimension—it is portable. Because of the "once a member always a member," policy of AltaOne, many members who have moved from Kern County still bank there. The nine original members who opened the "desk drawer" credit union in 1947 could not have foreseen just how big their creation would become. Surely these members would be pleased that the community spirit in which it was created is a living legacy of AltaOne Federal Credit Union.

✧

AltaOne Federal Credit Union Corporate Branch.

NICKEL FAMILY, L.L.C.

"Empire" is the only word that can be used to characterize the vast holdings of Henry Miller whose partnership with Charles Lux became a cattle kingdom encompassing more than a million acres in three states. Miller & Lux are a key element in the history of Kern County where Miller's legacy is the Nickel Family, L.L.C. The stories of Henry Miller and his great grandson, George W. Nickel, illustrate the beginnings, falls, and rises of empire.

Henry Miller was born Henry Kreiser in the tiny village of Brackenheim, Germany in 1827. He learned to raise, slaughter, and market livestock from his father, and set off for the New World as a teenager. In New York City the young man took a job cutting meat in a dingy butcher shop that he worked to transform into a sparkling success. The California Gold Rush attracted him to the west in 1850, and he bought the ticket of his friend, Henry Miller, who had decided against going. The ticket was non-transferable, so Henry took the name of his friend for the voyage, and it stuck until the end of his life. Henry crossed the isthmus now called Panama, survived yellow fever, and arrived in San Francisco with six dollars.

Miller chose not to leave the city and head for the mines, but employed his remarkable skills as a butcher to build his own business in booming San Francisco. Eventually, Miller opened his own shop on Jackson Street between Dupont and Kearney. California cattle were limited in those years, and Miller turned his attention to cattle production and the country where cattle came from. A trip into the San Joaquin Valley led to the purchase of 8,835 acres of land with cattle and the Double H Brand. Back in San Francisco, Miller formed a partnership with his chief competitor in the meat trade, Charles Lux, and Miller & Lux became an empire of steadily increasing cattle lands.

In Kern County, Miller acquired land along fifty miles of the lower Kern River including the areas of Panama, Buttonwillow, Buena Vista, Chester, and Adobe. The overflow of the river was tamed by Miller's construction of a fifty-mile channel turning swamps into productive farm and cattle land. In time, conflict over the water with upstream landholders led to a landmark Court decision in favor of Miller & Lux, upholding California's adoption of English common law and its concept of riparian rights. Even though victory in the case assured Miller rights to all of the riparian water from the Kern, Miller struck a deal to share it with Haggin & Tevis and other upstream landholders in exchange for

construction of the Buena Vista Reservoir. Miller & Lux retained rights to one third of the water from the flow of the Kern. Miller died in 1916.

Under the direction of Miller's son-in-law, James Leroy Nickel, the great cattle kingdom suffered. "It took my grandfather just ten years to put the company in debt to the tune of $28 million," says George Nickel. Land was sold to pay the debts, and the Miller Empire slowly crumbled. During these years, George Nickel was growing up cowboying on the ranches and eventually worked his way through the University of California at Berkeley. After graduating in 1939 he moved to Los Banos and was appointed to oversee operations for the Miller & Lux ranches.

Nickel, who was born just a year after Henry Miller's death, seems to have inherited his great grandfather's love of the land and passion for developing it. He slowed the land sales, and all company debts were paid off by 1943. By 1954 Miller & Lux holdings were down to forty-five thousand acres, which Nickel blames on corruption. That year, Nickel and two other Miller great-grandchildren sued for control of the company and subsequently divided the assets among seven Miller grandchildren. Nickel concentrated on water, farming and ranch business in Kern, Merced, and Fresno Counties.

When asked, George Nickel will tell you he is "in the water business, farming, and real estate development." Nickel pioneered engineering techniques for making use of sloping lands by drip irrigation and developed a genius for water distribution and conservation through underground storage of water. By using the waters of the Kern River to replenish the underground water table, there are vast savings in loss due to evaporation that was an ongoing problem with the enormous Buena Vista Reservoir. More than a century after the great battle over riparian rights, managing the company's share of the Kern River is an important aspect of what the Nickel family does. Nickel's purchase of the Olcese Ranch east of Bakersfield in 1965 led to his development of the famed Rio Bravo Resort, the Rio Bravo Golf Course and Club, much subdivision activity and three thousand acres of citrus growth.

Today, George Nickel is joined by his children in the Nickel Family, L.L.C. in the farming and water operations in Merced, Fresno, and Kern Counties and in his subdivision activities at the Olcese Ranch. Even with his ongoing battle with arthritis, Nickel puts in full days on all activities as further follow up to his great grandfather, Henry Miller.

✧

Left: George Nickel with his wife, Dodo Nickel, is ready for a little tennis competition at the Rio Bravo Resort.

Below: George Nickel stands before the Rio Bravo Resort he developed overlooking the Kern River. The development included a beautiful hotel facility, excellent dining areas, 19 championship tennis courts, q championship swimming area plus adjacent exercise facilities.

BEAR CREEK PRODUCTION CO.

Kern County is home to the world's largest rose "farm." Bear Creek Production Co. grows twenty-two million rose bushes on 5,300 acres in Wasco. In season, the millions of roses in bloom create a fragrant, technicolor ocean that is a delight to the nose and eye. Bear Creek Production Co. is the exclusive producer of Jackson & Perkins® roses, which have been prized above all others by gardeners for nearly a hundred years. Although the Wasco farm is the heart of Jackson & Perkins® rose production today, the earliest Jackson & Perkins® hybrids were grown in New York during the nineteenth century.

In 1872 attorney Charles Perkins partnered with his father-in-law and retired cheese maker, Albert E. Jackson, to begin a small truck farm operation in Newark, New York, specializing in strawberries, raspberries, and grapes. Attracted to rose propagation in 1884, Perkins bought new acreage, built a greenhouse out of recycled church windows, and hired horticulturalist Alvin Miller to experiment with rose hybrids. The Jackson & Perkins Company achieved fame in 1908 when Miller's magnificent Dorothy Perkins rose (named for Charles Perkins' granddaughter), a pink climber that grew to twenty feet and produced double blooms, won top honors at England's National Rose Society. By 1920 Jackson & Perkins was selling 250,000 rose bushes per year.

The next big leap for Jackson & Perkins came at the 1939 World's Fair in Flushing, New York, where the company presented a ten-thousand-square-foot garden called the "Parade of Modern Roses." More than forty thousand visitors inquired about a unique red floribunda, aptly named Worlds Fair, and left their names and addresses. This list became the foundation of Jackson & Perkins® mail order catalogue business. By the 1950s Jackson & Perkins was America's largest rose producer, growing twenty million rose bushes on sites in six states including California.

Harry and David, the world's largest mail order fruit business, purchased Jackson & Perkins in 1966. Six years later, the Bear Creek Corporation was formed as an umbrella organization over Harry and David and Jackson & Perkins. Rose growing was consolidated in Wasco where the permanent staff of 200 swells to 1,300 during peak season. Interestingly, wheat, corn, carrots, garlic, and other vegetable crops are alternated with the roses every few years to help keep the fields weed free. Bear Creek was concerned that the greatest roses in the world find just the right location for cultivation. "We located in the Wasco area because of the long growing season, good water, and excellent soil," said Dave Stump, who reorganized rose production for Bear Creek. "It's the finest land to grow horticultural crops in the world."

The land now occupied by Tejon Ranch has played a colorful role in California's history since the first Spanish soldier journeyed across "El Tejon" (Spanish for "badger") in 1772. Traversed by fur trappers and explorers from Jedediah Smith to Kit Carson and John C. Fremont, El Tejon was first formed into cattle ranches under Mexican land grants in 1843. The legendary General Edward Fitzgerald Beale—hero of the Mexican-American War and the first to bring news of California's gold discovery to our nation's capital—acquired and consolidated four Mexican land grants into what is now Tejon Ranch. A man with grand dreams, Beale instigated the establishment of Fort Tejon, which became the site of the experimental U.S. Camel Corps and way station for the Butterfield Overland Stage Line.

Following Beale's death in 1893, his son, Truxtun, maintained the ranch, selling it in 1912 to a group of Southern California businessmen led by the Sherman and Chandler families. In 1936, the ownership group formed Tejon Ranch Company and placed the Ranch in corporate ownership. Over time, the stock came to be traded over the counter until it was listed on the American Stock Exchange in 1973. Tejon stock commenced trading on the New York Stock Exchange on July 28, 1999. Currently, over thirty percent of Tejon Ranch Company shares are owned by two highly regarded investment firms—Third Avenue Value Fund and Carl Marks Management Company—and eighteen percent of the shares are owned by the descendants of the Sherman family, with significant additional holdings by numerous institutional investors.

During the twentieth century, Tejon Ranch generated revenues primarily through live-stock and farming operations, and since 1940 from oil and mineral royalties. By the mid-1990s, however, saturated population in the Los Angeles Basin and industrial growth in the Central Valley highlighted the value of the Tejon Ranch property itself. To develop the land responsibly, in 1996 the Tejon Ranch Company board of directors named Robert A. Stine, an experienced real estate developer, as president and chief executive officer. Under Stine's stewardship, corporate management committed to grow the Company's three core businesses—real estate, livestock, and farming—with greater emphasis on real estate development, particularly along the heavily traveled Interstate 5 corridor. Today, Tejon Ranch Company is well on its way to implementing its plans for growing the Company, increasing earnings by 67 percent per year and revenues by 50 percent per year over the past three years.

Entering the twenty-first century, Tejon Ranch Company is dedicated to building value for its shareholders while preserving the unique character and beauty of Tejon Ranch land for future generations.

TEJON RANCH COMPANY

❖

Below: Tejon Ranch Company, in addition to real estate development and farming, remains a major national livestock producer, maintaining more than thirty-five thousand head of cattle on its vast lands.

Bottom: Included in the Tejon Ranch's 270,000 acres is a natural, private 320-acre lake.

BEST WESTERN HILL HOUSE

When G. J. Zala purchased the Best Western Hill House in 1998, he knew he was investing in a special part of the history of Bakersfield with an eye to its future. He discovered people who had been coming to the hotel for decades since it opened under the name Vagabond Hotel in the 1960s. "People love this place, whoever comes, whether for the first time or the twentieth." In its first decade, the Vagabond offered the only first rate accommodations for travelers in Bakersfield.

As the city grew around it, the Best Western Hill House became a prime location for banquets and special events as well as a perfect spot in downtown for visiting businessmen. The construction of the Civic Center less than a block away has made the hotel a destination for convention attendees. With its colonial styling, Hill House offers a pleasing alternative to a stay in a high-rise building. Guests of the hotel enjoy the charm of sliding doors that open onto quaint patios bordered by trellises of flowers.

Of course, there is a lovely pool and restaurant on the premises, but many fine downtown restaurants and good shopping are just a few blocks away—an easy walk on a nice day.

Zala is a CPA and had been a payroll director for a prominent Los Angeles university when he decided he wanted to go into business for himself. He looked in Los Angeles for opportunities, but was drawn to Bakersfield for a combination of reasons including the business climate, the chance to live in "the heart of California," and the prospect of turning such a fine local establishment into a family business. He shares work with his wife, Gaytri, and the couple lives at Hill House with their two young children.

"Our goal was to maintain the history of Hill House while restoring it to its better days," says Zala. In late 1999, Hill House received Best Western's Directors Award and highest possible rating, three diamonds, after a rigorous inspection. Even with the high distinction of the award, the Zala family has plans for adding more trees, flowers, and a water fountain to the park-like grounds. "We plan to be in business here quite awhile." The Best Western Hill House is a Bakersfield tradition that future visitors and guests will be able to rely upon.

Cox Communications, Kern County's first cable television provider, is something of a paradox. Although it is part of Cox Enterprises, Inc., a large, reputable national corporation, it is also very involved in the local community in ways one would expect from a homegrown business. Based upon examination of Cox Enterprise's 102-year history, one sees over and over again that at Cox Communications, they have a vision "to be the recognized leader in the communications business, driven by quality, and committed to its customers, employees, shareholders, and communities through innovation and growth." At least in Kern County, this vision is becoming a reality.

Cox Enterprises, Inc. itself grew from the ambitions of Ohio farm boy James Cox, to become a newspaperman. Cox's purchase of the *Dayton Daily News* in 1898 led to the acquisition of other newspapers and media businesses in the twentieth century, which grew to include the Kern County cable system. Along the way, Cox also served three terms as governor of Ohio, served in the U.S. Congress, and was the Democratic Party nominee for the President of the United States in 1920 with the young Franklin Delano Roosevelt as his running mate. Clearly, it was Cox who planted the seed that produced the legacy of strong leadership and commitment to the communities served at Cox Enterprises and Cox Communications.

The Cox Communications cable system in Bakersfield dates back to a 1965 agreement with the City of Bakersfield to provide cable television services. By 2000, Cox was maintaining in excess of six hundred miles of cable and fiber, either buried in trenches or running along utility poles. Rapid advances in communications and computer technology have been cause for equally rapid upgrading to accommodate broader bandwidths and two-way communications capabilities. Cox has stayed abreast of the technology and anticipates the imminent addition of digital television and high-speed data services. As new neighborhoods spring up and businesses begin to need service, Cox expects their system to grow by forty to fifty miles per year.

Cox employs forty people working in their Bakersfield office or out in the field. J. D. Power & Associates has ranked Cox Communications the best at providing customer service among all cable companies in the U.S. for the past four years, and Cox Enterprises has ranked Cox Communications' Kern County operations as the best at providing customer service among all Cox locations evaluating installation and repair, customer billing, and customer care provided to customers who use the retail and call centers. People in Kern County know they will receive prompt, courteous, and capable service when they call on Cox Communications.

Beyond the best service to their customers, Cox employees in Kern County are involved in the community. The lobby at 820 Twenty-second Street has walls covered with plaques, trophies, awards, and letters expressing gratitude to Cox Communications and its employees for their community service. In 1998, the year of the Bakersfield Centennial, which coincided with Cox Enterprise's 100th year in business, the Cox Communications employees in Kern County launched the "Supporting Our Community" program and set a goal to get a high percentage of employees involved in local non-profit organizations. Employees responded with an involvement rate greater than ninety percent in 1998, and more than ninety-five percent in 1999. In the first two and a half years of the "Supporting Our Community" program, Cox employees in Kern County volunteered over 6,000 hours and contributed more than $1 million in cash and in-kind services to over seventy-five local, non-profit groups. In the last two years alone, Cox Communications and its employees have received more than twenty-five awards, including two Greater Bakersfield Chamber of Commerce Beautiful Bakersfield Awards, the United Way of Kern County's "Quality of Life Award," the Mexican-American Opportunity Foundation's "Aztec Award," and the Kern County Hispanic Chamber of Commerce's "Corporation of the Year Award." Director of Operations Keith Crossley says, "We did not decide to become involved in our community to receive any of the awards. Rather, we continue to give back to our community because we want to make Kern County even a better place to live. All of us at Cox are proud of what we have accomplished together and will continue to strive to make a positive difference in our community." Strong leadership, customer service, and community involvement all remain traditions at Cox Communications.

COX COMMUNICATIONS

SAN JOAQUIN BANK

✧

Top: Principal founder and current Chairman of the Board Bruce Maclin.

Above: San Joaquin Bank President and CEO Bart Hill, 1987.

Right: The original San Joaquin Bank officers in 1980. Left to right: Perry Carter (operations), Richard Northey (loans), Bruce Maclin (chairman), and Stan Perisich (president).

For exceptional banking service provided by people who really know Bakersfield and Kern County, customers and businessmen have been coming to San Joaquin Bank since 1980. At the festive opening of the bank in December of that year, San Joaquin Bank took in its first million dollars in assets and has since grown to become Kern County's largest locally owned bank with assets in excess of $220 million. "The key is service and quick turnaround," says principal founder Bruce Maclin who is chairman of the board at the bank today. He further attributes the bank's impressive string of sixteen consecutive years of record profits to San Joaquin's record of "attracting fabulous people to our staff."

The quick turnaround on loan applications that the bank prides itself on is possible because San Joaquin Bank is so closely oriented to this community. The loan committee meets on Tuesdays and drives around looking at real property. "It's easy to evaluate a loan when we can drive out and look at it," says Maclin. "We don't loan against property we haven't looked at." Decisions are made in a few days and loan applicants can be sure their applications have been given thorough scrutiny. As a business bank, this efficiency and thorough knowledge of the local area makes San Joaquin Bank uniquely able to serve the business community.

Service at San Joaquin Bank goes beyond the friendly, capable tellers at the bank's locations in downtown Bakersfield at 1301 Seventeenth Street, Delano at 1613 Inyo Street, and the original location at 4600 California Avenue. Service means a bank representative going to an interested customer's place of business to help with the necessary paperwork to open a new account. It also means a messenger service for picking up deposits from regular business customers and offering full, one-stop service for clients who come to any bank location. San Joaquin Bank makes it their business to know its customers and how best to serve their varying needs.

As members of the community, San Joaquin Bank and its employees are very involved in activities that benefit Kern County. Their broad ranges of commitments include supporting the Bakersfield Museum of Art, the Mercy Hospital expansion, and the Kern County Museum. The bank annually sponsors the Up on the Roof, Down on the Street Festival for the Downtown Business Association, and it organized a group of banks to provide financial service to the Bakersfield Music Theater for relocation.

Already a thriving institution, San Joaquin Bank looks to keep growing with the community. "We are successful because we know and understand Kern County, its economy and its people," says President and CEO Bart Hill. "San Joaquin Bank satisfies the need for a locally owned and operated bank which can respond quickly to the community."

The accounting partnership of Hocking, Denton, Palmquist & Co. began as a small office in Delano but has grown to include 8 partners and 37 associates who serve most of the communities in Kern County. Senior partner Thomas Hocking was living in San Francisco, California in 1958 when his brother, William, who was a schoolteacher in the area, suggested there were opportunities in Delano. "It's a nice, friendly community," says Thomas Hocking today. "I've never regretted settling here, I love the people."

Hocking began as "a little partnership" when he moved to Delano and bought Roberts and Associates when principal Harry Roberts was retiring. "From then, things just evolved," recalls Hocking. "In 1965 the firm purchased a two story office building at 1224 Jefferson Street in Delano and opened an office in Bakersfield in 1967. The accountants with the firm have always done a variety of accounting work including bookkeeping and income tax for individuals and local industries. In 1981 Timothy Denton and Phil Palmquist became partners at the firm. That same year Hocking, Denton and Palmquist built a new office building at 912 High Street in Delano and

acquired a building in Bakersfield at 3511 Union Avenue. A year later an office was opened in Visalia.

Mike Cebell and Clark Hurst became partners in 1985 and 1987, respectively. In 1994 Craig Swearingen came into the firm as partner at the Visalia office, located at 206 South Mooney Boulevard. That same year Hocking, Denton, Palmquist & Co. opened an office at 1485 East Valley Road in Montecito. Ben Rutherford became the seventh partner at the firm in 1995. Matt Dawson is the most recent accountant to become a full partner, joining the firm in January 2000.

Traditionally at Hocking, Denton, Palmquist & Co., partners work with a great deal of independence and are spread out across Kern, Tulare, and Santa Barbara Counties.

Hocking, Denton, Palmquist & Co. partners, associates, and staff are involved in a broad range of activities in the communities where they have offices. The members of the firm financially support Bakersfield Junior College, Cal State Bakersfield, Delano Junior College, the Delano Youth Foundation, and the Bakersfield Rescue Mission, and are members of many organizations devoted to improving local communities.

HOCKING, DENTON, PALMQUIST & CO.

✧

Hocking, Denton, Palmquist constructed this office building in 1981 at 912 High Street, Delano, California.

CASTLE & COOKE

Above: The original offices of the Kern County Land Company, c. 1900.

Below: The master-planned community of Seven Oaks surrounding the magnificent Seven Oaks Country Club, a current development by Castle & Cooke.

Castle & Cooke, a corporation that has developed unique and beautiful communities from Hawaii to California to Florida, maintains its mainland communities headquarters in Bakersfield where the company's roots go back more than a century. The corporate offices at 10000 Stockdale Highway and the renowned Seven Oaks country club community rest upon property first acquired by Haggin and Tevis as part of a massive land acquisition that would become the Kern County Land Company. The verdant greens of Seven Oaks are a testament to the company's history of managing property and water in Kern County.

James Haggin and Lloyd Tevis were Kentucky attorneys drawn west by the Gold Rush. Their partnership in San Francisco created an enormous pool of wealth which they converted to a vast land holding of nearly one half million acres north of the Kern River. Haggin and Tevis operated through the notorious W. B. "Billy" Carr who used the Desert Land Act of 1877 to claim numerous sections of land in need of irrigation. After experimenting with corporate farming, the Haggin and Tevis holdings were incorporated into the Kern County Land Company, and their strategy shifted from grand-scale agriculture to "colonization" and development.

Throughout the twentieth century, the company was tied to the changes and growth of Kern County and Bakersfield from a remote, sparsely populated rural area to a diverse, thriving community. By 1960, Kern County Land held more than a million acres of management property in California and Arizona, the hundred thousand-acre San Emidio Ranch south of Bakersfield. Tenneco, Inc. acquired the company in 1968 and changed the company name to Tenneco West. Under its new banner, the company led the way in local residential and business development. The donation of 370 acres which would become the campus of California State College, Bakersfield symbolizes the company's involvement in the community which has been a constant trait throughout its history.

Today, Castle & Cooke has inherited the proud history begun by Haggin and Tevis. After acquiring Tenneco West in 1988, Castle & Cooke made Bakersfield its mainland communities headquarters controlling development projects from California and Arizona all the way to Florida. The elegantly planned beauty of Seven Oaks exemplifies the Castle & Cooke touch. The community integrates homes of various scale and diverse sub-communities (retired couples, young families with children) with facilities for community activity and commercial support. The 1877 Haggin and Tevis dream of making something special of the desert has been realized by Castle & Cooke in the year 2000.

The staff at Thorp's Harley-Davidson, Inc., 820-824 Eighteenth Street, Bakersfield, California is assured of expertise based on a half-century of experience and a dedication to helping make customers' motorcycling experiences fulfill their dreams.

When C. D. "Tex" Thorp and his wife, Pat, opened their own business, Merced Harley-Davidson, in January of 1962, he had already been associated with Harley-Davidson companies for ten years, beginning as a trainee for Walker and Hayford Harley-Davidson. In 1959 Thorp went to the Rich Budleier Company, managing their San Fernando Harley-Davidson until 1961. He and Pat opened their first dealership in Merced, California in February 1962. They purchased the Bakersfield business from Ross J. Wooten on January 19, 1964, and changed the name to Thorp's Harley-Davidson.

For the next decade the Thorps operated their dealership in the same location Wooten had occupied for thirty-eight years. When growth required more space, they expanded next door, retaining the original location as the service area. Thorp's Harley-Davidson now occupies 12,000 square feet, with a 3,000-square-foot expansion planned this year.

The Thorps' son, Dan, began working at the dealership during high school, joining on a full-time basis in 1972, and his wife, Vicki, in 1978. With a present customer base of 9,980 "and growing," the company has grown from a two-person operation by Tex and Pat to thirteen employees.

Extremely active in organizations for dealers, Tex served three years as president of the Northern California Harley-Davidson Dealers Association, and two years as president of the California Dealers Association. As a member of the Dealer Advisory Council for three years, he represented all Harley-Davidson dealers in California for the Harley-Davidson Motor Company in Milwaukee, Wisconin. He was chosen in 1990 as "Dealer of the Year."

Thorp's participates in many community events, and sponsors several. Over the past fifteen years the annual Ride for Life, the company's main charity, has raised over $444,000 to aid in the fight against Muscular Dystrophy. This effort includes both the annual ride in May and assistance in the telethon in September. Thorp's also sponsors the Harley-Davidson Owners Group in Bakersfield, helping with such events as the Bakersfield Christmas Toy Run, The American Lung Association, Bakersfield Centennial Ride, American Diabetes Ride, Peace Ride, and Denim and Diamond Dance. Both Tex and Pat have been active in civic and service groups and in Northminster Presbyterian Church.

They attribute much of their business' success to their adherence to the company's mission statement: "To be the best we can every day and serve our customers to the best of our ability.

✧

*San Joaquin Light and Power Company is
now known as Pacific Gas and Electric
Company (PG&E.) This wagon is one used
by SJL&P during its years of operation and
is currently located in the collection of the
Kern County Museum.*

COURTESY OF GREG IGER.

Industry & Manufacturing

Kern County's construction, engineering, and energy industries shape tomorrow's skyline, providing working and living space for the people of Kern County and fuel for the state

Special Thanks To

BC Laboratories, Inc.

Kern Delta Weedpatch Ginning Company

S. C. ANDERSON, INC.

❖

Above: The Kern County Building, built by S. C. Anderson, is home to a twenty-two thousand-square-foot FBI-certified crime lab.

Bottom: Shell Plaza, the tallest building in Bakersfield.

More than five hundred buildings in Bakersfield and Kern County have been built, refurbished, or remodeled by S. C. Anderson, Inc., one of California's premier construction companies. Locally owned and operated, S. C. Anderson opened its doors in 1983 and undertook the construction of a small dental clinic on Stockdale Highway as its first project. Sing Lum Elementary School was the company's first large assignment, and the business has steadily grown and diversified for seventeen years. S. C. Anderson has built housing, offices, and infrastructure in Siberia, restored hurricane-damaged high-rises in Puerto Rico, and constructed landmark buildings in Bakersfield and Kern County.

Leigh Ann and Steven Anderson met in Sacramento where he was supervising a construction project for Robert G. Fisher Contracting and she was in charge of the business that was to occupy the building. They married with the dream of opening a business together. A native of Bakersfield, Steven had supervised the construction of the city's tallest building, Shell Plaza, while still with Fisher and wanted to open the business in his hometown. A full and active partner, Leigh Ann applied her business experience to sales and marketing, human resources, payroll, and workers compensation. The young company's "first world headquarters" was a jobsite trail-

er, in less than a year, the Andersons opened formal offices on District Boulevard on the south side of Bakersfield. Today, the Andersons have adjoining offices in the S. C. Anderson Building at 2160 Mars Court.

A few recently completed local projects demonstrate S. C. Anderson's versatility. The company managed the building of Liberty High School in Bakersfield, S. C. Anderson's largest single project ever. Construction included a gymnasium and performing arts center within a design integrating multiple buildings, and, typically, the $27 million project was completed on time and within budget. The newly constructed Bakersfield Heart Hospital and the Kern County District Attorney's Office Forensic Science/Family Support Building are also S. C. Anderson projects which presented unique challenges in creating state-of-the-art scientific facilities. The Heart Hospital is California's first privately held cardiac specialty hospital and the Kern County Building is home to a twenty-two thousand-square-foot FBI certified crime lab.

Meeting unique challenges has been the hallmark of S. C. Anderson. In 1994, S. C. Anderson was working with Southern California Edison in Santa Clarita when the Northridge Earthquake did major local damage and physically isolated the Edison crew at the site. Within five hours, S. C. Anderson was in action arranging for helicopters to fly its own crews to Santa Clarita to repair damage and to carry food and necessities to the stranded SoCal Edison crews. Such swift response and aggressive action led many businesses and

building owners in Santa Clarita to seek S. C. Anderson for major reconstruction work. S. C. Anderson spun off a new company, Anderson Group International that specializes in disaster response such as rebuilding the hotels and multiple housing units of Puerto Rico after a devastating hurricane.

In 1996, work on the Kern Medical Center's Emergency Center and Neo-Natal ICU stalled when the contractor they had hired went bankrupt. With the accreditation of the hospital on the line, the county turned to S. C. Anderson to take over the troubled project. S. C. Anderson took up the challenge and completed the job ahead of schedule and under budget; the county's accreditation was saved. "We do a bit of everything these days, you've got to be versatile to survive and excel in this business," says Leigh Ann Anderson. Kern County churchgoers attend services in

dozens of churches built by S. C. Anderson, just as shoppers go to stores and leave their cars in parking structures that are S. C. Anderson-built.

The S. C. Anderson approach to business involves crisp professionalism, co-operation with clients, and teamwork with employees and subcontractors. The offices of S. C. Anderson are shirt-and-tie where more than half of the staff wears rings signifying ten years with the company. Monthly education courses offered to employees broaden their knowledge and qualify them for promotion. These and other opportunities encourage existing employees to stay at S. C. Anderson and attract top-quality recruits. The Andersons are proud of the people with whom they work.

Even with its brilliant reputation, S. C. Anderson is always looking for ways to improve and grow. The company uses the assistance of a business consulting firm bi-annually in quality improvement meetings to improve performance. With licenses in five western states and Florida, and a growing reputation abroad, S. C. Anderson is poised to continue growing and adapting as a leading general contractor and construction manager. Whether building a parking structure for a local business or a Siberian highway or a housing facility for Occidental Petroleum, S. C. Anderson is committed to meeting client's needs while maintaining the highest level of integrity.

❖

Top: Liberty High School, is one of S. C. Anderson's largest single projects.

Left: Bakersfield Heart Hospital is an example of S. C. Anderson's ability to build state-of-the-art scientific facilities.

ENRON WIND

Wind Power is by no means a new idea. For centuries, wind has been used to power mills, draw water from the earth, and propel boats and ships. The thought of harnessing wind as an energy source in the Space Age, however, struck many people as quaint or even hopelessly idealistic. Many lumped wind power with solar and tidal power generation as a fringe idea, labeling it an "alternative" energy source. Even so, a boom in wind generated power ventures in the early 1980s saw dozens of new companies erecting wind turbines in Kern County's Tehachapi Mountains. Much of the technology and many of the companies failed in those early years. But a pioneer and survivor of that era—Enron Wind—helped establish wind power as a cost effective, conventional source of power today.

Enron Wind began as Zond, a company founded by a hand-full of pioneering entrepreneurs—Jim Dehlsen, a successful businessman, inventor and renewable energy supporter; Bob Gates, a Newport Beach-based marketing professional; and Dan Reynolds, a south-land businessman. Like many others, they were drawn to this new field following the enactment of federal laws requiring utilities to purchase a percentage of their power from renewable sources. This legislation, put into place to assure new electricity from renewable energy sources would be added to the nation's electricity grid, came at the same time the U.S. and State of California governments enacted

generous tax credits to invite investment in renewables. About the same time, the State of California released wind studies that pinpointed favorably windy locations. In 1980, as the door opened for speculators, idealists, and business people to re-explore harnessing the wind, Zond began.

Kern County's Tehachapi, designated by the state's research as one of California's finest areas for wind power development, became home to Zond in 1981. That same year, the company erected it's first wind turbines and became the first company to sell wind generated electricity to Southern California Edison Company, one of the world's largest wind power purchasers. But in the first round of nature versus technology, nature was a big winner. Available technology from Europe had never faced such harsh conditions, and wind technology from the United States was still new and experimental. Tehachapi truly became a proving ground as wind turbine after wind turbine was tried and tested, with most models imported from Europe. The turbines of 1981 generated 40 kilowatts in a strong wind, enough power for about 20 typical California homes—in stark contrast to the giants of the new millennium with a capacity of 1.5 megawatts, enough to power about 600 American homes. "Technologically, it was like the computer industry at first, very experimental and exciting," recalls wind

Above: Quite a few of Enron Wind's first employees have remained with the company. Lloyd Herziger, the company's photographer, was one of the company's first hires during the early 1980s.

Below: Enron Wind, a pioneering global wind power company, began in Tehachapi in 1980 and installed its first wind turbines there the following year. More recently, at its Tehachapi location, the company assembles the largest wind turbines manufactured in the United States.

power advocate and industry writer, Paul Gipe. Despite the early challenges, a "wind rush" or "wind boom" gripped Tehachapi.

At that time, Zond was one of many wind power companies struggling to make this new venture work and become profitable. In 1982, Zond management made the decision to move their headquarters to Tehachapi. Although other wind company headquarters preferred sites in large cities, the Zond team knew that to make it work, they would need to live, sleep, eat and breathe wind power—and they did. Determined, in 1983, Jim Dehlsen, Bob Gates, and a new Zond executive named Ken Karas (brought on to provide financing expertise in the new world of wind power, and later providing several years of strong, driving leadership as the company's CEO), visited Europe in search of a better mousetrap. One of their many stops—Vestas, a small Danish company with a good reputation.

Representatives of Vestas, hoping to make a modest sale to Zond, received much more. The big, beefy Danish machines (65 kilowatt models) looked sturdier than anything tried so far. Zond placed an order for 150 and acquired exclusive North American rights to import Vestas turbines. This transaction proved to be a turning point for both companies. The new equipment could withstand the rough Tehachapi environment and soon became the standard for wind generation in North America. Thousands of the Danish windmills made their way across the Atlantic—a few were even Federal Expressed from port to port to assure they met critical installation deadlines.

The impact of the burgeoning new industry on Tehachapi was enormous. During the early 1980's wind turbines were being erected by dozens of companies opening offices in the area. Kelcy's and The Mountain Inn, local eating establishments, began to sound like lunchrooms at the United Nations. Sometimes local cowboys had to look pretty hard to find a conversation taking place in English. Representatives from companies in the Netherlands, Belgium, Denmark, Germany and others gathered in pursuit of American windmill contracts. Celebrity sightings became commonplace as movie people and other "well-knowns" visited the pass to take a

look at their investments. The wind that had been so often cursed by local residents was now evolving into a viable industry.

Wind power exploded in the local area. Zond experienced meteoric growth. Accelerated development brought a new element to Tehachapi—the unique men and women who came to work on the new machines. The "windsmiths" were an interesting blend of idealism coupled with blue-collar determination and know how. "I truly respect the people who put up and maintained those turbines," says Gipe. "They believed in the dream of wind, and they proved it could be done in California and in America. And they should be proud of what

✧

Left: In 1982 the standard size wind turbines being erected were about forty kilowatts in capacity versus the 1.5-megawatt giants manufactured during the early 2000s.

Below: In the early 1980s, some wind turbines were Federal Expressed from Denmark to the U.S. to assure deadlines were met.

they accomplished." In fact, once the technology proved it could survive in Tehachapi, there could be little doubt of its viability anywhere.

Leading the wind power pack, Zond provided development and construction expertise for over 1,900 turbines by 1985. Company personnel took pride in a strong work ethic and a warm, family-like culture. Early employees remember many cold, icy, wintery nights—crews working around the clock, and hot, homemade soup being brought in and served on site by managers and spouses. During that time, Zond developed, erected, operated and maintained more wind turbines than anyone in the world. At the time of this publication, the vast majority of these turbines

remain at work producing power in Tehachapi. Many of the original "Zond" crew, both executives and staff, have remained with the company over the years.

While the arrival of viable technology would ensure the survival and growth of a new industry, another hurdle lay ahead. At the height of the "wind rush" of 1985, federal tax advantages for wind investors ended. The bust cycle took its toll on the Tehachapi wind industry. Most companies and investors fled the field or declared bankruptcy as a result of this sudden shift in policy. But a hearty few remained.

The leadership of Zond strongly believed staying to be the correct business choice. "They were visionaries," says Gipe. "They had invested a lot of time and financial resources into the industry, and they believed the long-term prospects were good." As other wind companies in Tehachapi folded, Zond scaled back, but managed to keep a positive balance sheet and continue building wind projects. Fortunately, the industry revived by the mid-1990's. Energized by knowledge gained from operating and maintaining over twenty-five hundred wind turbines in various terrains and climates, Zond, designed and set up operations in Tehachapi to manufacture its first "Zond" wind turbines. Labeled the Zond 550 kW, the first new turbine rolled out of Zond's Tehachapi facility in July of 1995. With improvements in technology and the nation's growing reliance on wind power, Zond soon won contracts to

supply, install, and operate the world's largest wind power projects in Minnesota and Iowa.

By 1997, Zond greatly expanded its manufacturing operations and designed the next generation turbine, a 750 kW, patented variable speed model. Recognizing the wind industry's potential, Enron Corp, one of the world's largest natural gas marketers, based in Houston, Texas, purchased Zond. Renamed "Enron Wind" following its sale, the company has since grown to include manufacturing operations in the world's three largest wind power markets, the U.S., Germany, and Spain. At the time of this printing, the company employs over 1,500 globally, operates 14 offices around the world, and has developed and/or manufactured over 4,500 wind turbines, comprising more than 1,600 megawatts of capacity—a "real, true-life American success story" that started right here in Kern County.

Wind energy has come of age and many consider Tehachapi the birth place and proving ground of a world-wide industry. From the very beginning, Zond/Enron Wind was there. "There was a real sense of community at Zond in those early days," says Gipe. "A sense that everybody was doing something they could tell their children about. And the fact is, they can tell their children about this with pride. These people built something that has and will continue to have a positive influence on the world."

In the 1990s, standard windmills generated 10 to 25 times more power than the turbines of the mid-1980s. This means that a single modern windmill might generate 650 to 1500 kilowatts in a steady wind, enough for 200 to 600 homes. Considering that there are 5,000 windmills in Tehachapi; 11,700 throughout the State of California; 13,000 throughout the U.S. comprising 2,554 megawatts of capacity; and over 17,000 megawatts of capacity throughout the world (enough to generate 34 billion kilowatt hours annually, or enough to power approximately five million California households), it is clear that wind has proven its reliability and cost effectiveness as a conventional rather than "alternative" source of energy. In 1994 California produced half the world's wind-generated electricity with Tehachapi leading the way as the world's largest site for wind-generated power. At the beginning of 2000, wind generation produced $1 billion worth of electricity per year and $2 billion were spent annually in wind power development. Wind has become the fastest growing bulk power technology in the world, and has grown at an average rate of twenty-eight percent annually from 1996 to 2000. By the end of the millennium year, the U.S. installed wind generating capacity grew to about 2,500 megawatts, globally it reached 17,500 megawatts. The World Energy Council estimates that new capacity worldwide will total 180,000 megawatts to 474,000 megawatts by the year 2020. Wind power truly is big business. And Kern County is at its heart.

✧

Above: Enron Wind's Tehachapi wind power facilities are home to over seventeen hundred wind turbines. The entire Tehachapi Wind Resource Area boasts over five thousand wind turbines.

Below: Paul Gipe, author and writer for wind energy, came to Tehachapi during the wind boom of the 1980s. He currently resides in Bakersfield, California.

MORTON ENGINEERING AND CONSTRUCTION

Morton Engineering and Construction is a diverse company known throughout the State of California and beyond for its work in field construction, welding, concrete work, and other industrial services. However, the Morton story is centered in Taft where the Morton family has lived for generations and the company remains headquartered. It all started with Samuel Mahlan Morton and a tractor back in 1950.

After their families had moved to the Taft area in the 1920s, Samuel Mahlan Morton and Imogene Jameson were married in 1934. The young couple dreamed of a life spent raising their children on a farm, so Sam went to work in the oilfields until he could save enough money to move his family to Visalia. The Mortons purchased a dairy farm in 1943. For nearly seven years all went well for Sam and Imogene until a rusty nail permanently changed the course of their lives and the lives of their children. Their daughter, Cookie, stepped on that nail and contracted a critical case of tetanus.

Doctors were able to save Cookie, but the medical costs bankrupted the family. The farm was sold and the Mortons, now with five children, moved back to Taft with just a cow and a tractor. Sam went to work in the oil fields again to bring in a regular paycheck,

and, on his days off, he used his tractor to level home lots for extra money. The tractor work was more to his liking, so he bought a backhoe and dump truck with a partner and operated his own business from the family home at 101 South Street in Taft. Imogene kept the books in a bedroom converted to an office.

A lot of the early work was for Mobil Oil in the oil fields, where the drillers and foremen thought Sam had thrown his money away thinking he could use the backhoe for oil field work. He proved them wrong. The business grew, and it was not long before the five Morton children became involved. "I was

Above: Samuel Mahlan Morton gave up daily farming to start his own business.

Right: Bob Morton.

Left: Bob Morton re up in the business and has guided it to new places like metal and the Internet.

Below: An early photo of part of a fleet of Morton trucks.

raised working for this company," recalls Bob Morton. He and his brothers started by washing and servicing the equipment until they were old enough and experienced enough to operate it. They also took their turn with their sisters milking the remaining dairy cow. Family life was very intertwined with the family business. Imogene cooked three meals a day, "good meals," as Bob recollects, for her family in addition to housework, raising six children, and being the only secretary her husband ever had. "Dad couldn't have done it without her."

For Sam Morton, Taft was a beloved hometown. "Dad was the kind of man who never met a stranger," says Bob. "He could take two hours going to the post office just talking to friends." He took a Model A Ford in trade for some work he did and fixed up the car for his daughter Belva to take to school, and the car, named "Purnie," became the traditional form of travel for all the Morton children in high school. Friends were always welcome at the Morton home. Listening to Bob and his sister Debbie talk about their early days evokes images of happy and busy times.

Top: An aerial view of the Morton Engineering Yard in Valley Acres.

Middle: Water treatment vessels.

Bottom: End caps for water treatment vessels.

Brothers Bob and John Morton bought their father's business in 1973 and split it. Bob consulted his father regularly about business matters through the 1970s and their relationship was close. "He was my best friend," recalls Bob. Samuel Mahlan Morton died of a heart attack in 1979. A few days after his funeral, each of his sons received a gift in the mail that Sam had ordered some time before. The gifts were small plaques engraved as follows:

"The Morton name…you got it from your father; it was all he had to give. So it's yours to use and cherish, for as long as you may live. If you lose the watch he gave you, it can always be replaced. But a black mark on your name, son, can never be erased. It was clean the day you took it, and a worthy name to bear. When he got it from his father, there was no dishonor there. So make sure you guard it wisely, after all is said and done. You'll be glad the name is spotless, when you give it to your son."

Bob Morton's only regret is that his father did not live to see how far the business that bears the family name has come in twenty years. The Morton companies have grown enormously and in many directions. From earth and dirt moving operations in the oil fields that had been Morton's bread and butter for thirty years, Bob expanded into welding. The welding company became a twenty-five-thousand-square-foot ASME Code shop that constructs a variety of vessels for a broad spectrum of industries including oil refining, nuclear power, and food processing.

Morton Engineering and Morton Construction are the other thriving businesses operating out of the Taft area. "We can build just about anything," says Bob Morton. Morton diversified to offset the volatility of the oilfield business which remains an important part of what the Morton companies do, comprising nearly half of revenues. "It's not that we reduced the oil field work we do, we just added other things," says Bob Morton. His willingness to look at new opportunities and plunge into new projects has given his companies a reputation for flexibility in meeting customer needs.

In Kern County, Morton turned naturally to agricultural work, which uses all three Morton companies in food processing. For instance, processing carrots involves heavy use of pressurized water and conveyor systems for sorting, cleaning, freezing, and packaging often executed in large metal buildings. Morton is capable of meeting all of these needs by engineering conveyors; constructing metal walkways, ladder systems, and metal buildings; and welding pressure pipes and tanks. Morton has built processing plants for carrots tomatoes, garlic, and potatoes. Beyond Kern County, Morton has built plants for fish processing in Long Beach and San Pedro.

In the area of field construction, Morton has done concrete work developing canals, bridges, and walls. In the refining industry, Morton lays cement foundations for tanks and processors.

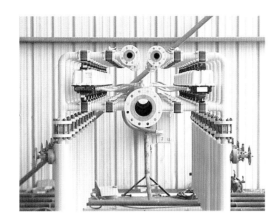

Morton welders put together the huge tanks that must withstand enormous internal pressure and the insulated pipes that are the cardiovascular system of a refinery. The pipe systems in refineries and oil fields come together in pumping stations built by Morton, and the complex and exacting requirements of header systems where pipelines come together to be monitored and controlled by computer sensors is a Morton specialty. But Morton also undertakes projects not as familiar to residents of Kern County as oil, refining and agricultural.

The anti-ballistic missile test launches at Vandenburg Air Force Base lifted off from a refurbished Minuteman missile silo adapted for the new rocket by Morton Engineering. The thirty-seven-foot-deep structure required near perfect workmanship with specifications to be met within 1/100,000th of an inch. Morton Engineering and Construction also excels in projects that help the environment like building a recycling plant in Indio that converts automobile tires into crumb rubber, using its fleet of heavy equipment and earth movers to clean up a contaminated industrial site near Magic Mountain, or repairing an oil pipeline leak near the Queen Mary in Long Beach. Morton bores underground tunnels for fiber optic cable and has undertaken construction projects in places as diverse as the San Francisco Airport, remote Indian reservations, and a manmade island for offshore oil production.

A new venture illustrates how Bob Morton's restless and opportunistic nature has led to such diverse growth. To give state-of-the-art service to far off customers, Morton set up a camera system in the welding shop so customers could go on-line and actually watch their projects being created. Customers visiting www.mortonengineering.com can control the camera to zoom in or follow any action in the shop. The system with a T-1 line dedicated to the cameras is a first on the Internet and Morton is marketing the system to other businesses whose customers might desire to check on projects and to operations like daycare centers where parents could look in on their kids. Morton is quick to share credit for the company's success, "You're no better than the people that work for you. We've got guys who've been here for twenty-six years."

Closer to home, Bob Morton was a founder of the Taft Bank and has had a thirty-six-year-long association with the R. M. Pyles Boys Camp. The camp was started more than fifty years ago to help at-risk boys in their early teens that might be headed in a wrong direction. Bob started as a volunteer at a barbeque thirty years ago but has since become a member of the board of directors which he chaired for four years. More than five hundred boys a year attend the camp forty miles north of Lake Isabella in small groups that camp and ride the wild country with a counselor who is himself a former camper. "It works," says Bob. "There are hundreds of success stories and the letters you get from mothers: 'I want to thank Pyles Boys Camp for giving my son back to me.' It's a great thing."

Sam Morton's little backhoe and tractor operation has come a long way to become Morton Engineering and Construction. It is strange to think that a rusty nail in the foot of a farm girl might well be the starting point for a great, family company. The move back to Taft was a good thing for the Morton family, and, it seems, the move was also a good thing for Taft and Kern County.

✧

Left: An automatic well test manifold.

Right: An industrial concrete project.

SERBAN SOUND AND COMMUNICATIONS

✧

*Above: Fred Brakeman, vice president,
and George Serban, chairman, reviewing
plans for a new high school now
under construction.*

COURTESY OF JODY SERBAN.

*Below: Mark Scatena, estimator/systems
designer, and Fred Brakeman programming
a sound cabinet for delivery to a new junior
high school.*

COURTESY OF JODY SERBAN.

From the year of its creation, 1968, Serban Sound and Communications has striven to be the leader in communications contracting by adapting to innovations in the industry and anticipating changes in the marketplace. Communications contracting is a broad field. The music in a restaurant, a video lesson in a public school or the computer network at the heart of a business are all manifestations of the variety of services in which Serban Sound specializes. Through decades of rapid change, Serban Sound has stayed in the lead through

smart business planning, selectivity in choosing the best personnel and by offering only the best product lines. The history of the company reflects the growth and diversification of communications over the last three decades.

George Serban was an engineer at a television station and his wife, Rita, a homemaker educated in business, when they purchased the local Muzak franchise in 1968. The Serbans still share the job of running Serban Sound. Although the company has broadened into other fields, Muzak remains an important element of the business serving several thousand subscribers throughout the area. The relationships Serban generated by going to businesses and institutions to help customers select the most appropriate Muzak service (audio architecture, audio imaging, video imaging, and system design, to name a few) led to repeat business when these same customers developed new needs. The solid reputation built through providing Muzak service has been a constant as Serban Sound has grown.

When the businesses and stores with Muzak needed paging or intercom systems, it was natural to turn to Serban Sound. This expansion marked the company's beginning as "low-voltage" systems specialists. Intercom, paging and data systems do not require the standard, higher voltage you find installed by electricians which feed wall plugs and appliances. Low voltage systems require a different expertise and the field has been rapidly growing as communications and data systems evolve. From intercom and paging systems for businesses, it was natural that Serban Sound would find work for hospitals and schools.

In recent years, Serban has done a great deal of work in Central California schools. The growth in this area typifies the salient characteristic of Serban Sound and Communications. Intercom systems work led to work on bell systems and clock systems. When the computer boom and multimedia came to education, Serban was ready with an organization of engineers, technicians, and planners to implement plans to bring education into the Information Age. "We try to be visionary," says George Serban, who is still very active with the company he founded. What his company has done within schools in the last decade exemplifies Serban Sound and Communications' capabilities.

Modern schools require a variety of communications systems including voice, video, data, and fire alarm networks in order to educate, administrate, and insure the safety of students. Voice systems involve intercoms, telephone, auditorium sound, and even the master clock system that keeps classes running on time. Data systems and computer networking serve both administration in the office and education in the classroom. Classrooms are linked to each other and to the Internet through computers that open a new world beyond the walls of the building.

And video has come a long way since the days when a student rolled a television on a tall stand to a classroom for temporary use. Today, Serban Sound installs video systems in schools that offer diverse and flexible uses that most television stations were incapable of just ten years ago. A master control nerve center is set up in the school library with resources that include cable TV, VCR, and DVD. The library is linked to permanent television monitors in the classroom, which give teachers remote control over the source machines in the library. The teacher can access and control a tape playback; encyclopedia on disk or a lesson taught at a faraway place available over cable. With the video cart, essentially a movable studio, camera, and audio equipment can be rolled to locations on campus and plugged into the system for live transmission to other classrooms. A special lecture in one classroom can be carried to others via the system. The school principal can press a button and address every classroom via "video all call" to convey messages or news.

Serban Sound and Communications has installed these types of systems in dozens of school districts providing consultation, design, engineering, and installation. Since the world of data systems can be challenging, Serban stays connected with customers via their own website, www.serban.com, which provides links to educational websites and updates for educators in new, better ways to use computers. They bring this same expertise and service to the private sector for office computer systems and communications.

Serban Sound and Communications is proud to be a leader in setting high standards for a new and growing industry through its charter memberships in the National Systems Contractors Association and the Building Industry Consulting Services International Association. Locally, George Serban has been involved with the Bakersfield Business Conference for fifteen years. The first year, when the event was small, Serban Sound supplied sound equipment and support for the few hundred attendees. Now that the event has grown to 12,500 participants, Serban serves as technical coordinator for the conference which requires vast video walls, hundreds of speakers, and enough generated electricity to run a small city. "It's a fun project," says George Serban. His pleasure in the growing challenges of the business conference reflects his company's attitude towards the dynamic world of communications. Serban Sound and Communications does more than keep pace, it stays in the lead.

✧

Above: George Serban and Fred Brakeman reminiscing about the past thirty years with old equipment displayed in our growing museum.
COURTESY OF JODY SERBAN.

Below: Kevin DeBondt, general manager and president of the Muzak Division, setting up a new client.
COURTESY OF JODY SERBAN.

A-C
ELECTRIC
COMPANY

As World War II ended, a group of electricians who all worked together at China Lake Naval Ordnance Test Station spent long evenings making plans for their post-war futures. The men determined that they could each do "a little better" by staying together and forming a new company rather than by separating and working for other contractors. A-C Electric Company came into being as a modest operation with specific values and goals: create an organization of better jobs for better people; be firm but fair in business; give back to the community; create a family organization that attracts quality people from beyond the family; and create an organization that would last beyond a single generation. A-C Electric Company has become a large, diverse and accomplished modern business without abandoning a single one of those values.

The company name takes the last initials of the principal founders and owners, Joe Alexander and Tom Corr who were electrical superintendents at China Lake. The workforce at A-C was small when the first small shop opened in Delano in 1945. Before the year ended, Alexander and Corr moved the office to 601 Thirty-fourth Street in Bakersfield where the company's headquarters is located today. As with all start-up companies, the first years were tough, but it was in these lean years that A-C Electric developed an aggressive attitude toward taking on new and unusual projects. This led to work on the California Aqueduct, traffic signals, prison systems and

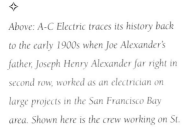

Above: A-C Electric traces its history back to the early 1900s when Joe Alexander's father, Joseph Henry Alexander far right in second row, worked as an electrician on large projects in the San Francisco Bay area. Shown here is the crew working on St. Francis Hotel around 1900.

Below: Founder Joe Alexander worked with his father doing "electric work of all kinds" around McFarland in the late 1920s and early 1930s.

missile stands for Edwards Air Force Base. "They were willing to learn about new needs," says current Executive Vice-President Tom Alexander, one of the second generation of Alexanders at A-C.

The Alexander family has been principal owners since 1965 when Corr sold his share of the company and retired. Tom Alexander and his brothers, Dan and Terry, grew up in the business starting as shop boys before entering the electrical apprenticeship program and becoming electricians, estimators and managers in the firm. Tom added a business degree from Cal Berkeley and runs the business. Dan is the Chief Estimator and oversees all estimating for the company while Terry is an Estimator and Project Manager specializing in traffic signal and lighting for street and highway projects. Joe's wife, Ruby Alexander, who became an active board member in 1975 when Joe passed away, designed the familiar A-C Electric logo. Tom's son, Daren, the third generation of Alexanders to join the business and now General Manager, has moved A-C Electric into the fields of high-end plant automation and industrial control.

One of the key projects that put A-C out in front of the brisk competition in the early years was its excellent performance in doing all the electrical work when Bakersfield College moved from downtown to the bluffs of Panorama Drive in 1956. A-C had always done residential and commercial work as well as work in the defense field, but the business began to grow significantly with high profile projects like lighting Memorial Stadium, St. Francis Church and the Meadows Field Air

Terminal. The increasing breadth of electrical experience gained from such diverse projects led to one of the company's earliest and longest lasting slogans, "A-C can do it because A-C has done it."

With increasing reputation, A-C Electric broadened its horizons. The Department of Water Resources turned to A-C in 1968 to do the electrical work for the Buena Vista and Wheeler Ridge Pump Plants. At about the same time, A-C was contracted for an addition to Tehachapi Prison. For thirty years, the prison system has relied on A-C for the complex requirements of lighting, locking and passage systems and the difficult specifications for construction. The Department of Water Resources has also continued using A-C Electric to update and upgrade vital systems.

Having established themselves in electrical contracting and cutting edge industrial automated systems, A-C Electric has refocused on residential and light commercial service with another innovative move. Although always capable of installing an outlet in a home or rewiring a circuit, A-C has taken a new look at what differentiates the requirements of a homeowner or small business owner from an industrial customer. A-C Electric will open several Mr. Electric franchises in Central California designed specifically for home and small business service. Special attention will be paid to making the entire Mr. Electric experience

customer-friendly by providing prompt, professional, clean and courteous service.

The evening gatherings at the close of World War II that led to the formation of a company also engendered a business philosophy that has endured far beyond the day when it was just a good intention. In seeking to do "a little better," A-C Electric Company has grown as a family-oriented business that includes its employees in ownership, has developed into a conscientious member of the communities it touches and shows all signs of thriving and continuing through many generations beyond that which founded it.

✧

Above: A-C did the electrical and lighting work on Bakersfield College including Memorial Stadium in the mid-1950s.

Below: A recent A-C project is the Amtrak Station, which opened July 4, 2000, in downtown Bakersfield.

EQUILON

Equilon's Bakersfield refinery has a long and colorful history. Despite the many different owners of the various parts of the plant, the refinery has grown steadily to meet the fuel needs of California's southern San Joaquin Valley. The most recent change, the alliance between Shell and Texaco, has created yet another round of opportunities for the plant.

What is today Equilon began as three different sites under three different operators. The earliest company, Mohawk, built a 1,500-barrel per day (B/D) refinery on the current site at 6451 Rosedale Highway in 1932 when "dustbowlers" from Oklahoma and Texas were

pouring into Bakersfield and the central valley. Despite the Great Depression, valley oil fields were being developed at a rapid pace leading Mohawk to expand its capacity to 12,000 B/D and eventually all the way up to 21,000 B/D. The plant had changed very little over the years when it was acquired by Reserve Oil and Gas, but it expanded again to meet the demand for low sulfur fuel oil used to power steam generators in the oil fields. Mohawk/Reserve built a new 40,000 B/D crude unit, vacuum flasher, naphtha hydrotreater, and fuel oil desulfurizer that were streamed in 1980 after the refinery had been purchased by Getty Refining and Marketing Company. Texaco acquired the refinery when it purchased Getty in 1984. Acquiring the Tosco refinery just across the railroad tracks would be Texaco's next move.

Tosco had originally been built by the U.S. Government during World War II to make hundred-octane aviation gasoline and was known simply as Area 2. After the war, except for a brief trial as an industrial detergent plant, Area 2 was idle from 1946 to 1950 until it resumed operation under the Norwalk Company. Its crude unit had only a 5,000 B/D capacity and its thermal crackers, used to make gasoline, were antiques. Bankline purchased and expanded the plant to 15,000 B/D in the 1950s and sold the plant to Signal Oil and Gas in 1959. Signal updated the plant by moving a new cracking unit and associated equipment to the site from Long Beach in 1961, started up the

first commercial hydrocracker in the western United States with a new hydrogen plant and made other improvements. Tosco purchased the plant in 1970 and saw peak crude production reach 40,000 B/D before shutting down in 1983. Texaco purchased the plant in 1986.

The youngest component of Equilon opened a mile and a half from the Mohawk/Tosco site in the late 1970s in response to a boom in valley crude production. The Independent Valley Energy Company (IVEC) was designed to make a "reduced crude" product from Kern heavy crude. The venture was not a commercial success and the units were closed down with Texaco purchasing the site in 1988. The acquisition of Getty/Mohawk and the two other sites, Tosco and IVEC, was part of Texaco's vision to both increase production in the San Joaquin Valley and increase the capacity of the Bakersfield refinery.

Texaco started up the HCU/Hydrogen Plant complex; two hydrotreaters and other associated equipment on the Tosco site in 1986 and immediately began integrating these units with the adjoining Mohawk plant. Pipelines connecting the IVEC cokers a mile and a half away with the Mohawk plant were completed in 1988, bringing the combined capacity to 45,000 B/D and establishing the basic configuration that characterizes the refinery today.

The 1990s brought many changes to the plant as expansion of the crude unit and corresponding expansion of downstream units were coupled with significant modifications in response to new fuel emissions regulations for gasoline and diesel and the need to lower emissions from the plant itself. The Heavy Crude Expansion Project increased the capacity of the crude unit to accommodate increased oil field production. In 1993 significant modifications were undertaken to make CARB quality diesel and meet new CARB gasoline benzene content requirements. Simultaneously, another significant effort made the plant an outstanding performer in reducing the amount of generated waste material and kept the plant in full compliance with tightening environmental regulations.

Today, the Bakersfield plant is in the beginning of a new and exciting era with the Texaco/Shell refining and marketing merger that created Equilon. The pipeline connection with the former Shell refinery at Martinez, California has made gas oil processing more profitable. Furthermore, under Equilon the plant has undergone another round of capacity expansions to bring it to its current 70,000 B/D crude along with incremental expansions of downstream units. The plant is also in line with the new CARB Phase 3 regulations. In short, Equilon has brought new opportunities to the field that will take the Bakersfield unit into the future as a strong and profitable plant.

COLOMBO CONSTRUCTION

✧

Above: Colombo Construction completed Tenneco's headquarters at California and Stockdale in 1968.

Below: The new Amtrak Station is another of Colombo Construction's projects in the Bakersfield area.

There are two ways to look at Colombo Construction Company, Inc.; one is to review the impressive number and variety of projects the company has completed over the years, the other is to listen to two generations of people reminisce about the company history, the same way that families will retell stories after a holiday meal. The pictures on the walls of Colombo Construction are of schools, office towers, malls, and other unique buildings constructed by the company. The stories start with Joe Colombo who founded the business in 1948 on a shoestring.

With his brothers, Natale and Fortunato, Joe left Italy at the age of nineteen and came to the United States. Making their way to California, the brothers found work on the farms around Shafter. Although the others moved to the Bay area, Joe stayed in Kern County and went to work for prominent contractor, Guy Hall, before eventually opening his own contracting company with John Tobisch. Colombo and Tobisch started by building houses and small business structures in the Bakersfield area. By 1958 business was going well enough that Lillian Valenti transitioned from keeping the books in her home to running the office on Nineteenth Street. In 1954, after Tobisch had left and the company had become simply Colombo Construction, Joe hired independent builder, John Lencioni, who insisted the job be only temporary while he waited for the plaster to dry on one of his own projects. He left after two weeks but returned again in a "temporary" capacity that has lasted more than forty years.

Toward the end of the 1950s Colombo and Lencioni began winning bids on school projects including Curran Junior High in Bakersfield. By the time Colombo succumbed to cancer in 1960 school contracting was a major source of Colombo Construction's income. Lencioni entered into a partnership with Colombo's widow, Teresa, and John Tobisch (who had returned to Colombo as an employee) to keep the company intact. The excellent reputation of Colombo Construction was bringing in business from Simi Valley, San Luis Obispo, and the central coast—places where Colombo Construction has since built more than twenty schools.

In 1968, the Kern County Land Company, then part of Tenneco, chose Colombo Construction to build their sixty-seven thousand-square-foot office building at California and Stockdale. Surprised by Lencioni's estimate of how swiftly the job could be done, the president of Tenneco bet that the project would not be

completed on time. In what was their biggest project to date, Colombo Construction graded the land in June and the building was ready for move-in by December. The delighted president of Tenneco flew in from Houston and hosted a celebratory dinner to pay the bet. Doing high-quality work on budget and on time is a cornerstone of Colombo Construction.

In the 1970s Colombo Construction continued to thrive and diversify, winning contracts for St. Phillips Catholic Church and the First Methodist Church and branching out to include pre-engineered metal buildings. Lencioni's son-in-law, Ken Altergott, and Joe Colombo's son, also called Joe, came to work for the company starting in the field and learning the business from the ground up. Another key name in the progress of Colombo Construction, Tom Eichman, joined the company from the County Planning Office. The three younger men eventually joined Lencioni and Valenti to become the corporation's key management team. The last quarter of the twentieth century saw Colombo Construction consolidate its position as one of Kern County's leading contractors.

Valley Plaza Shopping Mall, the new Amtrak Station, and the State Compensation Insurance Building are just a few of the projects Colombo Construction has completed in the Bakersfield area. World renowned architect Michael Graves has said of

Colombo Construction's quality work on his Institute of Theoretical Physics at UCSB: "This is the building by which all building's should be measured." The same meticulous execution that Colombo Construction applies to a Graves building is evident in their every endeavor from medical clinics in Brawley to Madera, Petro Truck Stops in California and Nevada, to John Deere retail facilities in Bakersfield and Fresno.

A rarity these days, Colombo Construction does its own concrete work, provides rough and finished carpentry, and steel erection without subcontracting. These in-house capabilities offer the reliable quality that has kept clients returning to Colombo Construction for decades. Colombo Construction is a distinctive combination of traditional values and qualities associated with the past and still thrives in projects going up today.

Above: Colombo Construction has built John Deere retail facilities in both Bakersfield and Fresno.

Below: The Institute of Theoretical Physics on the campus of the University of California-Santa Barbara.

BAKERSFIELD AIR CONDITIONING SUPPLY CO.

Maurice Glascock came to Bakersfield from Missouri after serving in the Navy as a corpsman between the World Wars. An enterprising man not afraid of a long day's work, Glascock tried a number of jobs including selling furniture for Montgomery Ward before turning his hand to heating and cooling. In 1943, he created a business that has become Bakersfield Air Conditioning Supply Company (BACSCO), a leading wholesale supplier of coolers, heaters, and all that those systems require. "He was a pioneer in this industry," says Maurice's son, Jim Glascock who swept the floors when he was ten years old. "Until the war, people were using fans and wet burlap to stay cool, but that all changed."

Glascock began in the business repairing swamp coolers, and then branched into sales and sheet metal services. In 1943, he opened Capital Heating and Air Conditioning. The original office was at 100 Sumner, and the original building, which survives today at the newer location at 215 Sumner, has aluminum duct work created by Glascock during the war when steel was unavailable. Genevieve

✧

Right: Maurice and Genevieve Glascock.

Below: Maurice Glascock, a pioneer in air conditioning in Bakersfield, stands beside a wood masticator that created excelsior from aspen wood to use in cooling pads for evaporative coolers.

"Jeanne" Glascock, who had been a legal secretary in San Diego before marrying Maurice, did the books and managed the office.

Jim's sister, Judy Thornberry, remembers: "[Dad] could figure out where the industry was going, and that kept this business alive. Cooler repair evolved into sheet metal, then manufacturing cooler pads, then wholesale supply." In the 1950s, Judy made float valve kits and cooler pads using excelsior (fine aspen shavings) in her father's store. Her sister, Joy Harvey, was secretary to her father before she went to college and remembers that her father went into wholesale supply with the realization that "when it's cheaper to buy something than to make it, it's time to change the business again." Joy, Judy, and Jim form the executive board that runs BACSCO today.

In the mid-1950s, the company incorporated under its present name as the one of the Central Valley's first heating and cooling wholesaler. Bakersfield Air Conditioning Supply Company remains one of the few independent wholesalers left in a very competitive industry. The store carries a broad inventory so contractors know they will find what they need at BACSCO; in fact, other wholesalers often resort to BACSCO when their own inventories are wanting. Until Maurice Glascock died in 1992, he came almost daily to the business he created and loved.

H. M.
HOLLOWAY

When the Great Depression took Los Angeles in its grip in 1931, sixty-two-year-old Harvey M. Holloway was working in construction but soon found himself without a job. Holloway was not a soft man. He had worked as a hard rock miner, Texas lawman, and many other things in his life, and he was not daunted by the grim prospects that surrounded him. His son Albert got Holloway a job with a Bakersfield oil company as a caretaker in a remote oil field in northwest Kern County near Lost Hills.

The oil fields needed someone present after the drillers left to lookout for natural gas leaks and fires. Holloway left his wife at home in Los Angeles and set up in the "doghouse" changing room of an abandoned drilling site. He fortified and insulated the walls of his "home" with scrap metal and cartons and even found an ingenious way to use the natural gas for heating and cooking. Saying, "if you can stand this, then I can, too," Holloway's wife joined him after six months. A self-educated man and naturally curious, Holloway noticed an outcropping of white crystalline material in a nearby hill. He took a sample of it to the Frank Hornkohl Lab in Bakersfield and found out the substance was calcium sulfate, commonly known as gypsum.

Gypsum, he found by doing research in the local library, had been used by farmers in other regions for soil treatment and was particularly useful in areas with alkali, water retention, and penetration problems. Benjamin Franklin had even written about gypsum's use in farming. In 1935, with the help of his son, Holloway obtained a surface mineral rights lease on the property near his remote home on the range and began shoveling the surface gypsum. At first he had to give the stuff to farmers who were skeptical just to prove the benefits. Soon farmers were coming to him in answer to his sales pitch, "Bring your truck to Lost Hills and we will shovel you on a load."

By 1939 Holloway's business was providing twenty thousand tons a year to local farmers and he was able to move his wife back into a real house. The business took his name, H. M. Holloway, and has been family-owned ever since. Today the company provides nearly seventy percent of all agricultural gypsum used throughout California, and the application of gypsum has made hundreds of thousands of acres of land on the west side of the San Joaquin Valley farmable. All from the perseverance of an "old" man weathering the Depression in a wind-blown shack beyond Lost Hills.

✧

Above: Loading trucks in 1947 prior to front-end loaders. Pictured are a Caterpillar D-4 and a BE-GE Scraper.

Below: H. M. Holloway's first mechanized mill/grinder, c. 1956. The company's first mechanized mill/grinder was the Petibone, which ground the gypsum and stacked it in windrows. A front-end loader was then used to load the trucks.

BC LABORATORIES, INC.

✧

Above: BC Laboratories, Inc. is housed in a custom-designed building that accommodates separate labs and ample refrigerated storage to guarantee control.

Right: BC Laboratories, Inc. remains a leader in the industry by constant reinvestment in technology including this state-of-the-art ion chromatography equipment for wet chemistry.

The largest family-owned, environmental laboratory in California's Central Valley began in a Bakersfield garage in 1949. What is today's BC Laboratories started as Bakersfield Core Laboratory in the garage of Joe and Bea Eglin's Quincy Street home specializing in analyzing oil well core samples. Joe, a chemical engineer, did the analyzing while Bea kept the books. Today, BC Laboratories is housed in a state-of-the-art, custom designed facility located at 4100 Atlas Court.

In the fifty years of its existence, BC Laboratories has evolved from an agricultural-petroleum based service into a full service environmental laboratory offering high quality analysis for a variety of federal and state regulatory programs including the Clean and Safe Waters Act, CCR Title 22, RCRA, NPDES and Superfund. The twenty-thousand-square-foot facility has three separate and carefully segregated departments

for wet chemistry, metals analysis, and organic analysis. Each department has a separate air system to prevent inter-laboratory contamination and OSHA standards are enthusiastically observed to insure the safety of BC's 85 dedicated employees. Enormous refrigerated storage space (twelve hundred cubic feet) enables BC to maintain high volumes of samples under carefully preserved conditions.

Joe and Bea Eglin managed the remarkable development of BC Laboratories with a combination of scientific innovation and business know-how. Joe Eglin remains vice president of BC with his daughter, Carolyn Jackson, serving as president and son, Richard Eglin, directing public relations. Bea Eglin, who was known throughout the community for her excellent business sense, passed away in 1996 and is missed by her family and the people who make up BC Laboratories.

As we enter the new millenium, BC Laboratories is in a unique position to continue its growth and success through their constant updating of equipment and investment in the education and well-being of their work force. They have a highly capable staff of engineers, chemists and environmental resource specialists working in a state-of-the-art laboratory complex focused on giving the best possible service in the industry. From a garage on Quincy Street, BC Laboratories has grown to become the leader in environmental investigation, compliance and remediation testing.

Irv Guinn started Guinn Construction back in 1952 as a partnership with his teenaged son, Gary. Gary's duties were largely taking care of their "fleet" of four vehicles when he was not attending school. In nearly fifty years, family-owned Guinn Construction has grown to include a fleet of more than 150 Caterpillar tractors employed in a variety of projects including oil field construction, landfill creation, and commercial site preparation.

Irv Guinn started with the Forestry Service supervising Civilian Conservation Corps (CCC) crews near his hometown of Springville. His crews made firebreaks and cleared roads; Irv ran the bulldozer himself and was noted for building the road connecting Roadsend with the Johnsondale Lumber Company. Ethel Bailey Guinn, Irv's wife, would bring him lunch, and baby Gary would sleep peacefully on the floorboard of the bulldozer. Irv became a charter member of the Operating Engineers Union Hall, Local 12 in 1939 and worked for ten years in Bakersfield with Rand Construction before opening his own business. "He was a self-made man," says Gary of his father. "He did it all himself."

The Russel Ranch oil strike and the Cuyama boom, meant that most of Guinn's early work was oil field related—building roads, preparing sites, pulling down derricks, and cleaning up drilling sites. Gary grew up in the business to become a full partner in managing the company through its years of remarkable growth. By the late 1970s and early 1980s Guinn Construction was very involved in prominent area projects like Cattle King Estates, the Hilton Inn, Red Lion Hotel and East Hills Mall, which are landmarks in the development of Bakersfield. Beyond the city, Guinn Construction excavated and lined the vast Chemical Waste Management Incorporated's Kettleman Hills Facility, which required the movement of 4.5 million cubic yards of material.

Guinn Construction has continued to diversify and is licensed in four states. Prominent projects today are the gold mine

leaching fields near Mojave, landfill/waste management projects and site construction throughout the west. The company has also donated time and equipment to build high school athletic fields and community raceways, to haul equipment for the West High School Band, and to set up the Kern County Fair. "We like to put back into the community," says Gary Guinn.

Irv Guinn passed away in 1985, but his legacy of a family business is in good hands. Joining Gary at the company are his son, Tim Guinn, who is CEO, and his sons-in-law, Jeff Alfonso and Dan Daniel, who are vice presidents and married to Gary's daughters Lori and Jana, respectively. The great tradition of Guinn Construction will continue for many years.

KYLE CARTER HOMES, INC.

Top: A beautiful home that typifies the care in design and building characteristics of a Kyle Carter home.

Below: The design supervisors, realtors, financial specialists, designers and staff of Kyle Carter Homes.

For nearly half a century, the Carter name has been unparalleled in the Bakersfield building industry. A leader in quality construction, the Carter reputation has been carried on since 1975 by Kyle Carter Homes.

Carter's philosophy for building a home starts long before the foundation is poured. He selects the best locations, within walking distance to shopping, excellent schools, neighborhood parks, and easy access to the freeways. Carter is a licensed engineering contractor and develops his own land, and then he sets out to build the neighborhood and communities that people want to invest their lives in. A Kyle Carter hallmark is the large park-like, tree-lined streets in each of his communities. They give the neighborhood a "homey" feel.

Kyle Carter Homes' in-house mortgage and escrow services offer a "one stop shop" approach to home buying that enables buyers to get a quality built home, in an easy to follow process, that takes some of the hassle out of home buying. Also Carter's on staff design team designs all of his plans to make the homes easy to change and then has a fully staffed, in-house drafting department to customize these plans within an affordable budget.

Another service that is unique to the Bakersfield area is Kyle Carter Homes' own state-of-the-art Selection Design Center for their new homebuyers. This is where knowledgeable interior design consultants not only decorate Carter's model homes, they take each new homebuyer through the exciting process of choosing the latest in flooring, tile, interior and exterior color selections and more. And Carter is a licensed swimming pool contractor. This provides his homebuyers with great savings by offering a built-in swimming pool that is constructed with their new home.

Kyle Carter Homes has been the recipient of top awards in Bakersfield with honors in landscaping, architecture and quality construction presented by the Kern County Building Industry Association. Also, according to The Bakersfield Californian's Best of Kern County 1998 and 1999 Reader's Choice Poll, Kyle Carter Homes was voted Best New Homebuilder, Best Customer Service, Best Mortgage Department, and for 1999, Favorite Swimming Pool Builder, Favorite Real Estate Agency/Agent and Best Local Website.

With Kyle Carter Homes' successful track record, repeat buyers and strong buyer referral rate, it comes as no surprise that each community developed and built by Kyle Carter Homes, assures a reputation for quality and integrity, and neighborhoods in which residents will continue to enjoy as the years go by.

For Rod and Bob Grimm farming had been part of their lives from childhood spent at their parents' chicken ranch and orange groves in Southern California. They began their own five-acre sweet corn farming operation together in the 1960s when Rod was a freshman in college and Bob was in the eighth grade. The brothers remained partners for decades in the farming business. Together they created the world's largest grower, packer, and shipper of fresh and frozen carrots, organic carrots, and carrot juice concentrate. They appropriately named their company Grimmway Farms.

The Grimms were attracted to Kern County in 1981 by the abundance of sandy loam soils and scant rainfall that is ideal for carrot growth and offers the opportunity for both spring and winter carrot harvests. The addition of massive harvesters, which can harvest upwards of seventy-five tons per hour, and the construction of a frozen carrot processing plant by 1985 vaulted Grimmway Farms into the elite of California carrot producers. The purchase of Belridge Packing Company and Mike Yurosek & Son Farms in 1990 and 1995, respectively, made Grimmway the producer of more than half of the carrots in California and the world leader in the carrot industry. Today Grimmway processes over forty thousand acres of carrots packed in four separate production facilities located in Kern County. Put in perspective, it would take a two and a half mile-long line of trucks each carrying twenty-five tons of carrots to handle the daily harvest at Grimmway Farms. Marketing and production of peeled baby carrots in various sized packaging has further propelled Grimmway's rapid growth. Grimmway Farms has growing operations in California, Nevada, and Colorado processing ten million pounds of carrots per day. These carrots are packaged under forty private labels and sold both domestically and in fifteen foreign countries.

While success was naturally the aim of the Grimm brothers, there was, however, particular attention given to conducting business in an open, honest, and respectful manner with customers and employees. The Grimms were known as Christian businessmen. They believed that their business was blessed by God,

and, along with hard work and loyal employees, was the reason for their success. Customers could rely on fair dealing with Grimmway where handshake deals were the norm. A handshake deal with the Juarez Brothers in 1976 sealed a trucking agreement that began with two trucks and today numbers over two hundred. Year-round planting and harvesting has created a permanent workforce at Grimmway numbering forty-four hundred employees, who meet in small groups twice a year with executives and general managers to discuss any work-related issues or concerns.

The Grimmway Farms mission statement has always been "To take care of our customers' needs everyday of the year with consistent quality, service, and competitive pricing." Today, according to Bob, "that is our goal and will continue to be our foremost challenge in the years ahead."

The partnership of Rod and Bob Grimm came to an end in January 1998 when Rod succumbed to cancer at the age of fifty-one. Thousands of people including employees, customers, and friends attended his funeral at St. John's Lutheran Church. The turnout was a tribute both to Rod Grimm as an individual and the type of business he and Bob built together at Grimmway Farms.

✧

Bob (left) and Rod (right) Grimm photographed on a catwalk above the Grimmway Farms two-inch, baby carrot processing plant.

CONCRETE CUTTING UNLIMITED

Concrete Cutting Unlimited came into being in 1989 when Gerald Ogden and a partner decided to go into business for themselves operating out of their adjoining garages. In twelve and a half years, Concrete Cutting has grown to employ twenty people and moved to a two-acre facility at 3747 Gilmore in Bakersfield. Ogden has since become sole owner, but his original partner, Randy Bradford, has rejoined the company.

Concrete Cutting are specialists in sawing through concrete and asphalt in projects that include work on roads, demolishing or remodeling buildings, treating concrete surfaces for safety, and precision work assisting plumbers and electricians both inside and out of doors. Since they do both hard (concrete/asphalt/tile) and soft (carpet/drywall) demolition, Concrete Cutting offers building demolition that is complete. Furthermore, the company has the capability to recycle asphalt and concrete.

The business has more than doubled in the last few years to more than $2 million in revenue, and Ogden takes pride in the quality of the work and service Concrete Cutting is known for and in the quality of the company's employees. He credits success to two things: God and just trying to do business honestly. Concrete Cutting has come a long way in twelve and a half years, and its future looks good.

❖

Gerald Ogden, owner, and Randy Bradford, project manager, stand in front of concrete collected from various projects over the past year. The concrete will be crushed and resold as recycled base.

❖

Taft's Gardner Field, as seen in this photograph, was a training facility for the United States military during World War II.

INDEX

SPONSORS